Ink and Watercolor

Ink and Watercolor

Learn to Create Quick, Stylized Sketch Paintings in 30 Days

Anastasia Kozlova

Cofounder of
Dream and Draw Art School

PAGE STREET
PUBLISHING CO.

PAGE STREET
PUBLISHING CO.

First published in 2024 by
Page Street Publishing Co.
27 Congress Street, Suite 1511
Salem, MA 01970
www.pagestreetpublishing.com

Distributed by Macmillan, sales in Canada by The Canadian Manda Group.

29 28 27 26 25 2 3 4 5 6

ISBN-13: 979-8-89003-154-9

Library of Congress Control Number: 2023952458

Edited by Alexandra Murphy
Cover and book design by Rosie Stewart for Page Street Publishing Co.
Artwork by Anastasia Kozlova

Printed and bound in China

trustees

Page Street Publishing protects our planet by donating to nonprofits like The Trustees, which focuses on local land conservation.

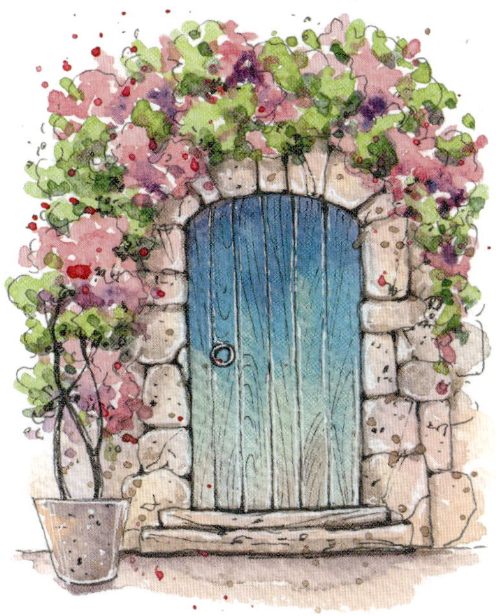

To my family, for believing in my vision and always encouraging me to keep creating. This book is a tribute to the love and joy you've given me.

Contents

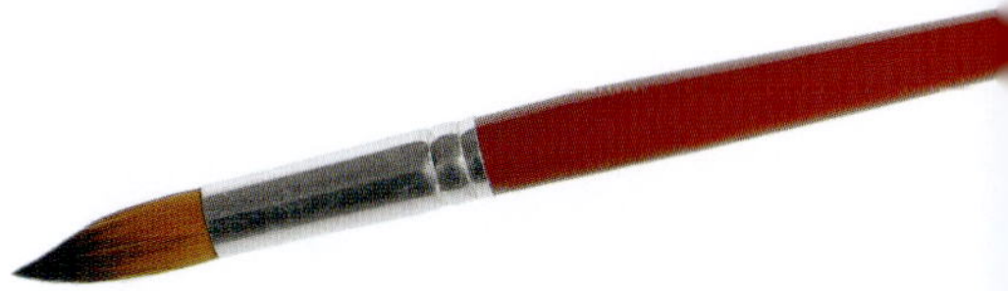

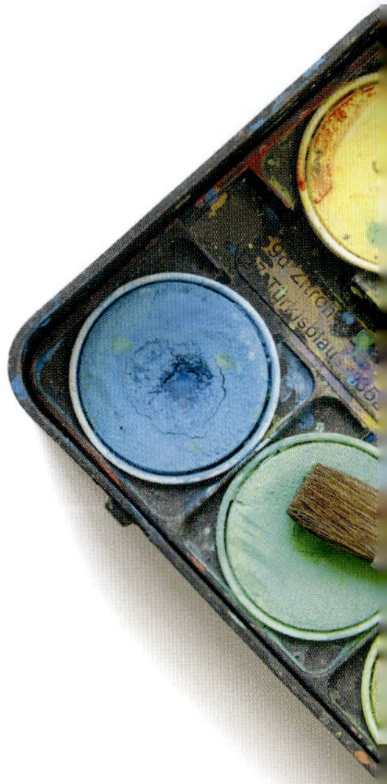

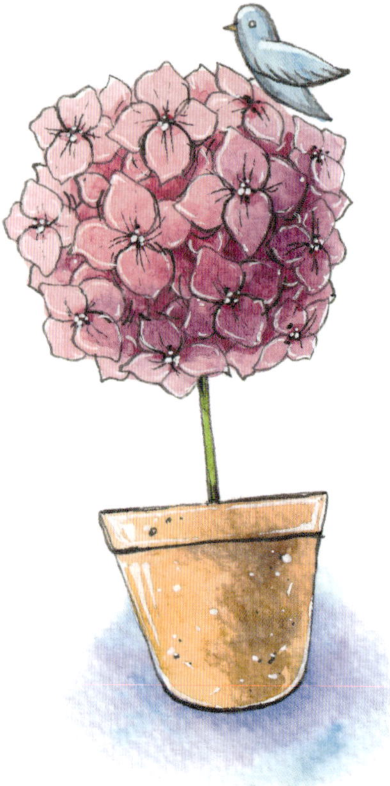
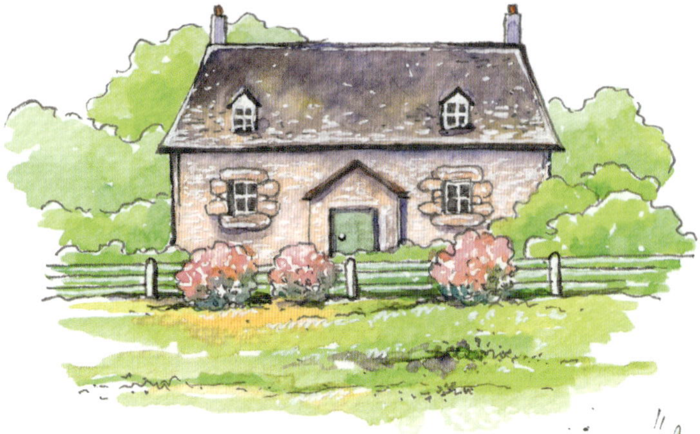
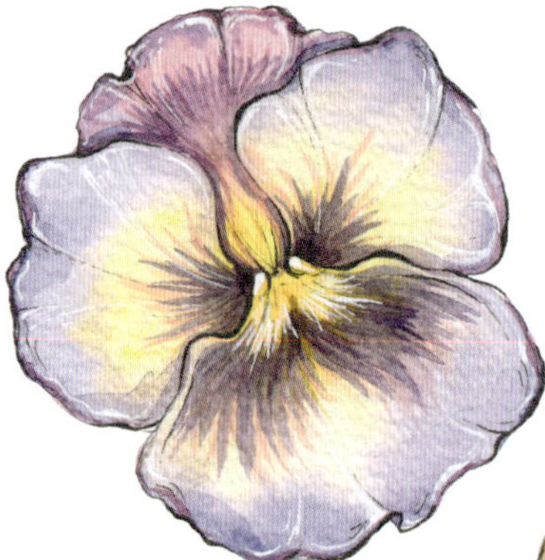
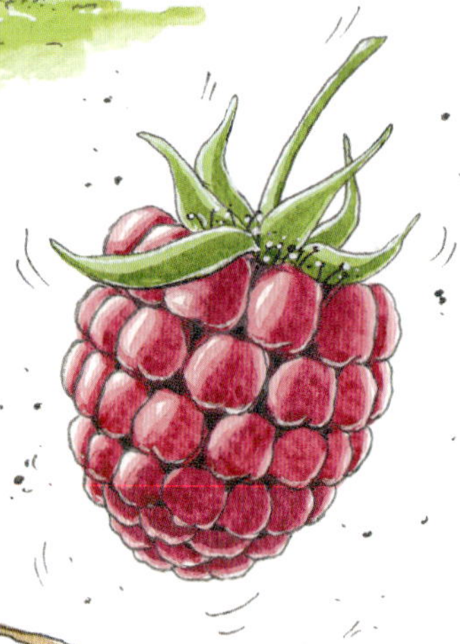
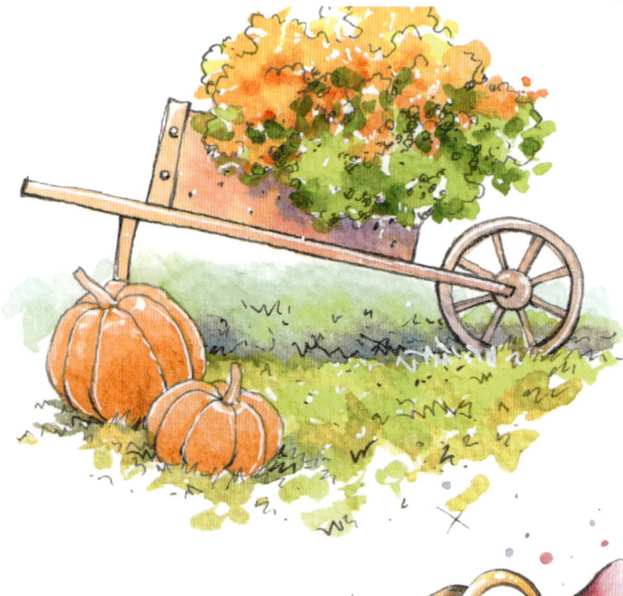
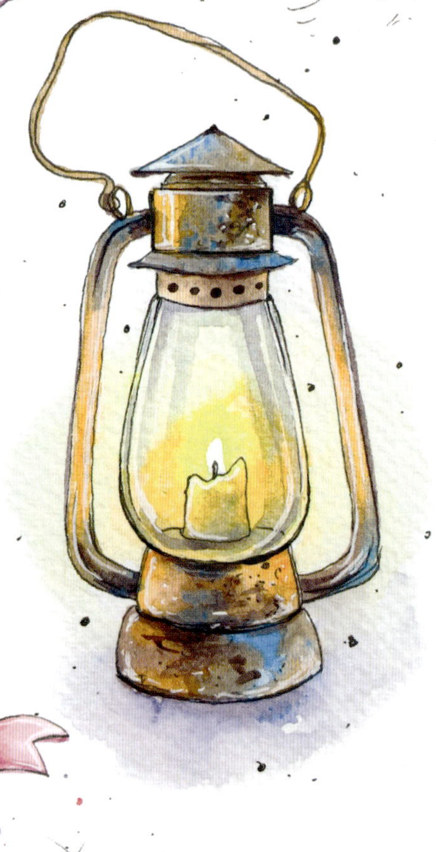
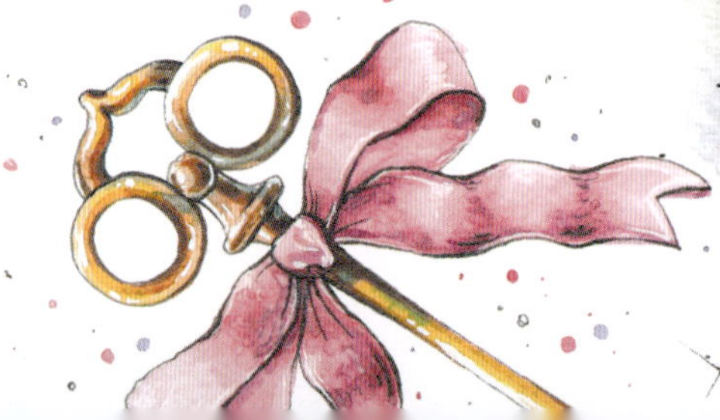

Introduction

From the first pencil lines to final vibrant artworks, get ready to embark on a voyage through the world of creativity. This book is the essence of my 11 years of teaching experience. It's more than just a collection of step-by-step lessons—it's a comprehensive learning journey tailored for beginners. Whether you're eager to explore a new style, enhance your art skills or perhaps find a new passion, this book is crafted just for you.

Many believe that drawing is all about talent or special abilities. Let me tell you a secret: That is not the case. Over 50,000 students have taken my online courses, proving time and time again that passion, interest and enthusiasm are far more important than talent.

My style of watercolor sketching combines detailed pen drawings with vibrant watercolor illustrations using a playful and forgiving approach. This style celebrates the beauty of flexibility and creative freedom. In this book, there are no strict rules—you are free to play with your artistic expressions, twist forms, stylize and infuse your artwork with personal touches. Every uneven line and splash of color, even the unexpected ones, adds a unique charm and character to your sketches. There are no mistakes in sketching—only opportunities for creativity.

This book was crafted to make the art of drawing accessible to everyone, unlocking the joy of creativity for each reader. It's my aim to inspire you to believe in your potential, to discover talents you never knew you had and to show you that you can create beauty with your own hands. Each chapter gently introduces a bit more knowledge and technique, so by the time you reach the final pages, you will find you have softly mastered the fundamentals of graphic and watercolor techniques. And each lesson has been designed to be short and simple; a perfect way to bring tranquility, relaxation and peace, and new energy into your daily life.

Set aside any self-doubt or hesitation, dive into my lessons and get ready to transform your dream to draw and paint into confident skills and stunning sketches.

Grab your pencil, pen and brushes, and let's begin!

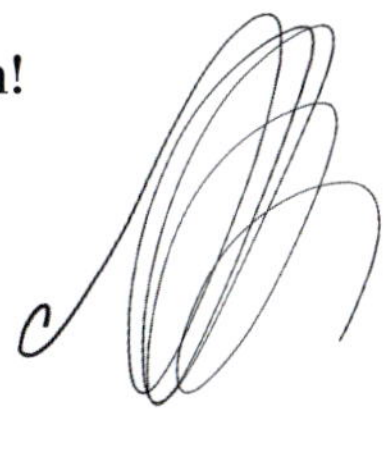

Materials

One of the many advantages to watercolor sketching is that it doesn't require many expensive or professional materials. Simple watercolor sets, basic watercolor paper, a single brush and a liner are all you need to start creating beautiful artwork. Plus, these materials are so lightweight and compact, you can take them anywhere—perfect for drawing in a cozy café, at a lively park or while enjoying the sun on vacation.

For the lessons in this book, you will need the following materials:

1. Pencil: Any HB pencil will do; I use a LAMY® mechanical pencil because it gives fine lines and doesn't need sharpening.

2. Erasers: Use any eraser you have. I use a Faber-Castell® kneadable eraser because it does not damage watercolor paper. I also recommend a white Koh-I-Noor® eraser with an elephant logo.

3. Waterproof Black Liner: A liner is a special marker pen with a fine metal sleeve, available in various thicknesses. I recommend using 0.1, 0.2 or 0.3 mm. Choose liners with waterproof ink, such as Pigma® Micron, Uni® Pin or ShinHan Touch®.

Note: Always check whether your liner is waterproof by drawing a few lines on a separate piece of paper and applying a wet brush over it. If the ink smudges, the liner is not waterproof. You can use non-waterproof liners for outlining after the watercolor wash step is dry.

4. Watercolor Brushes: Choose round brushes with sharp tips made from kolinsky sable, synthetic kolinsky or synthetic squirrel. You will need a size 4 brush for these lessons.

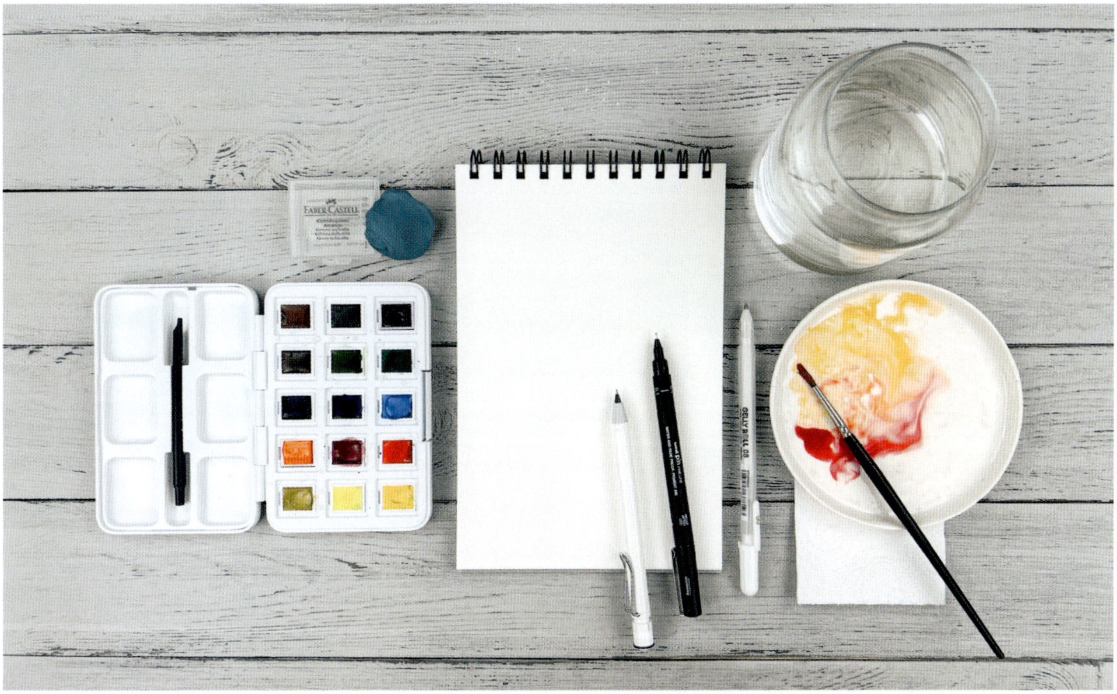

5. Watercolor Paper: I recommend choosing 200 to 300 gsm, medium grain/grain fin, 100% cellulose or 25% cotton, not/cold pressed. In this book, I use Fabriano® watercolor paper. You can also use other brands such as Canson® or Van Gogh®.

6. Watercolor Paints: You can use any student-grade or professional watercolors, such as Van Gogh, Winsor & Newton®, Daniel Smith®, Sennelier® or Schmincke®. The colors I use are Dioxazine Purple, Azo Orange, Quinacridone Rose, Phthalo Blue, Burnt Umber, Permanent Lemon Yellow, Permanent Red Light, Ultramarine Deep, Sap Green, Yellow Ochre, Azo Yellow Medium, Cerulean Blue (Phthalo), Phthalo Green and Burnt Sienna.

7. White Gel Pen: This is needed for highlights and various effects. I recommend the Sakura Gelly Roll® 0.8. Alternatively, you can use white gouache, acrylic paint or an acrylic marker size 0.7.

8. Palette: A palette is essential for mixing colors. Use a ceramic or plastic palette or a simple white ceramic plate.

Additionally, prepare a **cup or jar for water** and **napkins or a cloth** for brush cleaning.

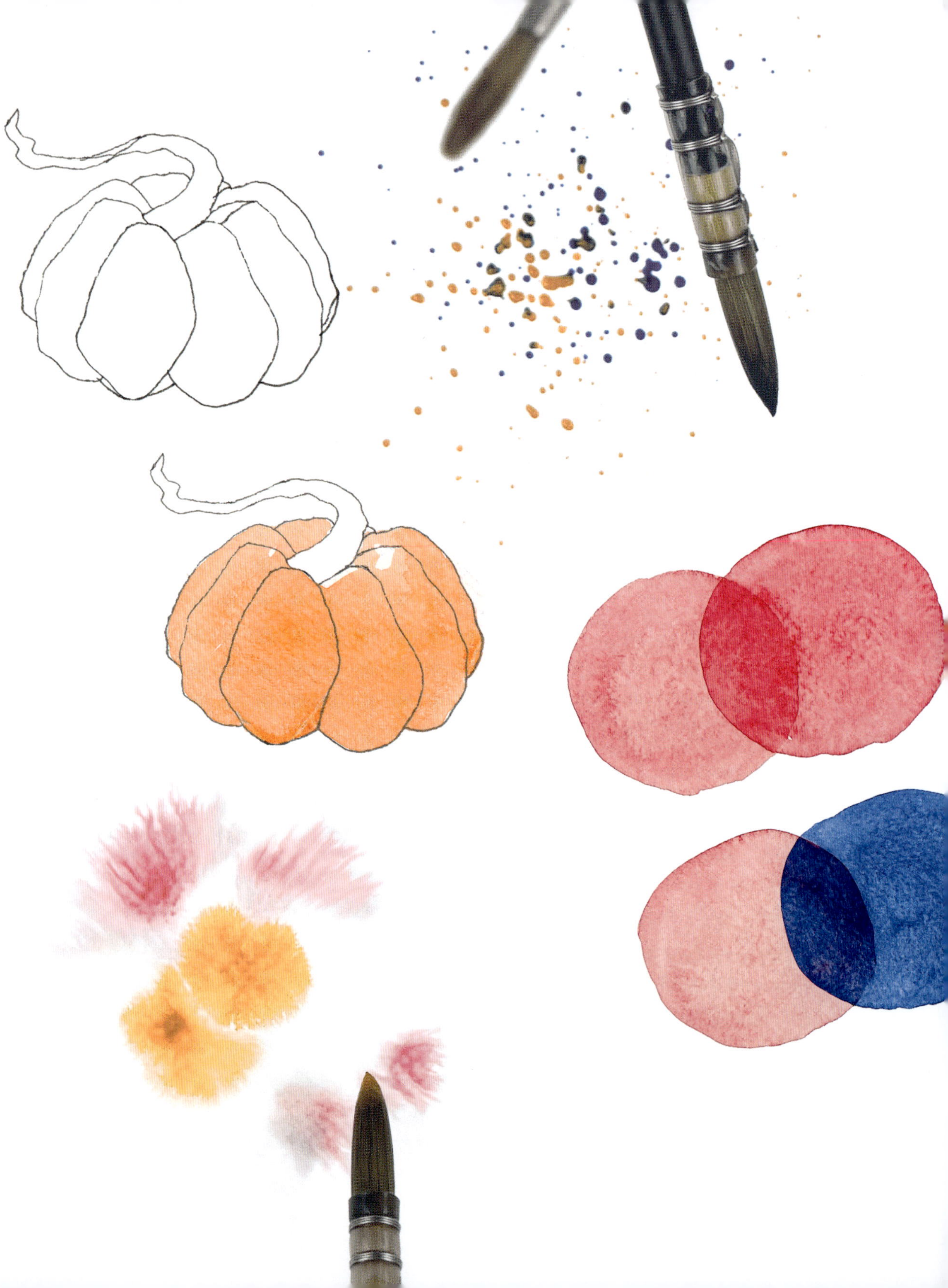

Watercolor Sketching Basics

Dive into the essentials of graphic and watercolor techniques in this exciting section! You'll learn the foundational skills of using liners and white gel pens, along with key watercolor methods. I'll guide you through each technique before showing you how to combine them later on in the lessons.

Though the techniques are simple and accessible to everyone, do not underestimate the potential of watercolor sketching—it's not just about simple drawings. This style can grow with you as you develop your skills, offering opportunities to explore intricate details, complex scenes and a variety of watercolor techniques. Whether you're capturing the simplicity of a serene landscape or the bustling vibrancy of city life, watercolor sketching can provide all levels of artistic expression. Get ready to learn useful skills that will fuel your artistic ideas and creativity!

Graphic Techniques with Liner Pens

Let's start with the world of graphic techniques, where you'll explore the nuances between lines and hatches. Every artist was once a beginner, so let's practice the basics! Explore each method in detail and practice these fundamentals to enhance your skills before progressing to more complex lessons.

Line and Hatch

A. Line: A line is drawn at one speed and with one level of pressure on the liner.

B. Hatch: A hatch is made with a quick motion of the hand. It starts using normal pressure, the same as a line, but ends by lifting the liner sharply off the paper, resulting in a thinner and sharper end.

A.

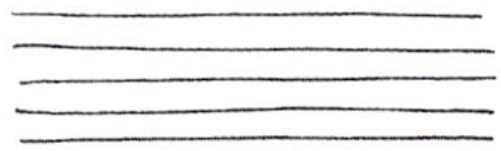

B.

Different Types of Lines, Hatches and Basic Graphic Techniques

1. Simple lines

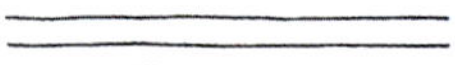

2. Thin lines

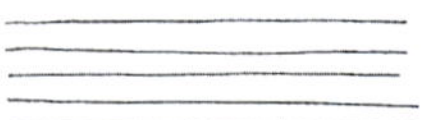

3. Uneven lines

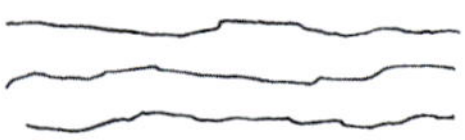

4. Uneven interrupted lines

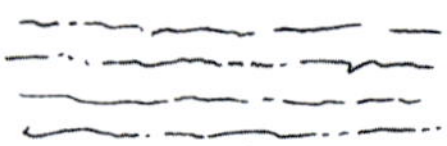

5. Curly interrupted lines

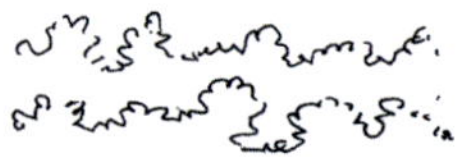

6. Zigzag lines

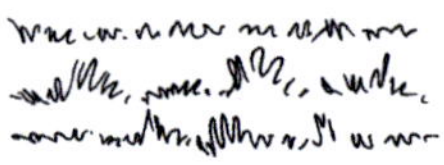

7. Short curved lines

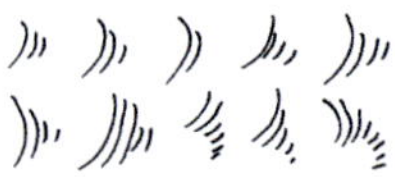

8. Dots, short hatches and doodles

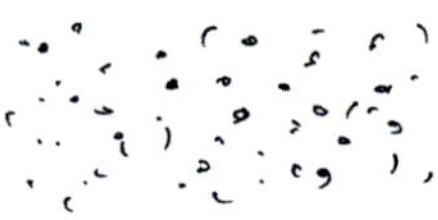

9. Smooth, wavy lines

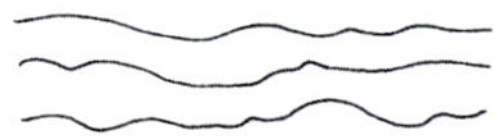

10. Lines with bolder areas

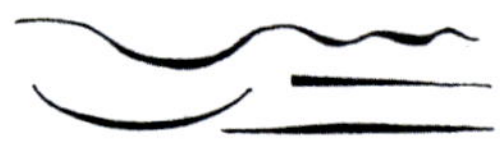

11. Short hatches

12. Semi-oval lines and hatches

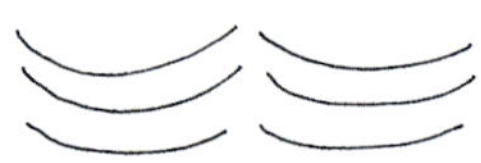

Textures

A. Rough Texture: This texture is used to depict greenery, flowers, fruit peels and stones. When creating this texture, it's important to make a smooth transition from darker areas to lighter ones; this can be done by gradually reducing the number of dots in the lighter part.

B. Wood Texture: This is best depicted with smooth, thin, barely visible lines. Lines can be closer together in some areas and further apart in others. Some parts of the texture can be made with semi-oval lines.

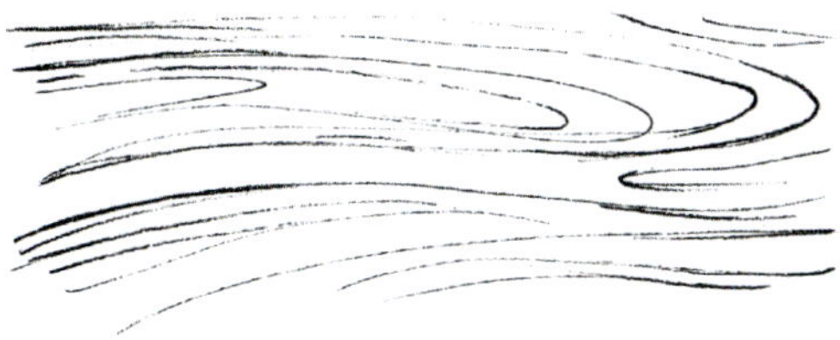

C. Shiny Metal Texture: To show the shine of metal, draw black-colored, vertical, straight stripes of shadows and reflections without roughness. Stripes can vary in thickness.

Using the White Gel Pen

The main rule is to only use white gel pen on dried watercolor. And my own favorite tips are:

1. Do not press too hard on it. Pressing too hard leaves uneven white lines and there may also be gaps in the pigment.

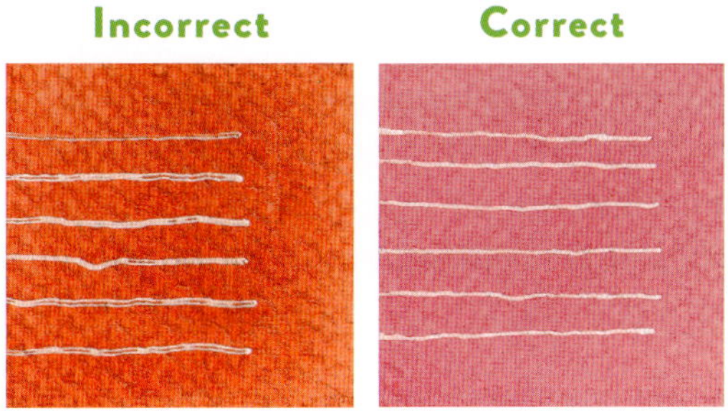

2. It can work as a corrector by covering extra paint and liner. In the first row, the left pumpkin has uneven lines that can confidently be covered with white to achieve the desired drawing result. In the second row, there are areas on the pumpkin where the watercolor went over the edges, which can also be easily covered with the white pen.

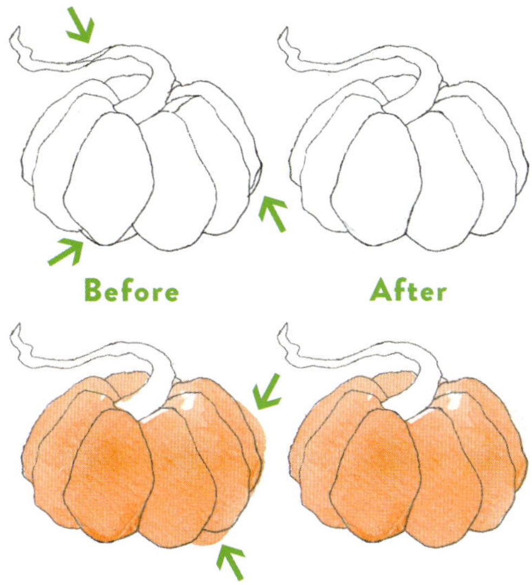

3. You can cover it again with watercolor if you have overdone the whites.

Watercolor Basics

Time for some magic watercolor basics! You'll learn about its translucency, layering abilities and gorgeous color gradients. Watercolor stands out for its ability to blend and flow, offering a unique palette of possibilities. Every masterpiece begins with a single brushstroke. Your journey is just beginning!

Preparing Your Paints and Palette

Before you start painting with watercolors, prepare your paints by adding a drop of water to each color pan to activate them. This makes it easier to pick up the paint with your brush. Also add a bit of water to your palette—this will make it easier to mix colors. Always mix the paint on the palette with water before painting. The amount of water you use will depend on the shade you want. For a lighter shade, dilute the pigment with a lot of water. For a flat wash, use an equal amount of water.

Using a Cloth or Napkin

Always prepare a cloth or napkin before starting to paint so you can remove extra water from the brush. You can also use it to remove extra water or paint directly from your painting.

How Much Water to Use

Watercolor is inherently water-based, so mastering the balance of water and paint is key to achieving stunning, vibrant results. Ensure your brush is not too dry or overly wet—too little water will make your paint difficult to manage, while too much water can cause it to run wildly across your paper.

To get the perfect balance, bathe your brush in water, give it a gentle swirl, then gently wipe it on the edge of your jar to shake off any extra drops. This will keep your brush neat and finely pointed, suitable for the strokes needed.

90% Water + 10% Paint | 65% Water + 35% Paint | 50% Water + 50% Paint | 35% Water + 65% Paint | 20% Water + 80% Paint

Brightness and Tone in Watercolor

We'll explore not just the vibrant colors straight from the pan but also their different tones. If you're looking for a lighter tone, something that is more pale and transparent: Add a bit of water to your color on the palette. Like magic, the more water you mix in, the lighter the tone becomes. Want it darker? Do the opposite—use less water in the mix, and you will get a richer and deeper color.

Mixing Colors

We will also mix colors together, creating gradations. For example, let's mix a dark purple color. By combining Quinacridone Rose and Ultramarine Deep, you can experiment with different proportions to discover your perfect shade. Whether you mix them in equal parts or adjust the ratios, each blend unveils a unique color. This technique helps expand your palette and enhance your watercolor paintings.

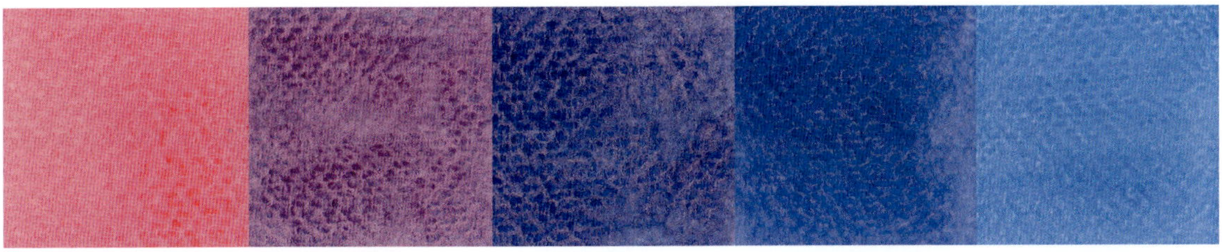

100% Quinacridone Rose | 75% Quinacridone Rose + 25% Ultramarine Deep | 50% Quinacridone Rose + 50% Ultramarine Deep | 25% Quinacridone Rose + 75% Ultramarine Deep | 100% Ultramarine Deep

Watercolor Techniques

In this section, we'll explore some fundamental watercolor techniques that will be the backbone of our upcoming lessons. It's a great idea to get comfortable with these methods first by giving them a little practice. This way, when you dive into the main lessons, you'll feel more confident and ready to create your masterpieces with ease.

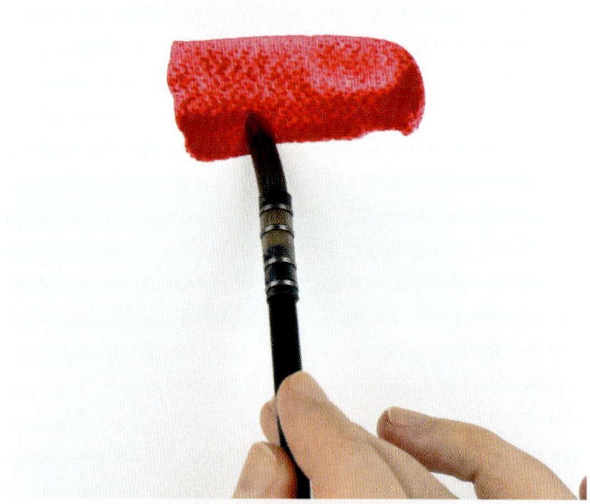

Simple Flat Wash

Prepare the color on the palette before painting. With a damp brush, grab some paint and begin painting wide horizontal strokes, gradually moving downward on your paper. Work your way down, and after a few passes, refresh your brush with more color and keep going. Make sure each new stroke slightly overlaps the previous one to create a seamless wash.

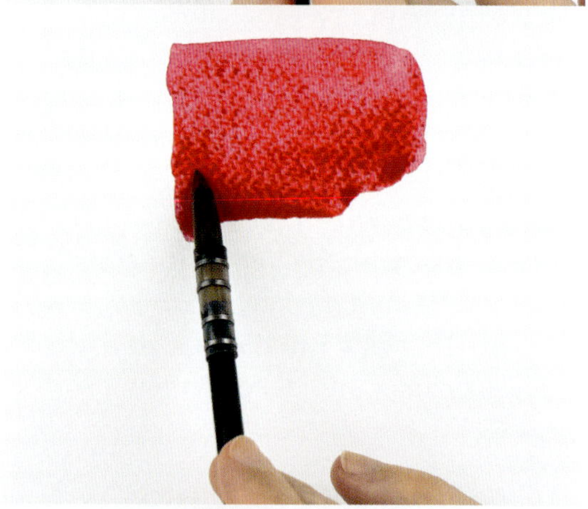

Continue this method until you've covered the entire area. Focus on moving downward only and avoid applying additional layers over the already painted area. When you're finished, you can use a slightly damp brush to gently lift off any remaining drops of water or paint.

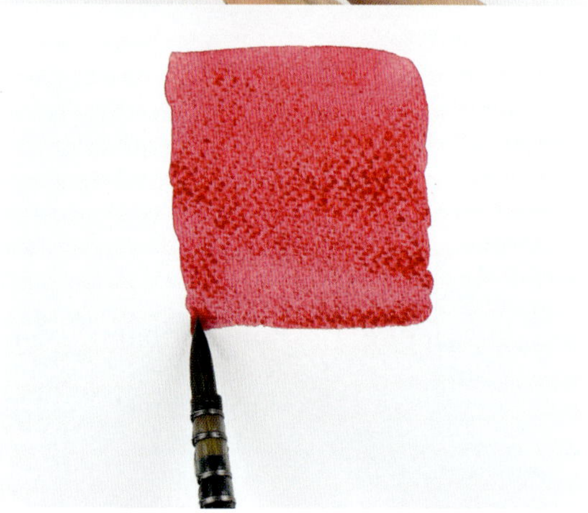

Glazing (aka Layering)

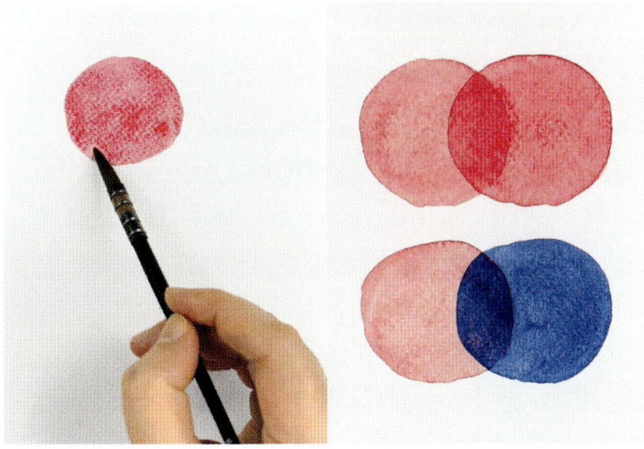

Glazing, also known as layering, is a magical way to blend colors in watercolor, where you layer two or three washes to create stunning optical effects or deepen tones. What is the key to successful glazing? Patience! Make sure each layer is completely dry before adding the next. Another rule of glazing is to not use too much water and to not press hard with the brush. Pressing too hard or using too much water can disturb the beautiful layers you've already put down.

Transition from Opaque to Transparent Color

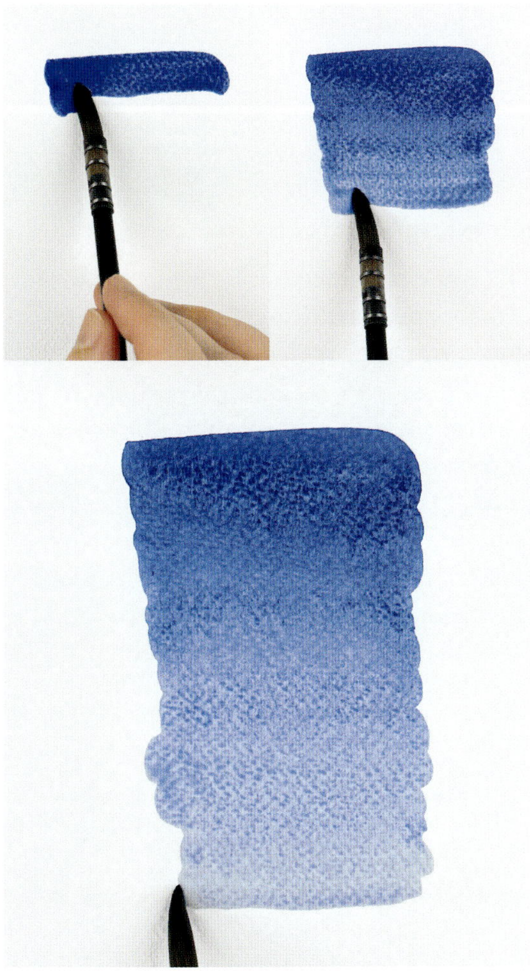

Prepare the color on the palette before painting. With a damp brush, grab some paint and begin painting wide horizontal strokes, gradually moving downward. Work your way down, and after a few strokes, add more water to the palette to lighten the shade. Continue painting by picking up this lightened color and make sure each new stroke slightly overlaps the previous one to create a seamless wash. Continue adding more water to the color on the palette and painting the entire area. Try to move only downward and avoid applying additional layers over the already painted area. When you're finished, you can use a slightly damp brush to gently lift off any remaining drops of water or paint.

Transition from One Color to Another

Prepare two colors on the palette before painting. Pick up a medium amount of water with your brush and take the first color. Begin painting wide horizontal strokes, gradually moving downward. Work your way down, and after a few strokes, pick up the second color with your brush from the palette and continue making strokes, slightly mixing the colors directly on the paper as you continue the wash. Continue this process, gradually adding more of the second color to the wash and covering the entire area. When you're done, you can use a slightly damp brush to gently lift off any remaining drops of water or paint.

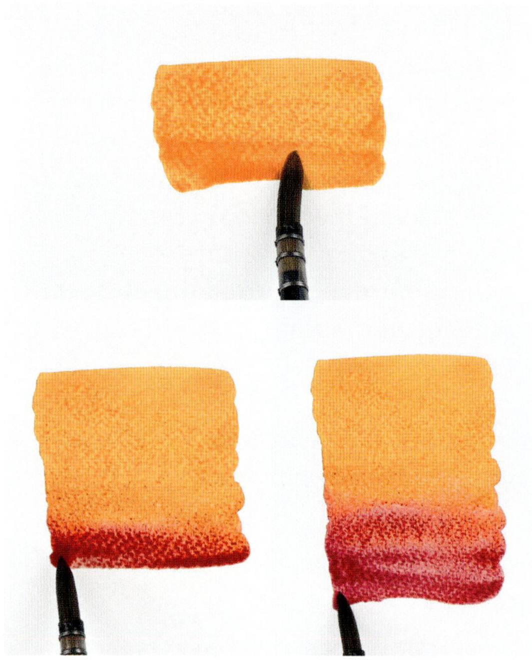

Wet-on-Wet Technique

The wet-on-wet technique is like a dance of colors on your paper. Start by prewetting your paper with clean water, which sets the stage for a beautiful performance. Then apply different colors so they merge into each other, creating stunning, vibrant gradients that flow across the paper. This method not only adds a touch of excitement to your painting but also brings out the spontaneous nature of watercolors. Dive in and let the colors swirl and play!

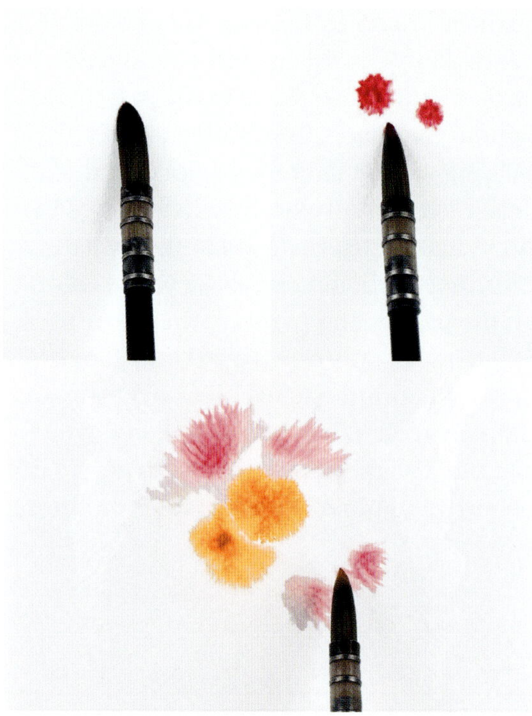

Softening Edges

Soft edges bring a gentle touch to your artwork! After making a wash, clean the brush in water, then wipe it slightly on the edge of a cup or a napkin. With this slightly damp brush, softly lift the paint from the edges of your wash, blending it out to create that soft look. Repeat this process: Clean the brush, wipe it and gently collect the paint from the edge of the wash. If the paint has dried, don't worry! It's still possible to create a soft edge by simply adding water to the edge, waiting about 10 seconds and then you can soften.

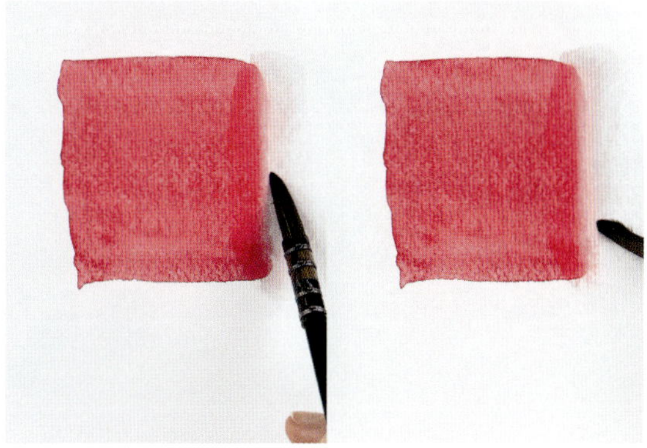

Splattering

Get ready to have some fun with color splatters! First, choose your favorite color and mix it on your palette with a little extra water for the perfect splashy consistency. Then load your brush with the color and give it a quick tap with your finger, another brush or a pencil to create random splatters across your sketch. If there are parts of your sketch you would like to keep clean, simply cover them with a napkin, a piece of paper or your hand. Also, if there is a splatter you don't like, just remove it gently with a damp brush or napkin while it is still wet.

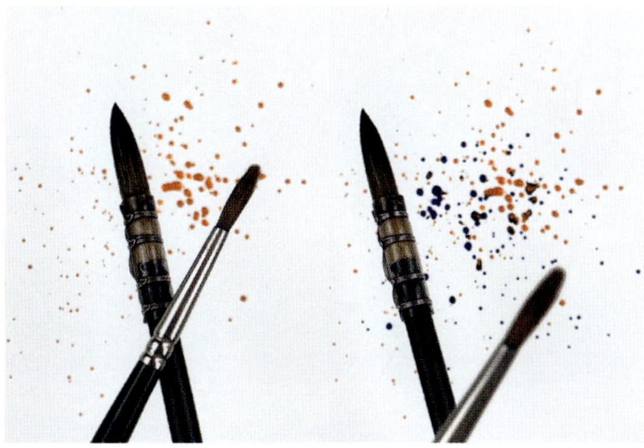

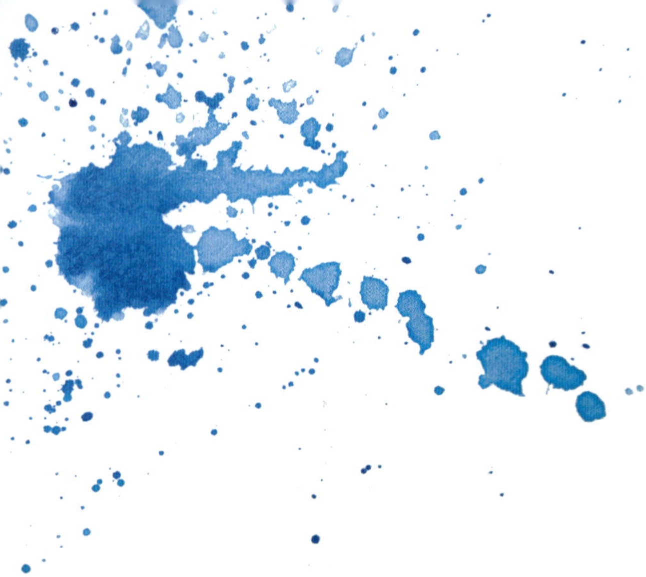

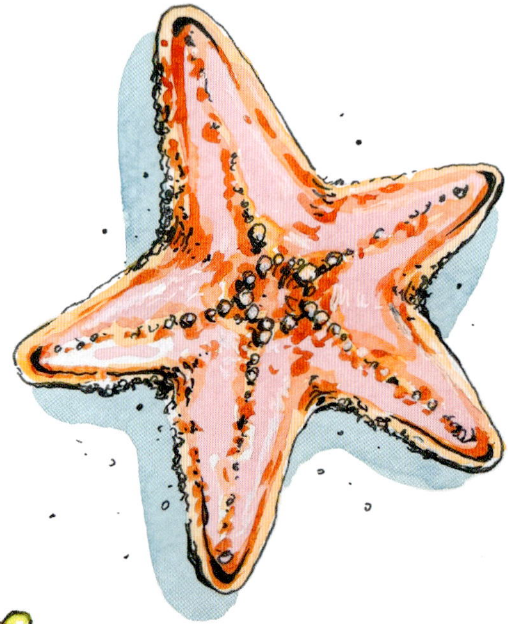

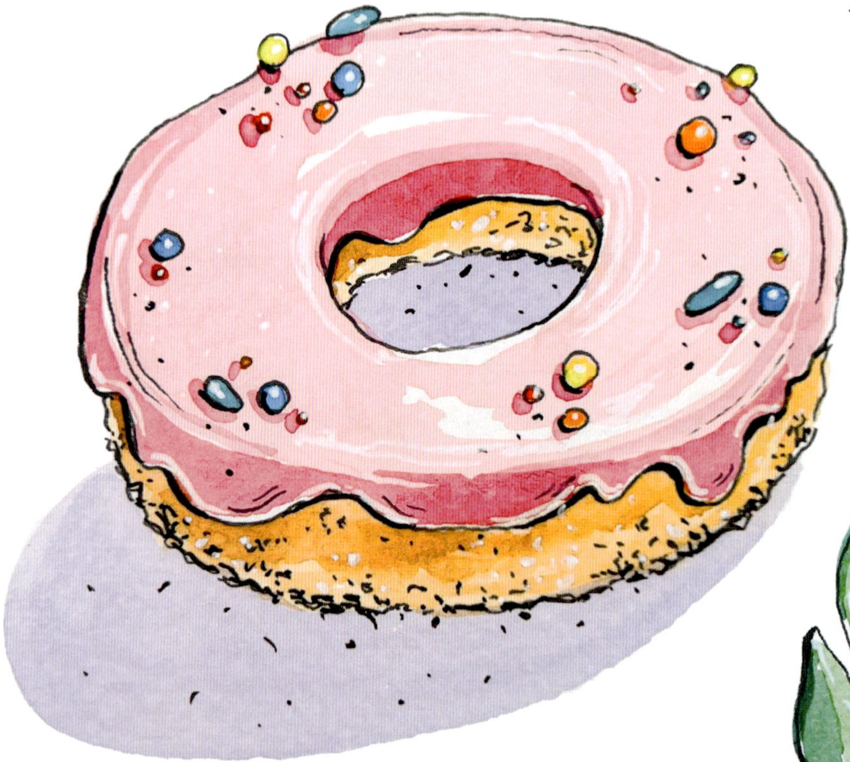

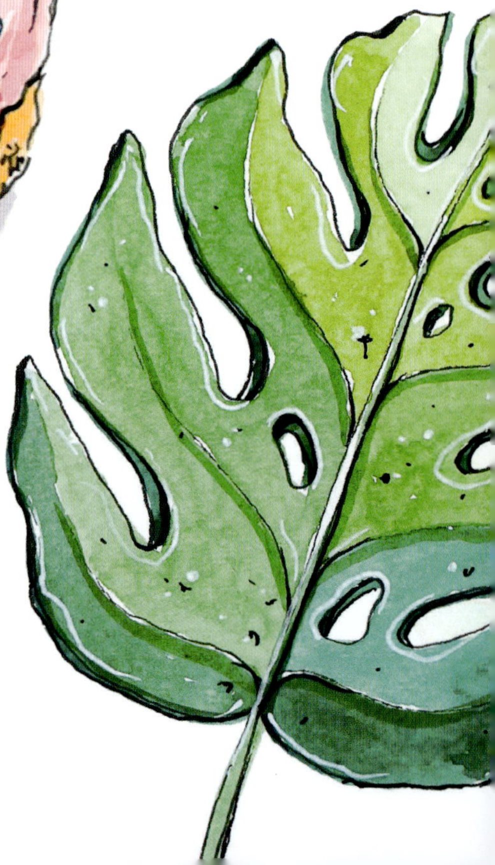

Simple Washes and Lines

Watercolor sketching is fantastic because, with even the simplest techniques, you can create many amazing and bright paintings! In this chapter, we'll learn different types of simple graphic lines and dots. We'll explore flat watercolor washes and how to use them to create a three-dimensional effect. You'll practice mixing various color shades, starting off with creating different shades of one color in the Magic Green Monstera (page 24) and then moving on to more involved paintings like the Ocean Jewel Starfish (page 32). And with the help of a white gel pen, you'll discover how to create a sparkling effect and emphasize volume.

Lesson 1. Magic Green Monstera

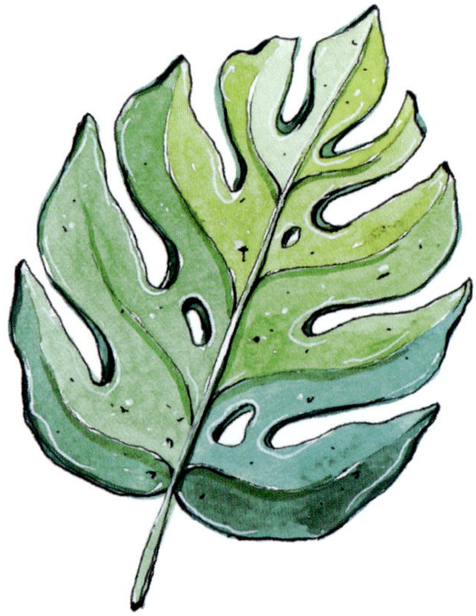

We are starting our journey into the bright watercolor sketching world! In this lesson, you will learn simple liner outlines, how to mix various shades of green and basic watercolor washes. Monstera leaves have a very interesting curvy shape with a variety of green shades. So, let's begin!

Paint Colors

Permanent Lemon Yellow

Yellow Ochre

Sap Green

Phthalo Green

Cerulean Blue

Phthalo Blue

1. Use a pencil to draw a droplet form of a leaf, and add central and side lines to divide the leaf into an equal number of sections.

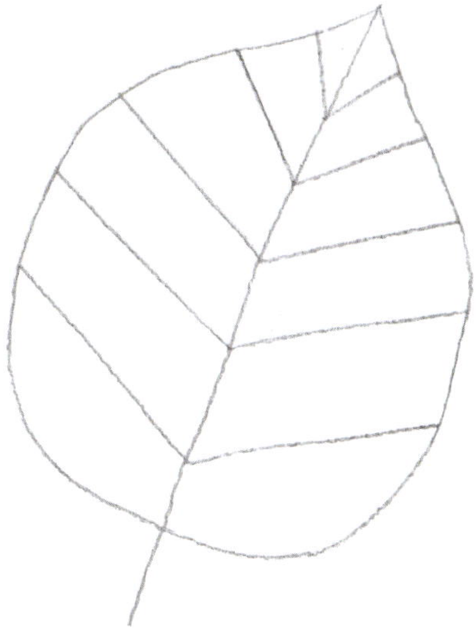

1

2. Make the outline with a waterproof black liner with a curvy line. Monsteras have pointy edges and a wavy contour between the leaf veins. Use the pencil lines as a guide and draw an equal amount of leaf curves on each side. Then add a few random ovals, curvy veins and a stem. Erase the pencil.

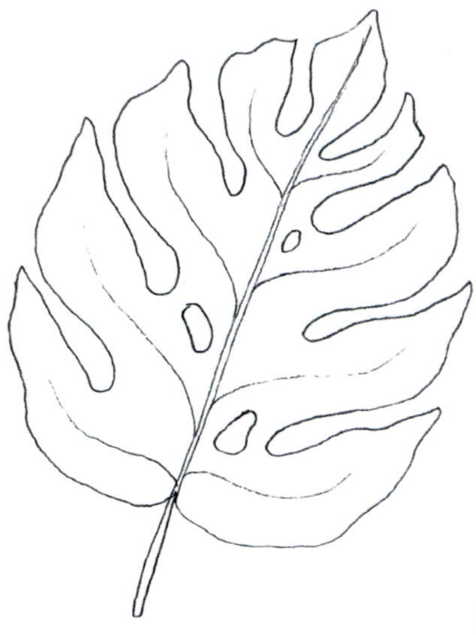

2

3. Mixing colors can be challenging but so much fun! Let's mix and play with colors! Prepare the watercolors and add several drops of Permanent Lemon Yellow and Yellow Ochre on the palette to mix different variants of green. In the first mixing, add just a small amount of Sap Green to Permanent Lemon Yellow and you will get a light yellowish-green. Use this one to make a simple watercolor wash on the top right part of the leaf and paint until the first vein line.

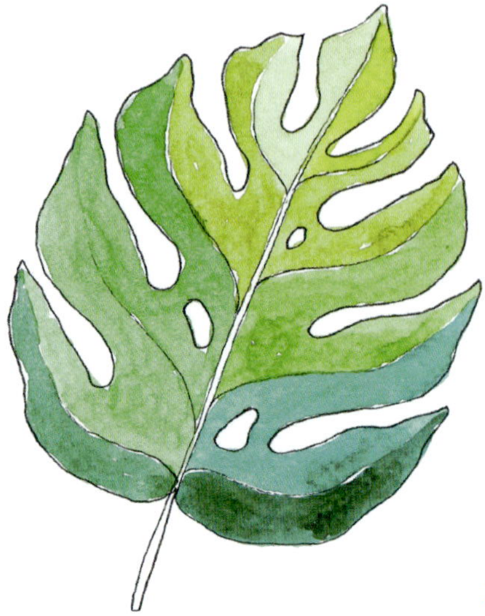

3

sap green + permanent lemon yellow

Dilute the same color with water and paint the left top part also until the first vein line.

Mix a new green using Yellow Ochre and Sap Green in an equal proportion and paint both sides of the leaf from the first small veins to the second veins. Leave the central vein white.

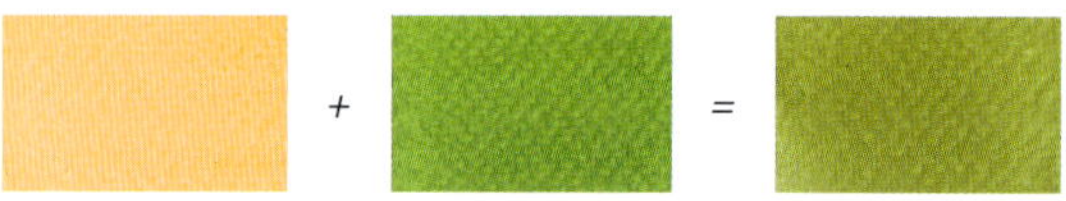

yellow ochre + sap green

Continue mixing different greens and painting within the vein sections. The next mixture is Phthalo Green and Sap Green in equal proportions. Use it to paint the left side. Then add two drops of Permanent Lemon Yellow to the mixture and paint the opposite side of the leaf.

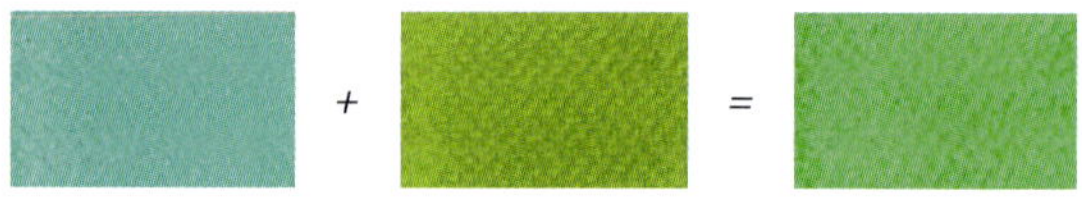

phthalo green + sap green

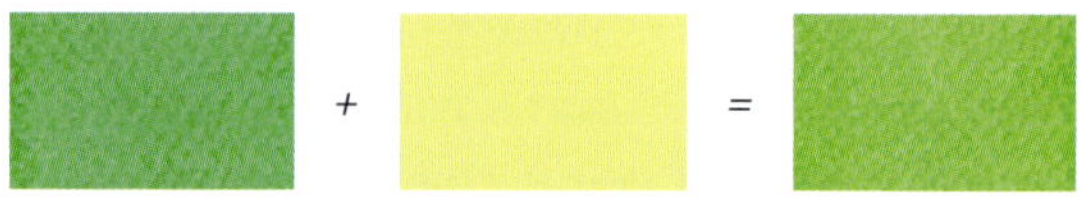

mix 3 + permanent lemon yellow

Then try mixing a new green with Phthalo Green and Cerulean Blue. The last mixing is Phthalo Green plus Phthalo Blue for the bottom parts, but one is darker and the opposite one is lighter because it's diluted with water.

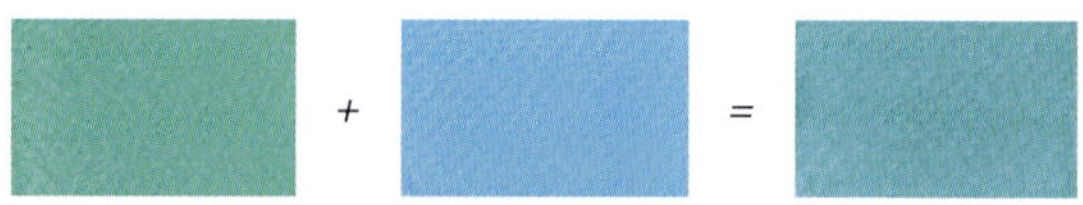

phthalo green + cerulean blue

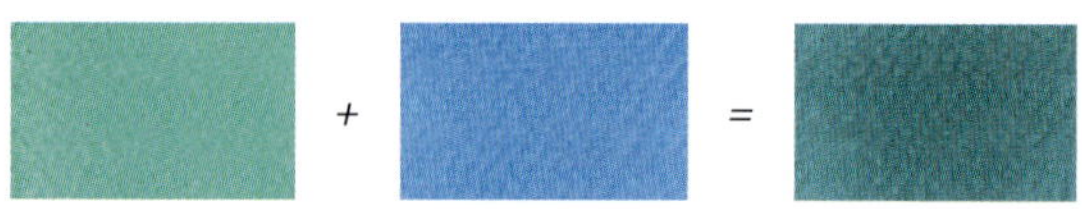

phthalo green + phthalo blue

4. You are doing great! Just imagine how many green shades you can mix using different yellow, blue and green colors! I love all these magical mixes! When the paint is dry, use the darkest color (Phthalo Green and Phthalo Blue) and paint lines along the contour, mainly on the bottom of each leaf curve. Add lines inside the ovals as well, but only along the side closest to the center. Use Sap Green to enhance the veins: Just make one stroke next to the liner outline.

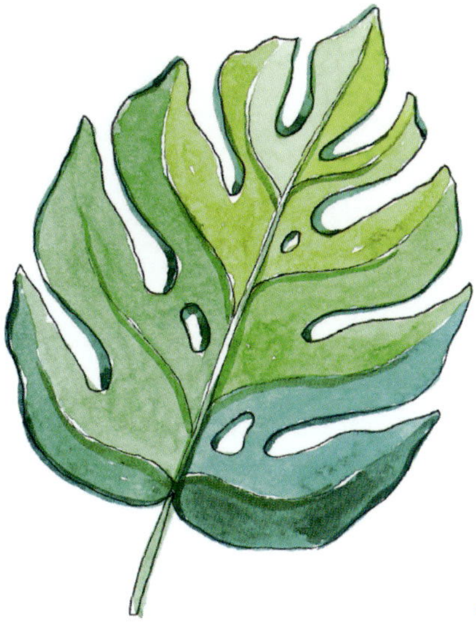

4

5. Use a white gel pen to draw lines along the contour of the leaf curves, veins and ovals. Feel free to make them in a loose way; it's okay if they are a bit messy. Put several small white dots and short dashes on the leaf randomly. Then use the black liner to make the pointy edges of each leaf darker and outline the dark green strokes on the sides. Do the same with the ovals: Add an outline to the dark green watercolor strokes. Make veins closer to the central vein darker and put small dots and short dashes randomly, and sometimes next to the white dots.

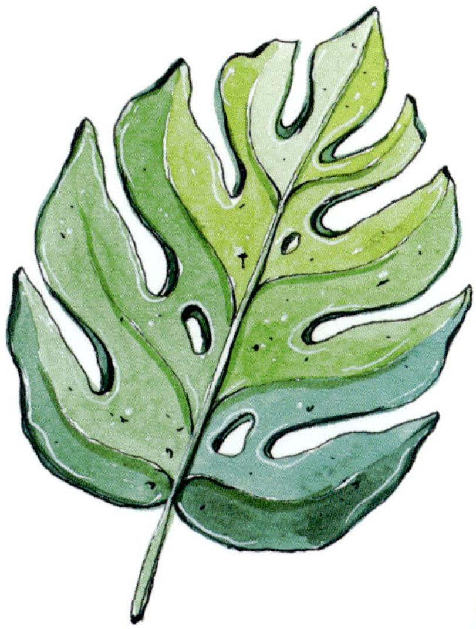

5

Wonderful! Our sketch is ready!

Lesson 2. Sweet Donut Treat

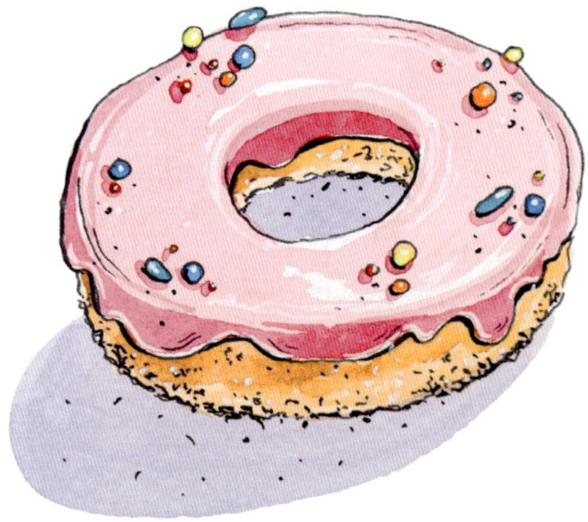

Take your brushes and get ready for some watercolor magic! In this lesson, we'll be painting a delicious and tasty donut with shiny icing and colorful sprinkles. You will learn how to create three-dimensional volume and the texture of dough. You'll also practice drawing wavy lines and ovals. So, let's begin!

Paint Colors

Quinacridone Rose	Yellow Ochre	Dioxazine Purple	Cerulean Blue
Azo Orange	Permanent Lemon Yellow	Phthalo Green	Permanent Red Light

1. Use a pencil to draw a large oval and then a smaller one inside it in the center. Then make uneven wavy lines to show icing. Draw the first wavy lines on the top half inside the small oval. Draw the second wavy line at the bottom of the large oval on the outside. Add thickness to the donut with a semi-oval line at the bottom of the large oval and also inside the small oval.

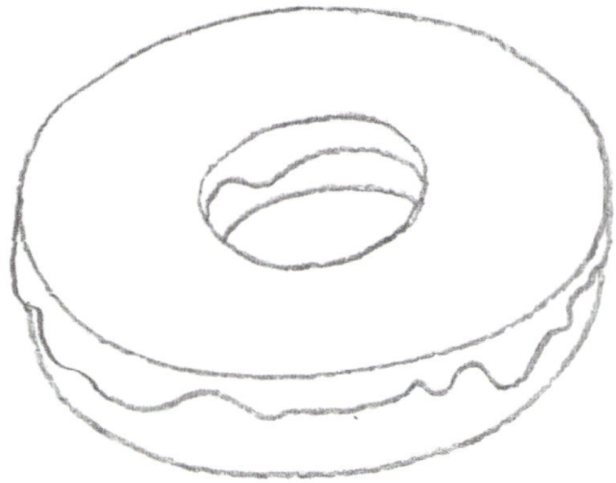

1

2. Make the outline with a waterproof black liner with a curvy, uneven line. On the small inner oval, add two short lines on the sides going upward. Add sprinkles in the form of small ovals and circles of different sizes in various places on the icing. Great! Outline the dough with an uneven dashed line. Add dots, lines and dashes at the bottom part of the dough to show shadow and texture. On the icing add smooth, wavy lines along the edges. Erase the pencil.

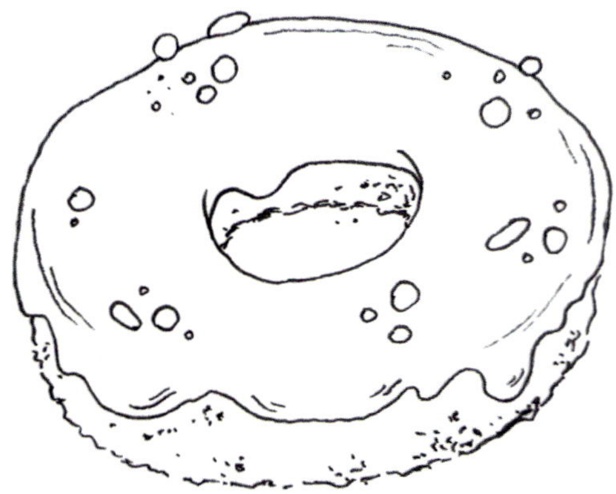

2

3. Mix Quinacridone Rose with water to get a light pink shade. Paint the icing, leaving some white paper spots at the top and a bit more on the drooping part of the icing. Then mix Yellow Ochre with water to get a light shade and paint the dough of the donut at the bottom, leaving some white paper spots next to the icing. Dilute Dioxazine Purple with water to make it lighter and paint a shadow in an oval shape on the left side below the donut. Color the space inside the small oval as well.

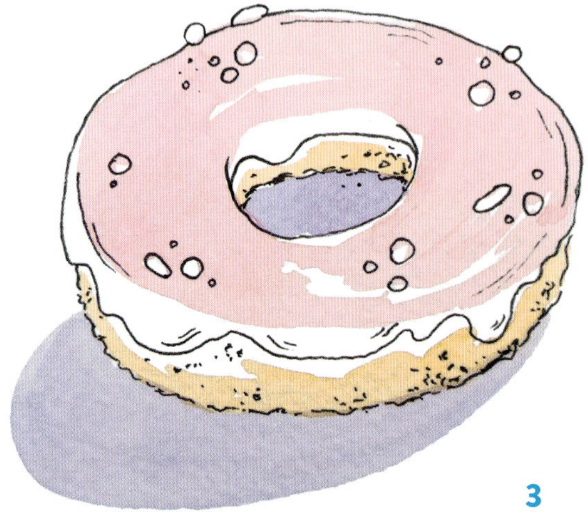

3

4. Use Cerulean Blue, Azo Orange, Permanent Lemon Yellow, Phthalo Green and Permanent Red Light (or any colors you like) to paint the sprinkles. Use Yellow Ochre to paint the remaining dough parts with small, short strokes to show the dough's texture. Slightly overlap the light Yellow Ochre from the previous step with more small strokes to create a beautiful transition from dark to light Yellow Ochre. Well done!

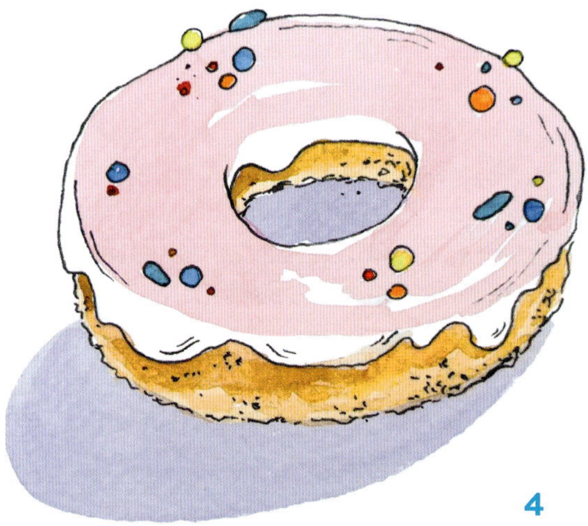

4

5. Slightly dilute Quinacridone Rose with water to get a darker shade than the one used in step 3 and apply it to the edges of the top part of the icing with long, curvy strokes. Then use an even less diluted Quinacridone Rose to paint the bottom part of the dripping icing outside the donut and inside the small oval. Leave a thin white outline at the very bottom of the dripping icing. Also add dark Quinacridone Rose shadows under the sprinkles on the bottom left side. Amazing! Now we should wait for everything to be completely dry.

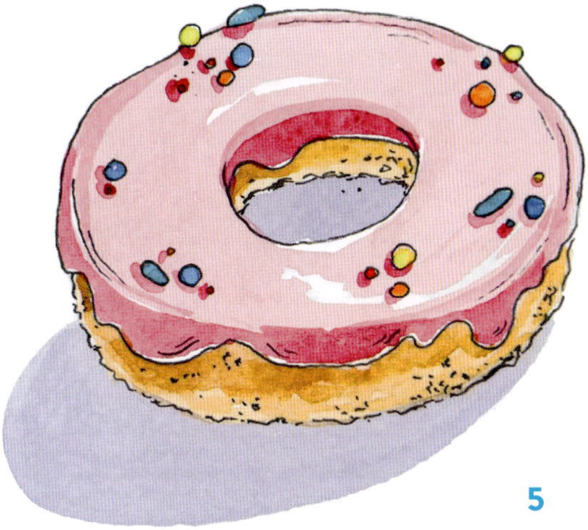

5

6. With a white gel pen, make one dot on each sprinkle's upper right side. Randomly add dots and short comma-like lines on the dough in various places to show the texture. On the pink icing, add long, curvy lines along the edges and at the bottom of the dripping icing. Also add a few random dots on top of the icing. Use black liner to outline the bottom part of the dripping icing to make a smooth line that's bolder in some places. Enhance the shadow under the dough with dots and short lines. Add a few dots and small lines to the purple shadow in random places.

Great! Our sketch is ready!

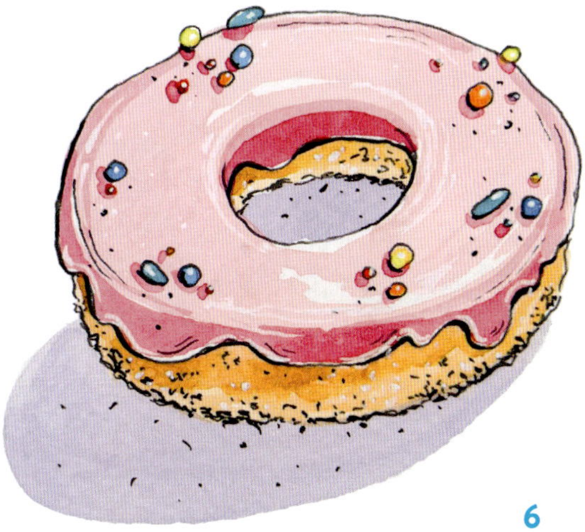

6

Lesson 3. Ocean Jewel Starfish

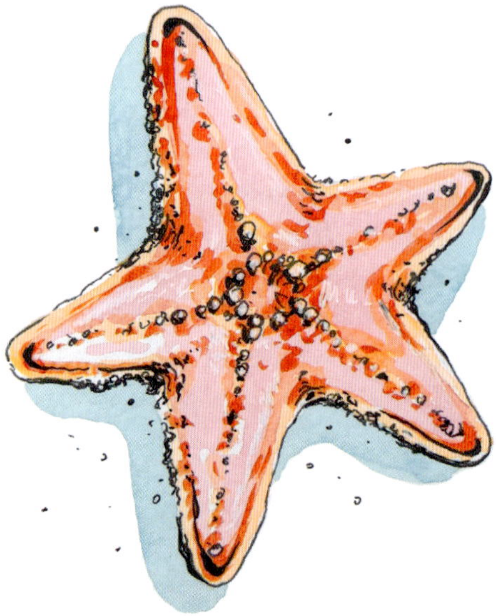

Let's dive into the atmosphere of the ocean depths by creating a watercolor sketch of a starfish, as a symbol of the beauty and jewels of the underwater world! In this lesson, we will continue exploring simple flat washes, choosing lovely color combinations and creating volume and texture. Let's begin!

Paint Colors

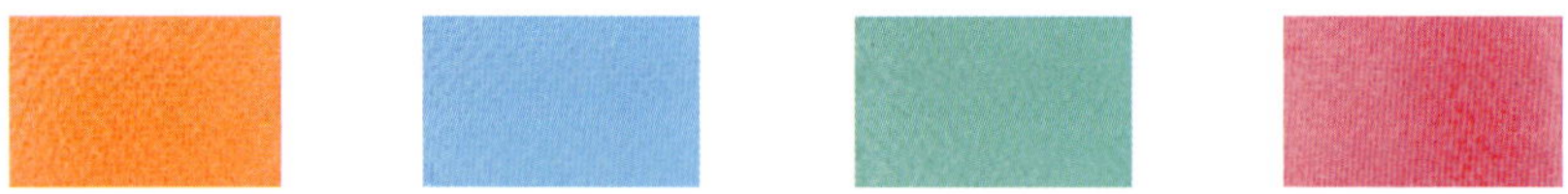

Azo Orange | Cerulean Blue | Phthalo Green | Quinacridone Rose

1. Draw a small circle in the center of the paper with a pencil. To create your starfish's points, draw five straight lines in different directions going out from the circle: Draw the first line upward, slightly slanted to the left, the second and third to the sides and the fourth and fifth downward and a bit to the sides. Draw the starfish's contour with a smooth line based on the lines' direction.

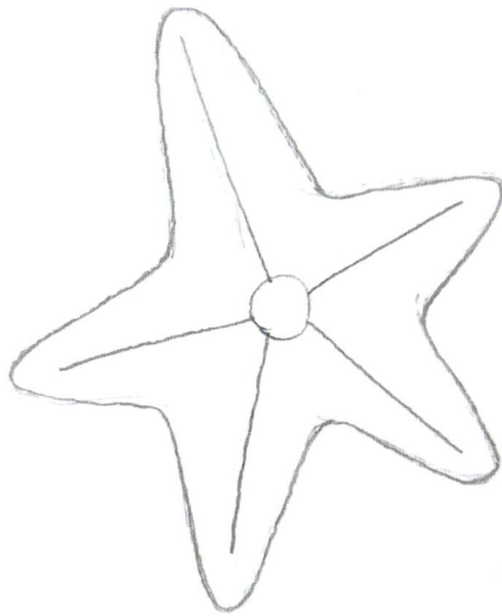

1

2. Outline the starfish with a waterproof black liner with a combination of smooth and uneven lines. Make the line interrupted and detached in the areas closer to the center. On the small central circle, draw small, uneven and irregular circles of different sizes. For the five lines, draw several small circles of different sizes and add dots, semi-ovals and small lines. Add curvy lines inside on the inner angles of the starfish. This will create the effect of volume and texture. You are doing great! And now, let's erase the pencil.

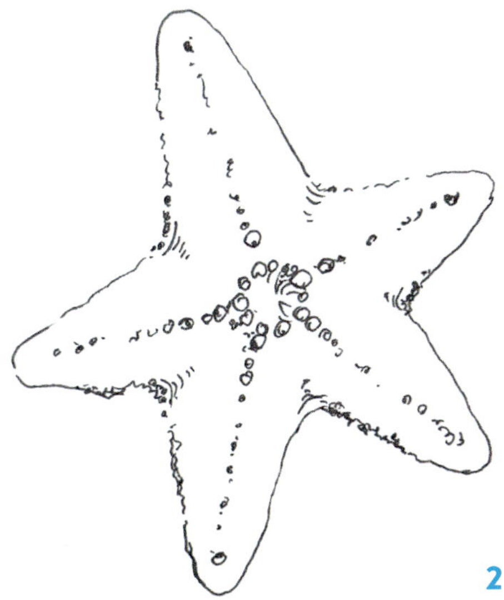

2

3. On your palette, use Azo Orange and dilute it a bit with water to get a light orange color. Use this color to paint an uneven line following the inner contour of the starfish. Then with short, small, random strokes, color the middle space of the starfish, leaving some white paper uncovered. Also make uneven strokes along the central lines of the starfish. Great! Then wait for the paper to dry completely. Now let's mix a light turquoise color. Add equal parts Cerulean Blue and Phthalo Green on the palette, mix them and add some water to lighten the color. With the light turquoise, make flat, smooth washes to paint the shadow under the starfish. Wait until the paper is dry.

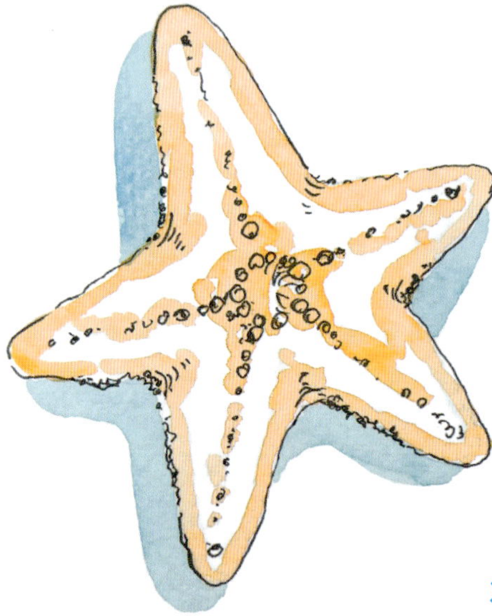

3

cerulean blue + phthalo green

4. Mix Quinacridone Rose with a bit of water to get a light pink. Use this color to paint the leftover parts of the starfish, slightly overlapping the orange contour and covering the central orange area a bit more. Leave some areas of the paper white. Again, let's wait for the paper to dry before moving on.

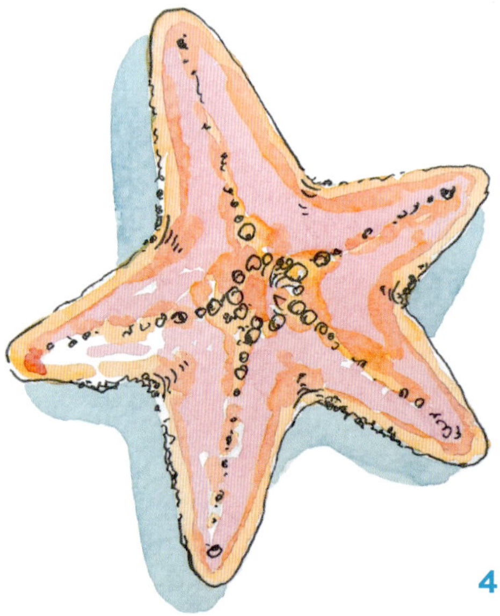

4

5. Mix Quinacridone Rose and Azo Orange in equal parts on your palette to get an orange-pink color. Apply this color with short, small strokes along the contour where the pink overlaps the orange. Also add small random dots and strokes in the center and along the central lines of the starfish. Well done! Make some strokes with this color on the inner corners of the starfish.

quinacridone rose + azo orange

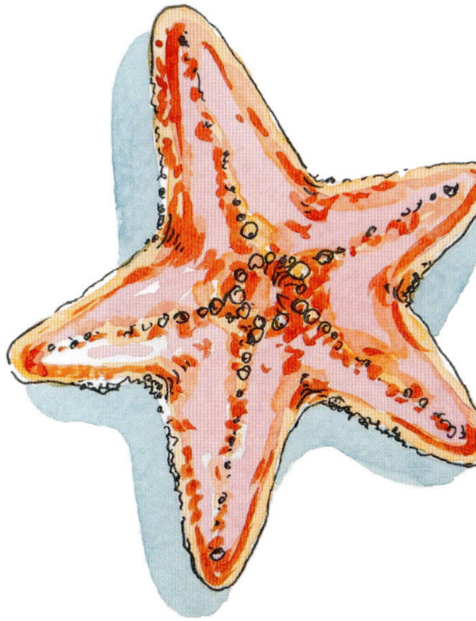

5

6. After the paper is dry, use a white gel pen to randomly draw lines on the light pink parts of the starfish. Place dots in the small circles at the center and in some circles on the lines of the starfish. Make the outline darker with the black liner in some areas. Make the lines of the outline bolder at the inner and outer tips of the starfish along the contour. Also draw curvy, comma-like lines at each of the starfish's tips. Draw lines and curls to show the shadows and texture on the inner sides of the starfish. Also darken the outline of the small circles in the center of the starfish on their left side. Add random dots, circles and lines on the background around the starfish.

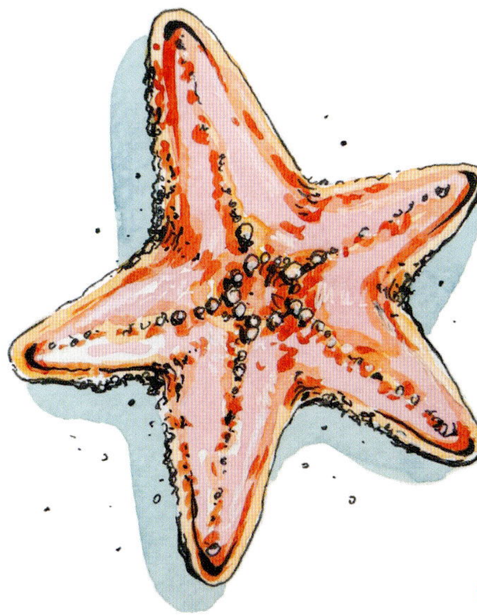

6

Excellent! Our sketch is ready!

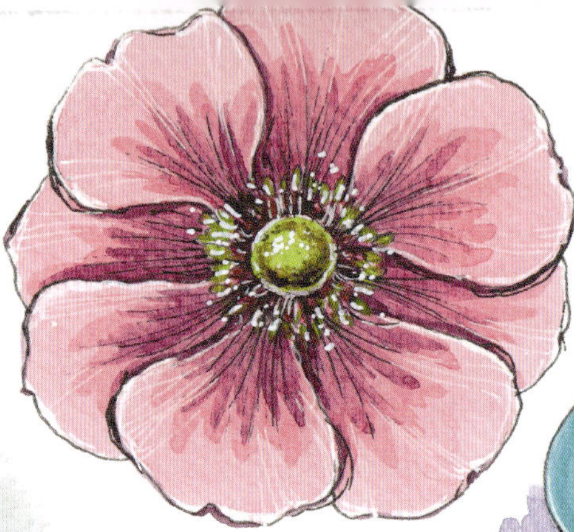

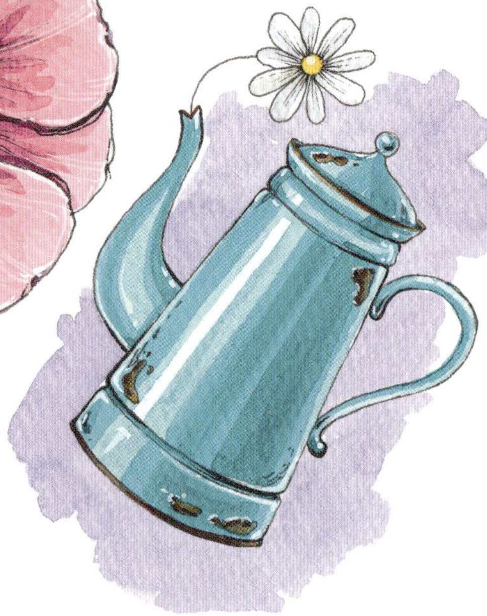

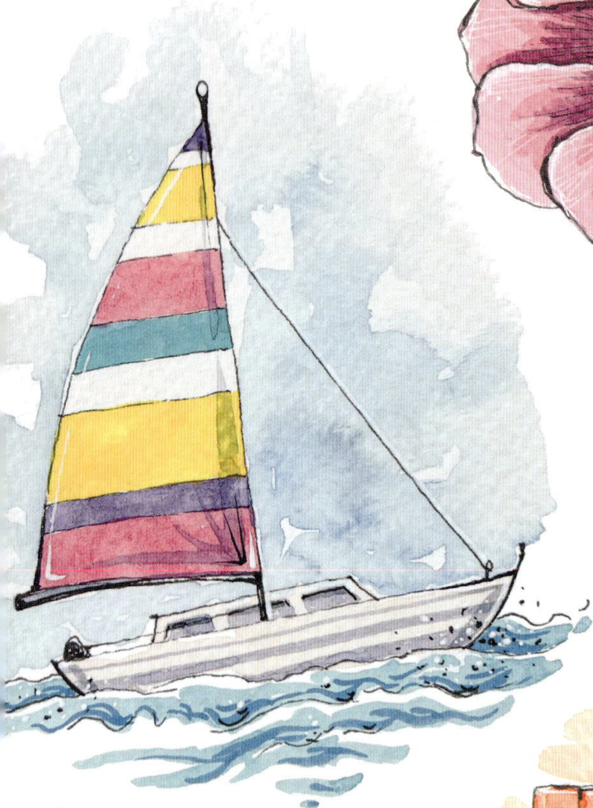

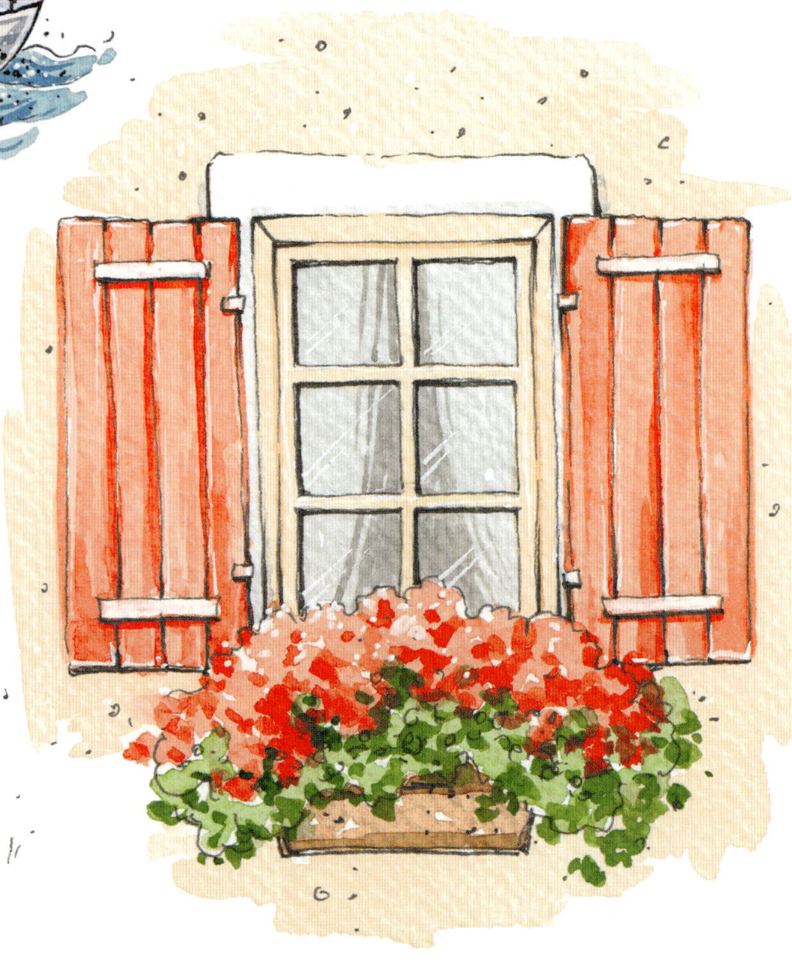

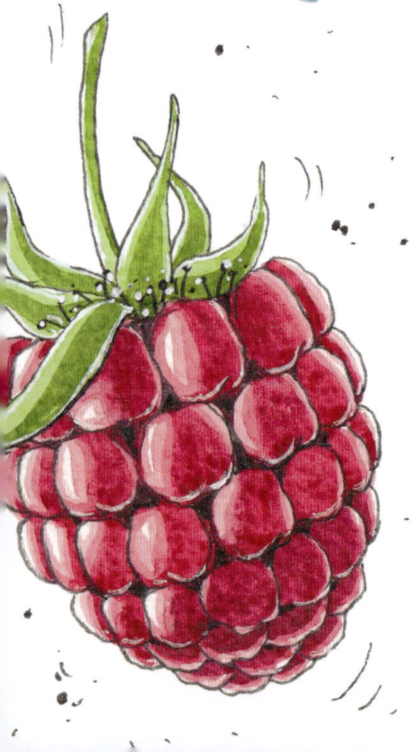

Layering and Hatching

This chapter is dedicated to the practice of the watercolor glazing technique. With glazing, you can create incredibly realistic, bright and dimensional sketches, as in Raspberry Berry Bliss (page 42) and It's Teatime! (page 50), by simply layering watercolor strokes one on top of the other. Master this technique, and you'll be able to depict and show a lot of effects and textures in your sketches, like in Window Floral Bloom (page 58). It's a simple and very powerful technique that I use in almost every sketch. As for the graphics, we'll enrich our arsenal with various new hatches that will help us draw different effects, from the delicate veins of flowers in Colorful Fairy-tale Anemone (page 38) to the shine of glass and folds on fabric in Coffee Journeys (page 54).

Lesson 4. Colorful Fairy-tale Anemone

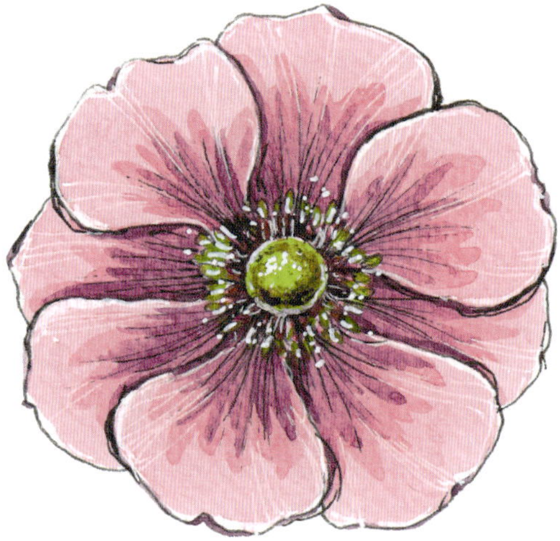

Get ready to uncover the secrets of using glazing as a powerful and delicate tool for creating incredibly airy images. In this lesson, we'll draw an elegant anemone flower, showing the lightness of its petals through layers of watercolor. We'll explore new types of liner hatches for veins that will add uniqueness and volume to your sketches. So, let's begin!

Paint Colors

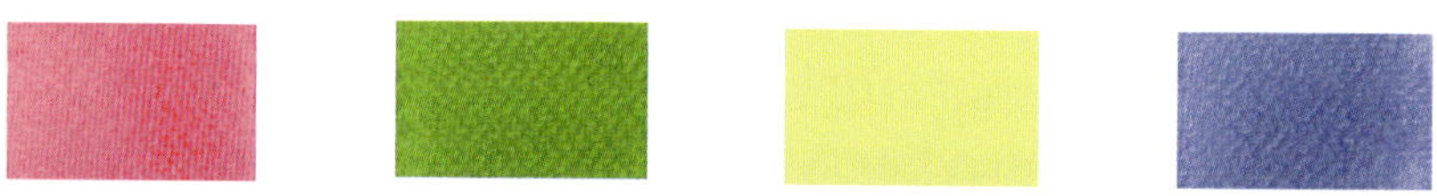

Quinacridone Rose	Sap Green	Permanent Lemon Yellow	Dioxazine Purple

1. Draw a large circle in the center of the paper with pencil. Then draw a small circle inside it and an even smaller one within the small circle. From the center circle, draw three lines at roughly equal distances from each other. Draw curvy and irregularly shaped teardrop petals along these lines. Great! These are the top petals. Then draw one vertical line from the center circle toward the top, between the two upper lines, and add two lines between the lower side lines. Complete the petals, making some overlap others.

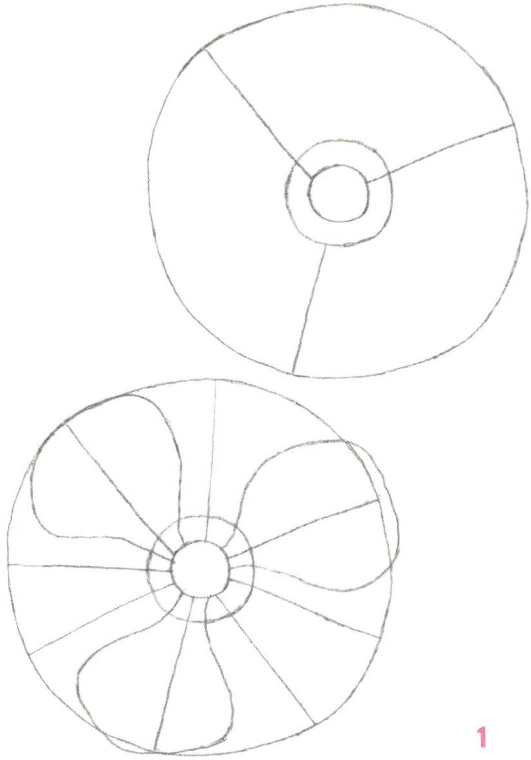

1

2. Outline the smallest central circle with a waterproof black liner. Draw small dots and short lines on the lower right side and slightly around the rest of the inner circle. On the middle circle, randomly draw small ovals of slightly different sizes and shapes. Connect some of these small ovals to the small central circle to depict the stamens. Outline the petals with smooth, slightly wavy lines. Draw thin hatches in the middle of the petals with quick hand movements for the veins. Erase the pencil.

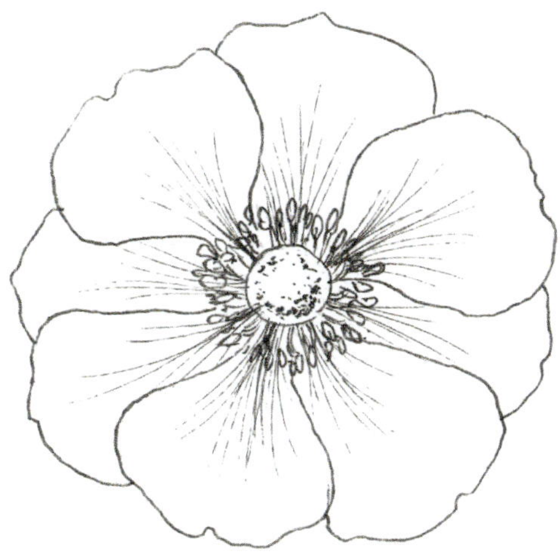

2

3. Great! Let's add some color! Prepare your watercolor palette and add a few drops of Quinacridone Rose and water to mix a light pink. Apply this color on each petal with a simple flat wash, leaving some white paper along the edges of the petals. Wait for the paint to dry completely. Mix Sap Green with a bit of Permanent Lemon Yellow on the palette. Color the center and the small ovals. Again, wait for the paper to dry.

sap green + permanent lemon yellow

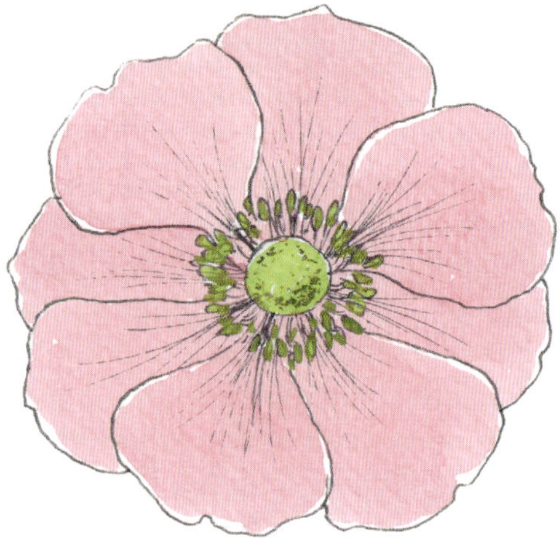

3

4. And now let's do some magic layering! Add more Quinacridone Rose to the light pink on the palette to get a medium pink shade. Paint with long, slightly curved strokes from the center of the flower to the edges of the petals, following their shape. Try not to cover the first light pink layer completely. Wait for the paint to dry. Mix Quinacridone Rose and Sap Green in equal parts and apply this color with small strokes around the outer contour of the small center circle of the flower. Then add small strokes of this color inside the central circle, close to the outline.

quinacridone rose + sap green

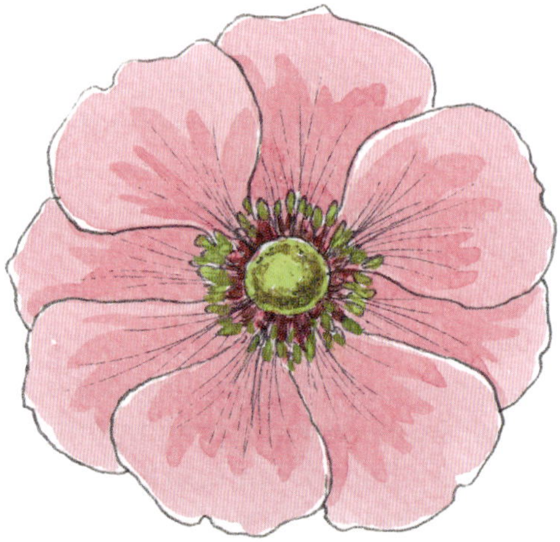

4

5. Mix Quinacridone Rose on the palette with a drop of Dioxazine Purple, then add a bit of water to lighten the mix. On the petals, make long, thin, curved strokes from the center. Leave the previous layers as they are, painting from the center of the petals. Well done! Wait for the paint to dry. Mix Dioxazine Purple with a bit of Sap Green and paint small strokes and dots on the bottom part of the central flower circle and between the circle and the oval stamens, leaving some of the previous layers visible. Add thin lines with this color in some places along the edges of the petals to show shadow and dimension.

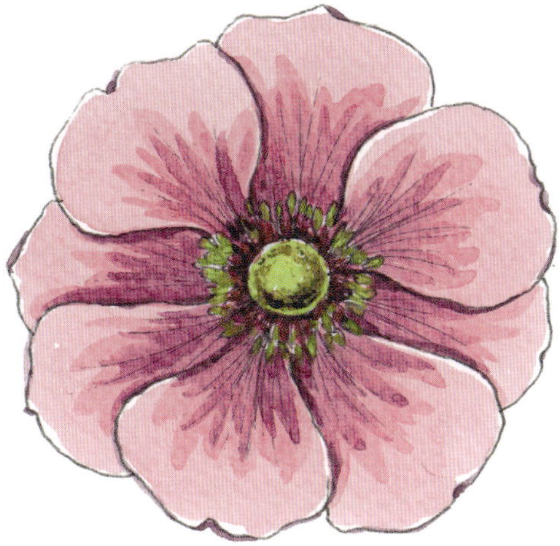

5

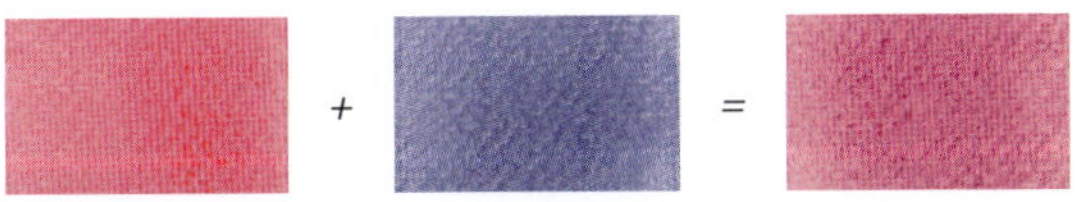

quinacridone rose + dioxazine purple

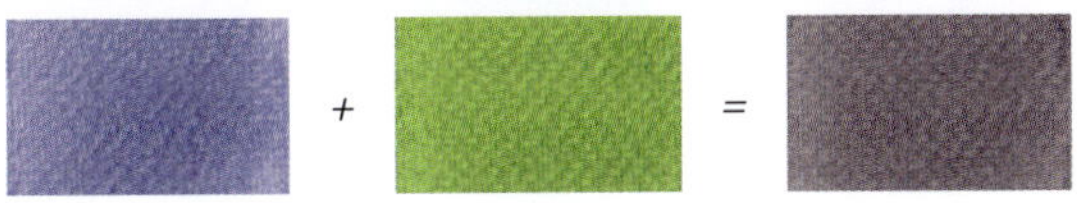

dioxazine purple + sap green

6. When the paper is dry, use the black liner to outline parts of the stamens, adding bolder lines on one side. Also add smooth lines in random places along the petal edges. With a white gel pen, randomly place dots on top of the flower's center. Draw dots and short lines around the contour of the small circle. Randomly add short, detached lines to the stamen lines and small dots to the stamen ovals. Along the inner contour of the petals, draw white lines that vary in weight. Great! Finally, draw long hatches from the outer edges of the petals toward the center of the flower.

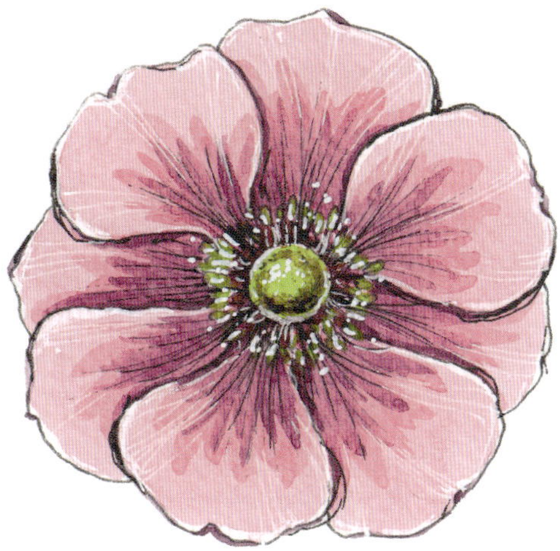

6

Excellent work! Our sketch is ready!

Lesson 5. Raspberry Berry Bliss

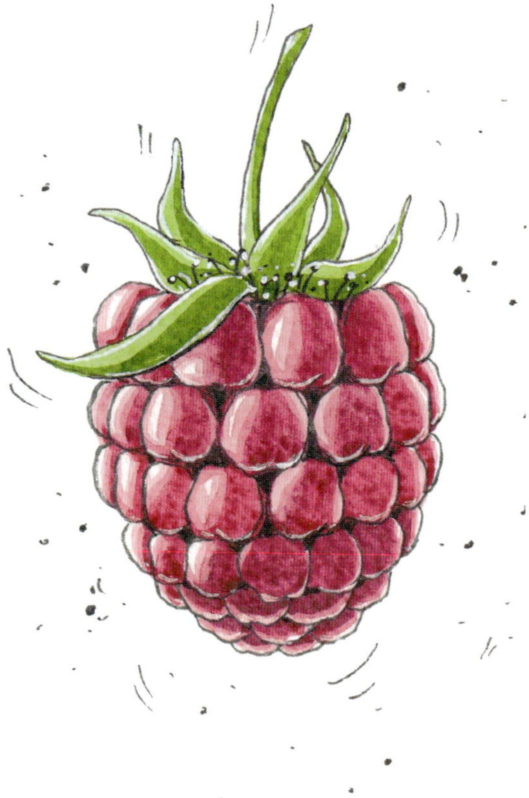

In this lesson, we're drawing a sweet and juicy raspberry as a reminder of the warm and sunny summer! We'll use only two colors, making it easy to focus on enhancing your technique. We'll develop our watercolor skills by combining simple watercolor wash and glazing techniques. You will continue to learn how to create dimension and add new decorative elements to the background, which will turn your work into a unique piece of art. Grab your brushes, and let's go forward with this creative adventure!

Paint Colors

Quinacridone Rose

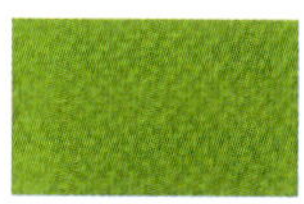

Sap Green

1. In the center of your paper, draw an oval droplet shape that is wider toward the top. Divide this shape into five roughly equal rows with curved lines. Divide the very bottom row in half again. Now draw the drupelets of the raspberry as ovals slightly overlapping each other. Draw larger ovals at the top and gradually make them smaller as you move downward and overlap them more like scales toward the lower rows. From the center top, draw a slightly curved line for the stem. Then draw six curved lines in different directions from that center area. Add second curved lines to them, making sharp tips and a wider base. Great! That is how we are going to show the leaves.

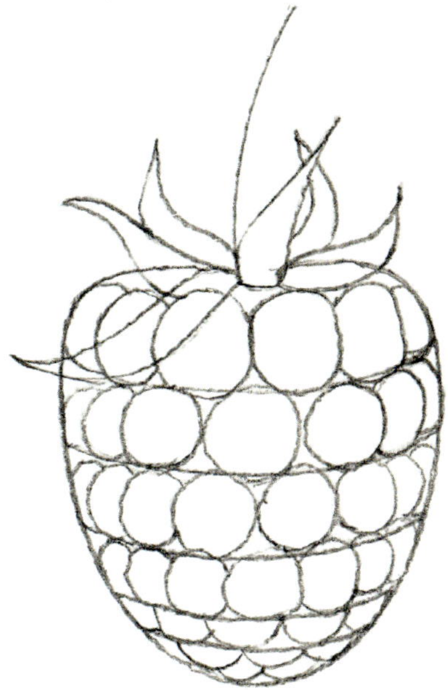

1

2. Mark the outline of the leaves with a waterproof black liner, making some of them overlap others. Add thickness to the stem by drawing one additional line next to the first one. Then outline the raspberry drupelets with an irregular and uneven contour, adding some inner bottom lines on central ones. Note that some drupelets overlap others. In the central part of the raspberry, you will have small triangular spaces between the drupelets. Great! That's just exactly what we need! Color these spaces with the black liner. Erase the pencil.

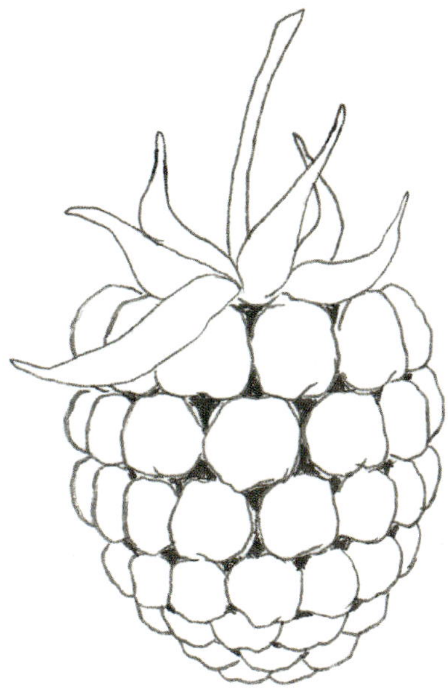

2

3. Dilute Quinacridone Rose with some water to get a light pink shade. Use this color to paint the raspberry. Leave spots of white paper on the top left of the left-side drupelets and a thin line of white paper along the contours of the drupelets on the right side of the raspberry. Mix the Sap Green with water to get a lighter shade. Paint the leaves and the raspberry stem with this color. Perfect! The first layer is done!

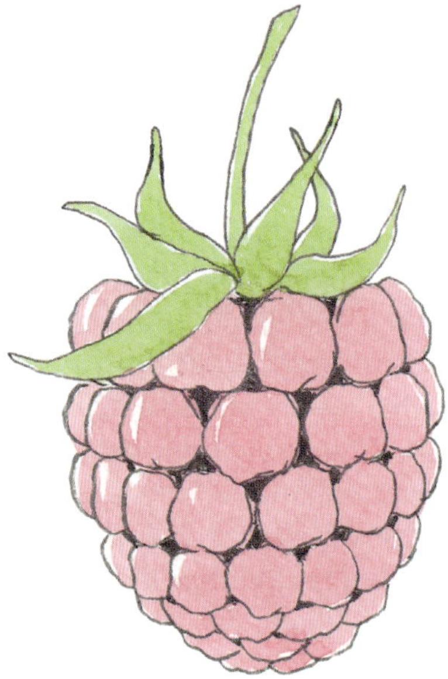

3

4. When the paper is dry, add more Quinacridone Rose to the light pink on the palette to get a medium pink shade. Paint the drupelets of the raspberry, leaving small areas of light pink on the edges of the drupelets and near the spot of white paper. Apply a second layer of Sap Green to the leaves and the raspberry stem, leaving areas of light green as well. At this stage, we're painting the second layer but leaving spots of the first layer of watercolor visible to create dimension.

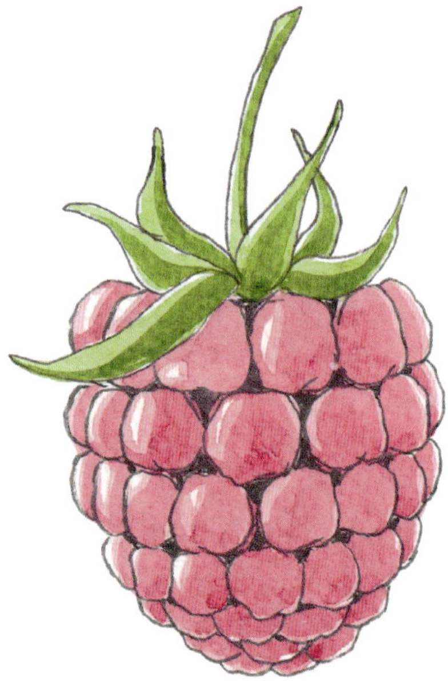

4

5. Wait again for the paper to dry, and then apply a third layer to the raspberry drupelets with a deeper pink by using less water, also leaving some spots of the first two layers visible. This is how glazing works! We are making this raspberry look more dimensional by simply painting one layer on top of another. That's true magic!

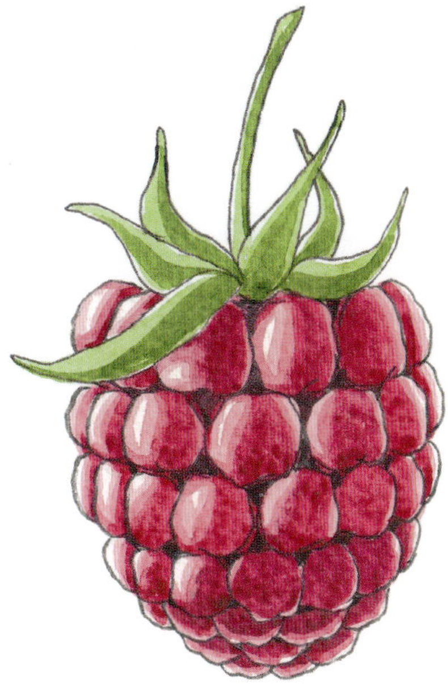

5

6. Once the paint has dried, use a black liner to draw small tendrils with a dot on top in different directions right above the raspberry leaves. Also add random curved lines and dots around the berry. Use a white gel pen to add a few light tendrils over the black ones, then draw curved lines along the bottom contour of some drupelets.

Wonderful! Our sketch is ready!

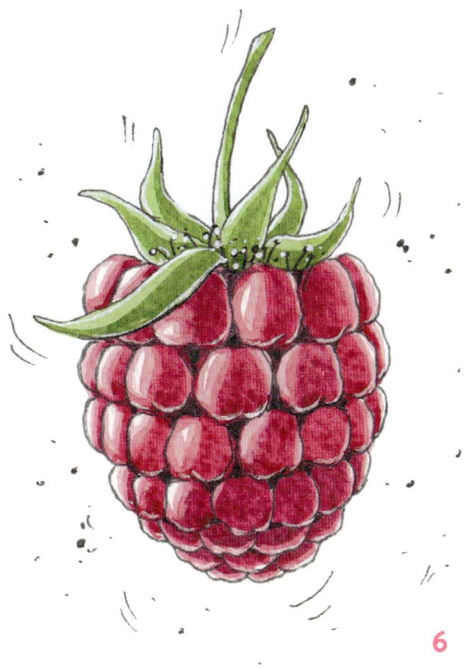

6

Lesson 6. Sailing into Colors

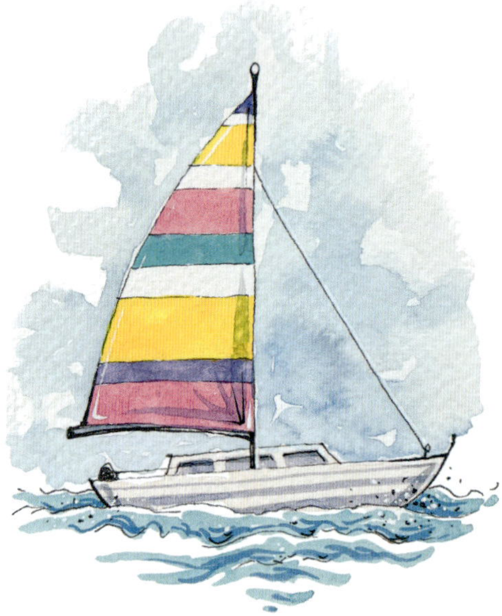

Let's go on a sea journey sailing the waves of inspiration! In this lesson, we will draw and paint a vibrant sailboat on the water, featuring a beautiful combination of colors and shades for the sail. We'll learn how to depict shimmering waves, water splashes and light, airy clouds. So, let's begin!

Paint Colors

- Cerulean Blue
- Phthalo Green
- Azo Yellow Medium
- Quinacridone Rose
- Dioxazine Purple
- Yellow Ochre
- Ultramarine Deep
- Burnt Umber

1. Draw a horizontal line with a pencil slightly lower than the paper's center; this will be the waterline. Above that line, draw a shorter line with a slight tilt to the left and downward. Connect the ends of this line with curved lines to the waterline on both sides to finish the boat. Above that, draw a trapezoid shape for the boat's cabin. From the center of the boat, draw a vertical line upward for the mast, then a horizontal line at the bottom of the mast. Connect the horizontal line to the top of the mast with an arc-shaped line to show the sail. Draw horizontal lines on the sail. Then draw a slanted line connecting the mast of the sailboat to the bow of the boat.

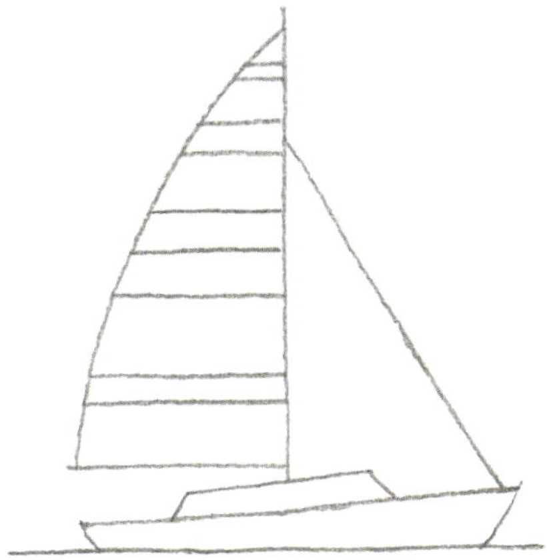

1

2. Use a waterproof black liner to draw several horizontal wavy lines to show the surface of the water. Start by using the first horizontal line you drew in the previous step as a guide to make your base waterline. Also, add wave lines from the sides of the boat (but not higher than it) and shorter wavy lines below the boat. Then outline the boat. Add small details to the mast and the bow of the boat in the form of lines and ovals. Draw a small semicircle at the back of the boat and color it in with the liner. Draw a line from the semicircle to the mast. Add thickness to the bottom of the sail with a heavier line. Great! You are doing well! Erase the pencil.

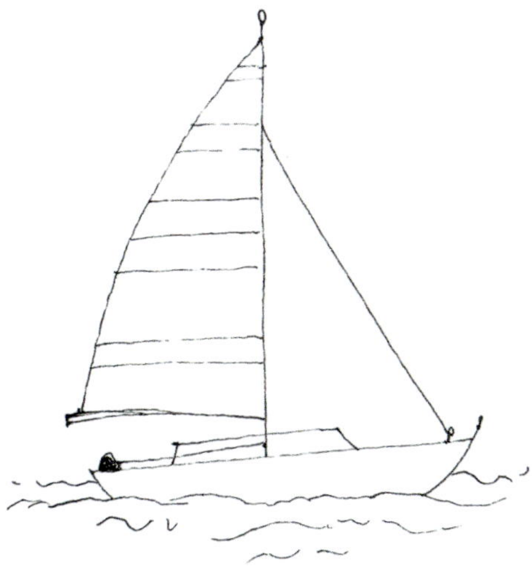

2

3. Mix Cerulean Blue and Phthalo Green in equal parts on the palette to get turquoise. Paint one of the stripes on the sail with this color. Add water to the turquoise to lighten the shade. With light turquoise, paint wavy lines on the water just below the liner lines, leaving spots of white paper. Paint the remaining sailboat stripes with Azo Yellow Medium, Quinacridone Rose and Dioxazine Purple (or any other colors you like), but remember to leave a few of them white. Mix Yellow Ochre and water to get a light beige color. The shade should be very light. Paint the entire boat with this color. Wait for the paint to be completely dry before moving on.

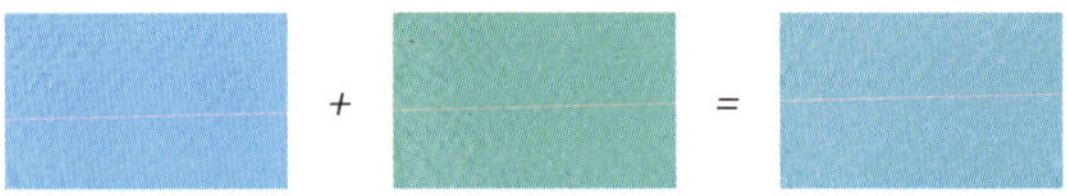

cerulean blue + phthalo green

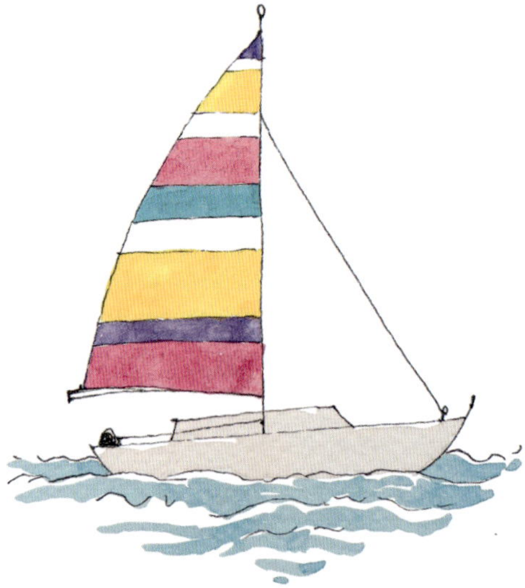

3

4. Use Cerulean Blue to paint thin, wavy lines over the turquoise waves, trying not to cover the white spots. Then dilute Cerulean Blue with water to get a lighter blue. Using this color, paint the sky with large strokes, occasionally adding water directly to the paint on the paper and leaving some areas unpainted. Mix Ultramarine Deep and Burnt Umber in equal parts on the palette and add water to get a light shade of gray. With this color, paint horizontal stripes of various thicknesses on the boat. Also paint three trapezoid-shaped windows on the cabin of the boat. Add shadows to the sail with thin paint lines along the mast and at the bottom with the same color. Perfect! Let's wait for the paint to dry. Then, with the same gray color, add shadow lines at the bow and the back part of the boat. Also add shadow lines at the top of the cabin windows.

ultramarine deep + burnt umber

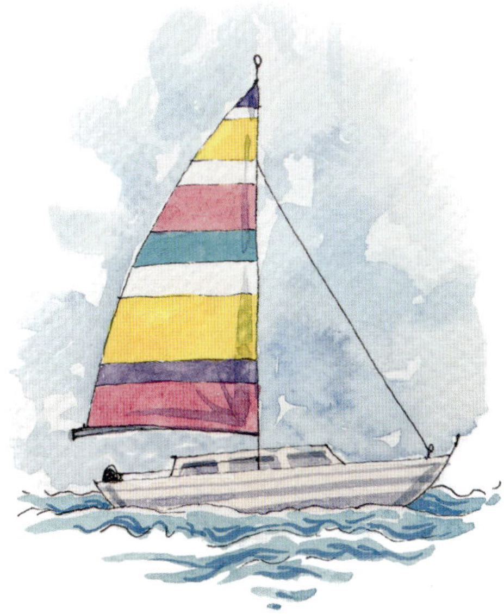

4

5. With your black liner, randomly draw water splashes using dots at the front and back of the boat. Draw semi-oval lines above the wave lines. Make the lines bolder at the bottom of the mast, at its top and under the sail. Add shadow hatches to the bottom right of the sail. Add lines to the windows. Darken the outlines of the bow and stern. With a white gel pen, add random dots to the splashes you made with your black liner. Draw a white line above the slanted line from the mast to the bow of the boat. Add white lines and hatches to the sail along the contour.

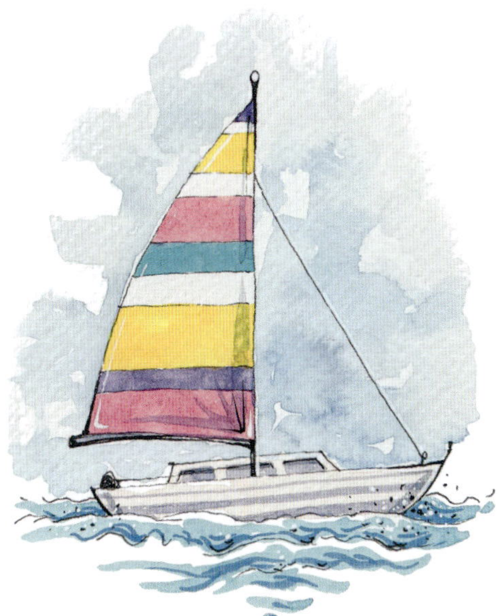

5

Well done! Our sketch is ready!

Lesson 7. It's Teatime!

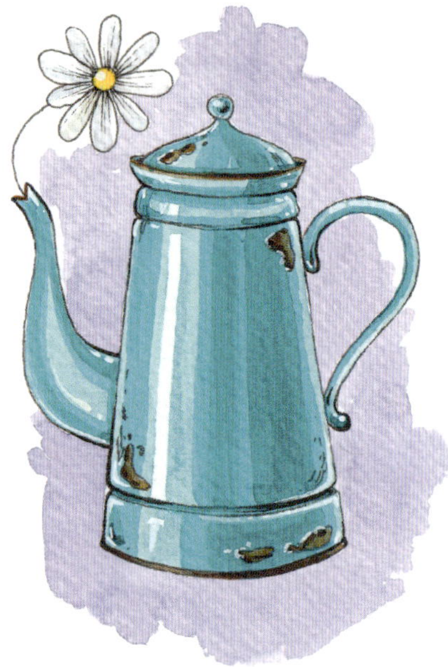

Let's capture the warmth of teatime moments by drawing an old vintage teapot! Continuing our practice with glazes, you'll learn to master the texture of shiny metal and how to create a vintage look by adding chips. We're embarking on a journey into a world of warmth, aromas and stories captured in each brushstroke.

Paint Colors

Cerulean Blue

Phthalo Green

Azo Yellow Medium

Ultramarine Deep

Burnt Umber

Dioxazine Purple

Yellow Ochre

1. Draw a vertical line in the center of your paper; this will be the central axis of our teapot. Draw a symmetrical, vertically extended trapezoid narrowing upward, with the axis line in the center. Draw one horizontal line at the top of the trapezoid and two lines at the bottom. At the top of the trapezoid, draw a small inverted trapezoid facing upward. Draw a small regular triangle on its top. At the top of the triangle, draw a small circle. Great! Then draw a smooth curved line for the teapot's spout on the left side of the large trapezoid. Add another curved line to show the thickness of the spout, making it wider at the base and narrower toward the end. On the right side, draw a smooth curved line for the handle. Add thickness by drawing another line next to it. Draw semi-oval lines on each horizontal line. From the teapot's spout, draw a line that curves upward. Then draw a circle at the end of the line and droplet-like petals from the center. Great! This will be a cute daisy flower.

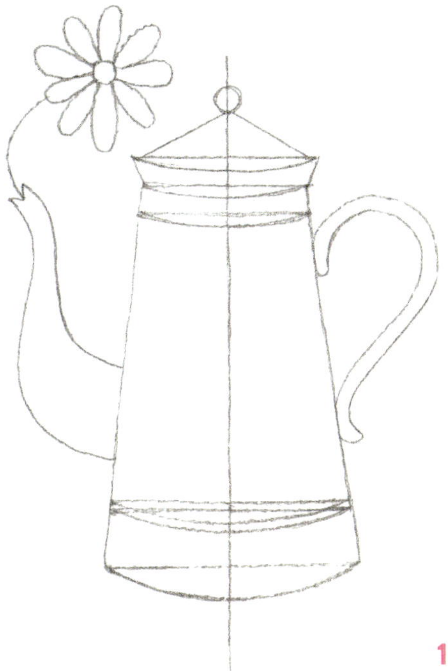

1

2. Outline the teapot with a waterproof black liner. Make the side lines of the teapot lid more curved. Add rounded edges at the semi-oval lines at the top and bottom of the teapot. Draw small, irregularly shaped areas of various sizes on the teapot in different places. Add short lines and dots to give the teapot a vintage look and show chipped spots. Outline the daisy. Erase the pencil.

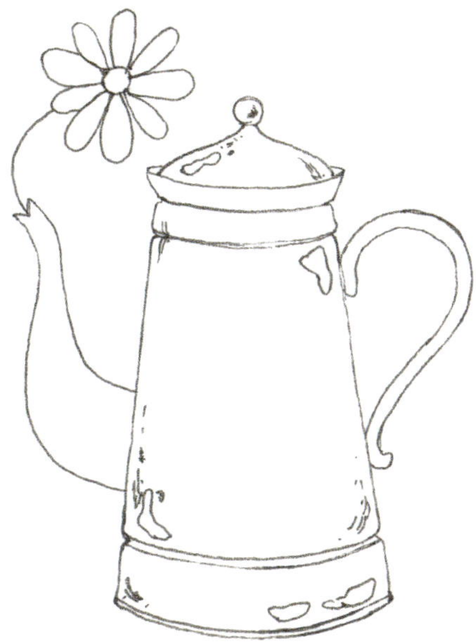

2

3. Mix Cerulean Blue and Phthalo Green in equal parts to get turquoise. Add water to the turquoise to lighten the shade. Paint the teapot with a simple flat wash, leaving a white highlight stripe on the left side. Paint the daisy's center with Azo Yellow Medium. Wait for everything to dry. Mix Ultramarine Deep and Burnt Umber in equal parts and add water to get a very light shade. Loosely paint the daisy petals. Mix Dioxazine Purple with water to get a light purple. Paint the background in a spontaneous shape around the teapot with this color. Perfect! Now wait for the paint to dry.

cerulean blue + phthalo green

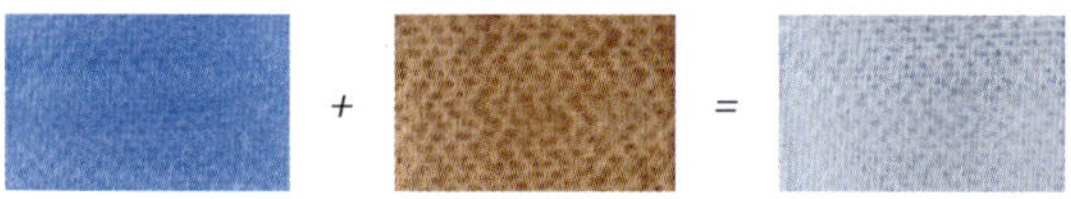

ultramarine deep + burnt umber

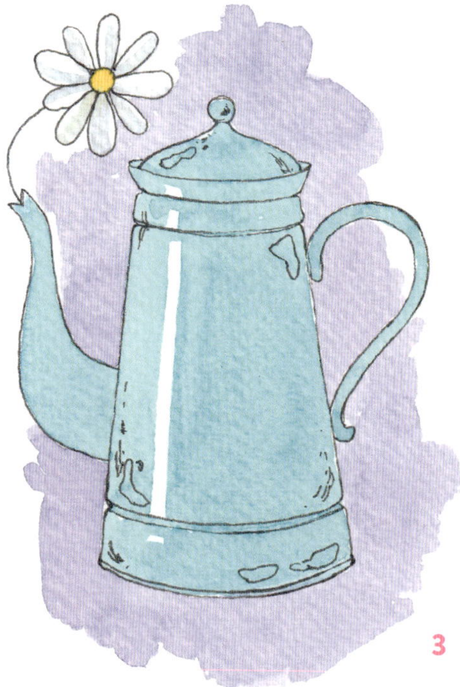

3

4. Let's create some magic with layering! Mix a darker shade of turquoise by using less water and paint a second layer, but leave the middle area on the spout and some space to the left and right side of the white stripe alone. Also leave a line of the first layer visible on the outside contour of the handle and a few areas on the top and bottom curves of the teapot. Wait for the paint to dry. Color the chipped areas with Yellow Ochre and then add small, random strokes with Burnt Umber over the Yellow Ochre. Then use the same colors for the spout's opening and the top and bottom semi-oval lines of the teapot.

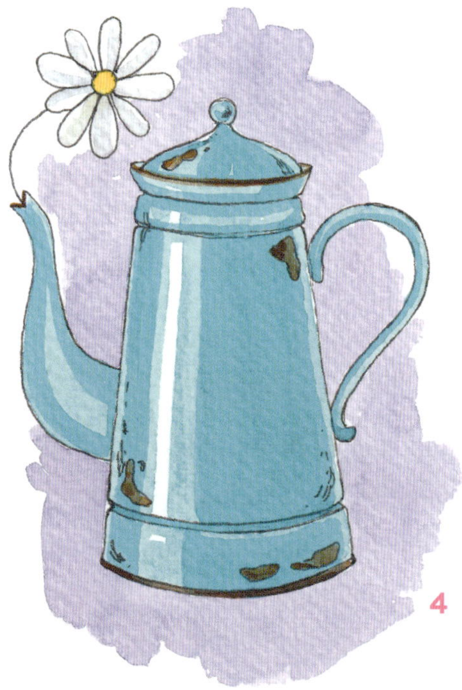

4

5. When the paint is dry, mix turquoise, but a slightly deeper shade by adding more paint and less water. Paint a third layer on the teapot with long, vertical extended stripes following its shape, leaving areas of the previous layers visible. When the paper is dry, use Burnt Umber and add random small strokes to the chipped areas and the semi-oval lines.

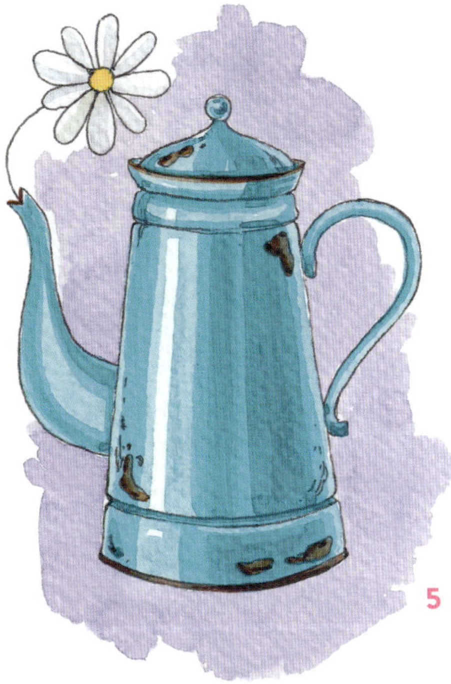

5

6. With the black liner, add thickness to the curves following the teapot's shape, especially at the bottom, as well as on the spout and handle. Make thin hatches from the center to the petals of the daisy to add volume and show veins. With a white gel pen, add highlights to the curves following the teapot's shape. Be sure to add semi-oval lines at the bottom near the base, on the spout and on the handle. Add small light areas, lines and dots to the left side of each chip.

Amazing! Our sketch is ready!

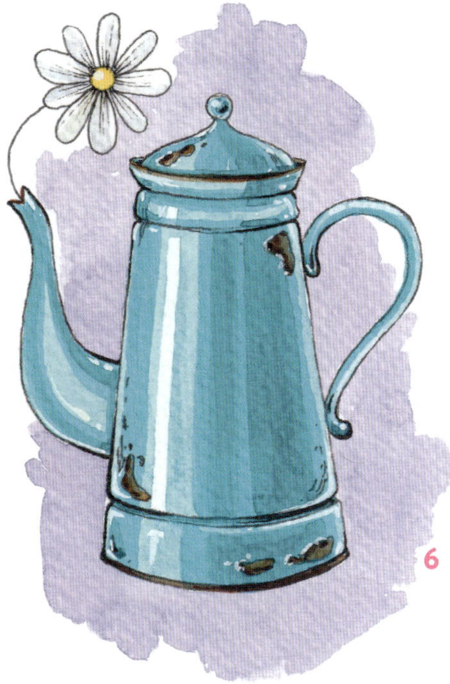

6

Lesson 8. Coffee Journeys

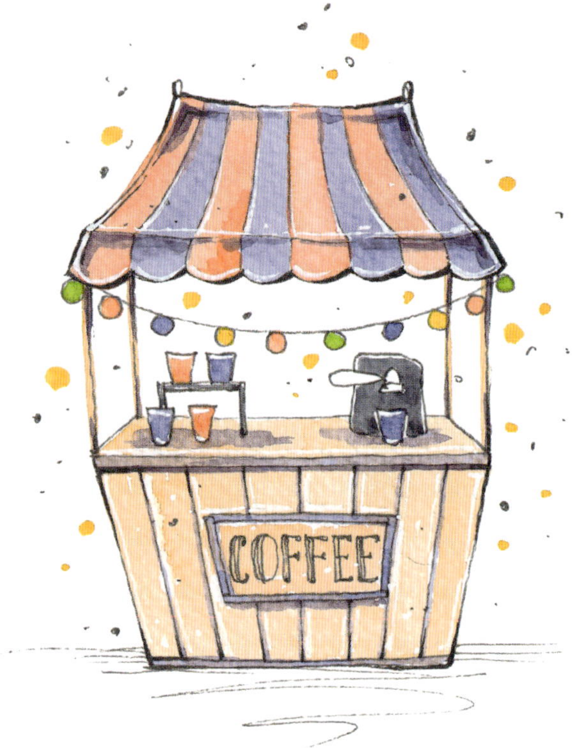

Get inspired with the aroma of freshly brewed coffee as you paint a vibrant and cozy coffee shop. We'll explore how simple geometric shapes gain dimension and how regular lines add a sense of ease and uniqueness to the story. In this lesson, you'll master playing with forms and shades and creating layers of watercolor that will bring every detail to life, from coffee cups to delicate garlands. Let each brushstroke be filled with warmth and coziness, just like a cup of morning coffee. Let's begin!

Paint Colors

- Yellow Ochre
- Quinacridone Rose
- Dioxazine Purple
- Azo Yellow Medium
- Sap Green
- Ultramarine Deep
- Burnt Umber

1. In the lower half of the paper, draw a regular trapezoid that is wider toward the top with a pencil. Draw a small trapezoid in its center; this will be the shop counter. Add a duplicate line inside to create a frame and write "COFFEE" inside it. On the larger trapezoid, draw a flatter trapezoid that narrows upward. Draw a new trapezoid, narrowing upward, about 1.5 inches (4 cm) above the base of the coffee shop. Then draw a narrow, flattened trapezoid in its lower part; this will be the awning over the counter. Perfect! Now from the corners of the lower narrow trapezoid, draw four vertical lines up to the upper trapezoid. Don't worry if your trapezoids are a bit crooked; you are doing great! This will add uniqueness and charm to your sketch.

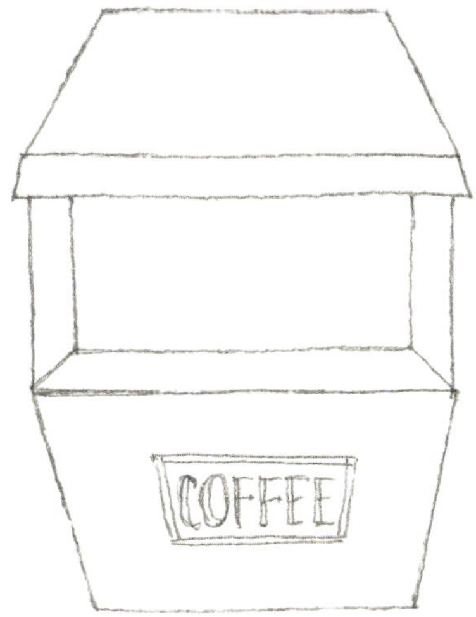

1

2. Make the side and horizontal lines of the upper trapezoid curved. Now, we're going to draw several stripes on the awning. To make it easy, first draw a line in the middle, then also draw lines in the middle of the left and right parts. Finally, divide the remaining parts in half again. Draw stripes on the lower counter in a similar manner.

Add scallops at the lower edge of the stripes on the awning. Draw a half oval-shaped garland line from the left edge of the awning to the right and randomly add circles along the garland's length. Draw a small rectangle on the counter on the right (a coffee machine), a slightly smaller rectangle on the left (a shelf) and several trapezoidal cups in various places.

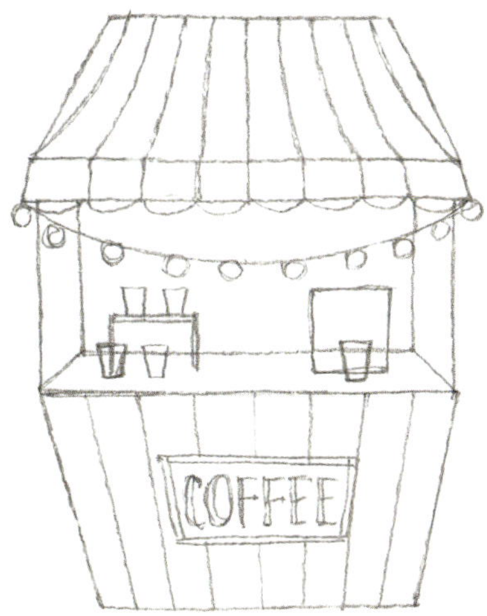

2

3. Outline the coffee shop with a waterproof black liner using thin, loose lines. Add two small ovals on top of the awning. Draw the handle on the coffee machine and then outline the machine, giving it round corners. Next, outline the cups and shelf. Draw one horizontal line at the bottom and top of the counter, then outline the sign frame and vertical stripes on the counter. At the bottom, draw thin, crooked horizontal lines and a couple of quick hatches under the counter. Put dots and small comma-like lines around the coffee shop background. Perfect! Erase the pencil.

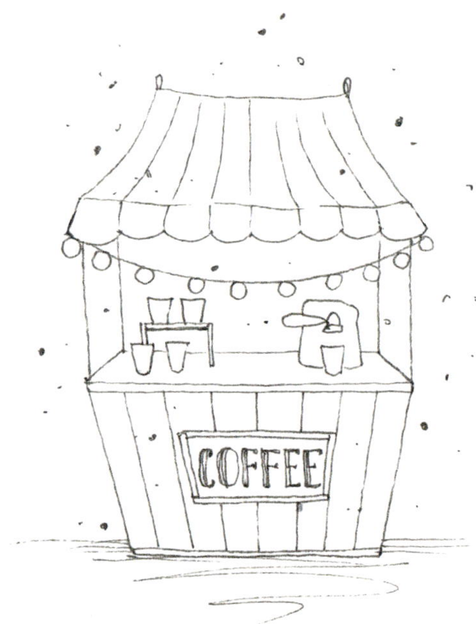

3

4. Mix Yellow Ochre with water on the palette to get a light ochre color. Paint the entire counter and sign with this color. Paint thin strokes along the vertical posts of the awning. To the light ochre, add a couple of drops of Yellow Ochre and Quinacridone Rose in equal proportions to get a light orange color. Use this color to paint some stripes on the awning. Also paint some of the garland bulbs and cups with this color. You are doing great! Now wait for the paper to dry. Mix water with Dioxazine Purple to get a light purple and paint the remaining stripes on the awning, horizontal and vertical stripes on the counter, the frame around the sign, cups and a few garland bulbs. Use Azo Yellow Medium along with Sap Green mixed with water to paint the remaining garland bulbs.

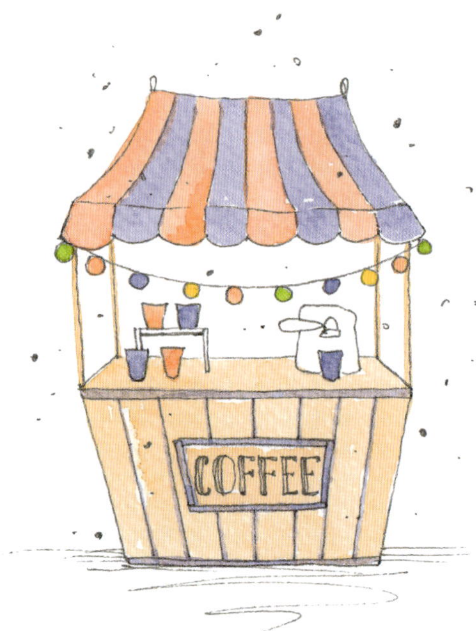

4

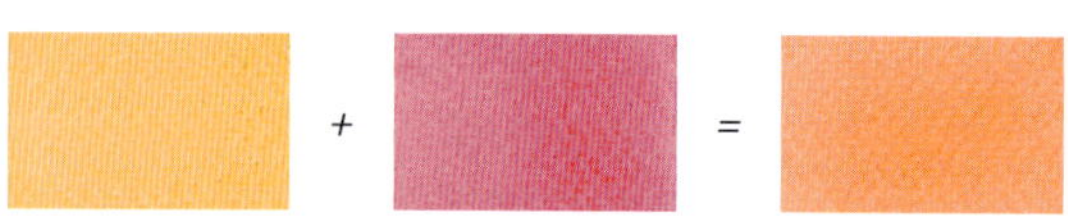

yellow ochre + quinacridone rose

5. When the paper is dry, mix Ultramarine Deep with Burnt Umber in equal proportions to get a gray shade. Paint the coffee machine with this color, leaving white contour areas, and the shelf on the counter. Use Dioxazine Purple to paint shadow lines on the awning, at the bottom and top of the awning rails and underneath the coffee machine and shelf. Paint small, loose dots with Azo Yellow Medium around the coffee shop background.

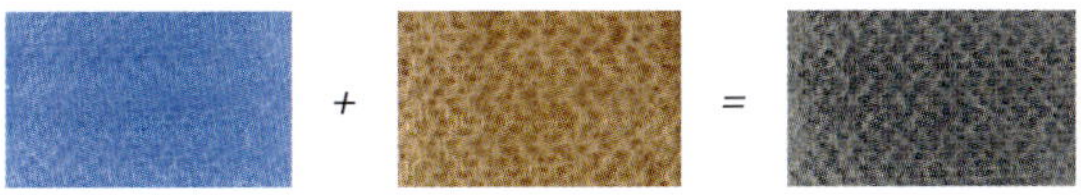

ultramarine deep + burnt umber

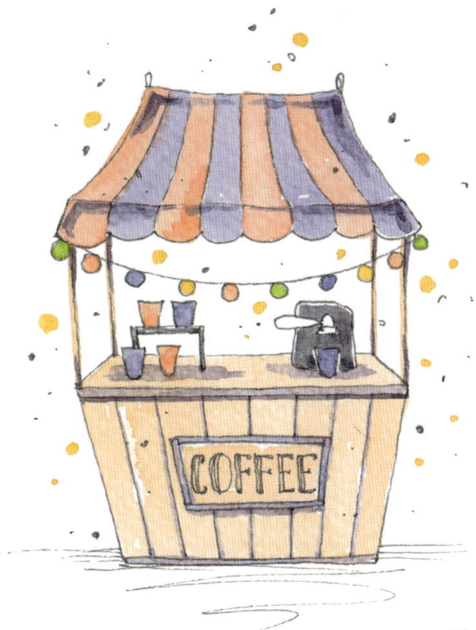

5

6. With the waterproof black liner, draw shadows at the bottom of the awning's rounded edges, and at the corners at the bottom and at the top. Also darken the counter corners. With a white gel pen, add lines along the stripes on the awning and semi-oval lines on the awning's rounded edges. Add white stripes and dots to the cups. Outline the sign on the outside and add lines next to the black vertical lines on the counter. Add a horizontal white line on top of the counter's edge.

This project has so many details, but I'm sure you did a great job! Our sketch is ready!

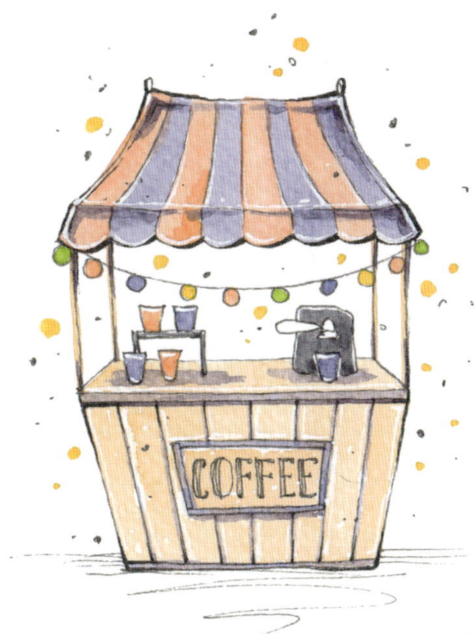

6

Lesson 9. Window Floral Bloom

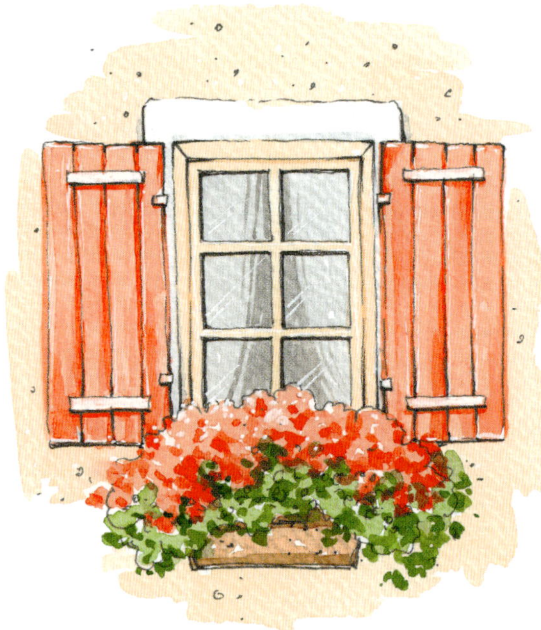

Get inspired by the beauty of simple moments, painting a bright and cozy watercolor window! Discover how pencil lines, liner and layers of watercolor can transform simple shapes into a vibrant sketch of a warm, homey atmosphere. You'll learn to draw vivid blooming flowers, wooden shutters and shiny glass. Prepare your paints and brushes and let's begin!

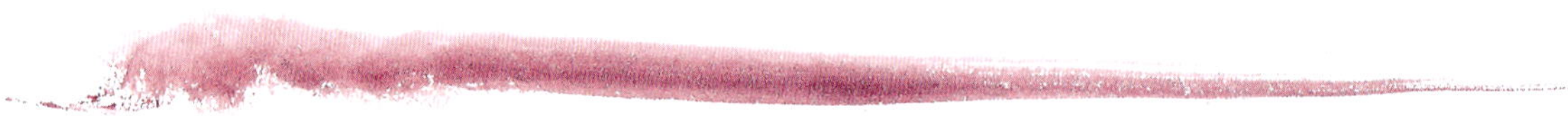

Paint Colors

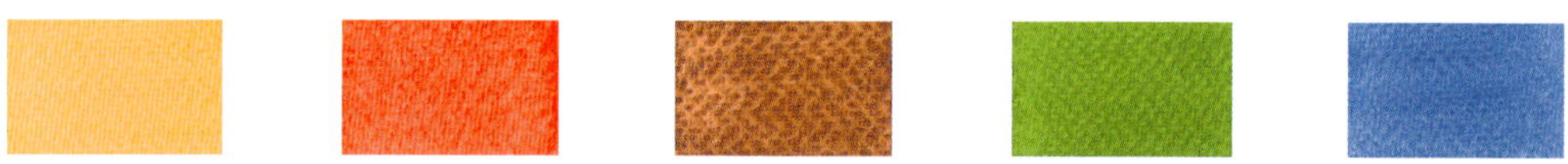

Yellow Ochre	Permanent Red Light	Burnt Sienna	Sap Green	Ultramarine Deep

1. Draw a rectangle in the center of the paper. Draw another rectangle slightly smaller inside it. Connect the corners of the rectangles with diagonal lines. Draw a third rectangle inside the second one. So, now we have three rectangles, one inside another. Great! Then divide the small one vertically into two equal parts and then horizontally into three equal parts. Draw additional lines next to the vertical and horizontal lines to create a window frame. Add two rectangles to the right and left, slightly away from the window; these are the shutters. Draw stripes for the wooden panels on each shutter and rectangles connecting the panels on the top and bottom of each shutter. Below the window draw a small horizontal trapezoid widening upward. With wavy, curly and cloud-like lines, draw flowers and foliage, overlapping the trapezoid and the window a bit. Draw a frame above the window. It's fine if your lines are not like mine; they can be a bit slanted or crooked.

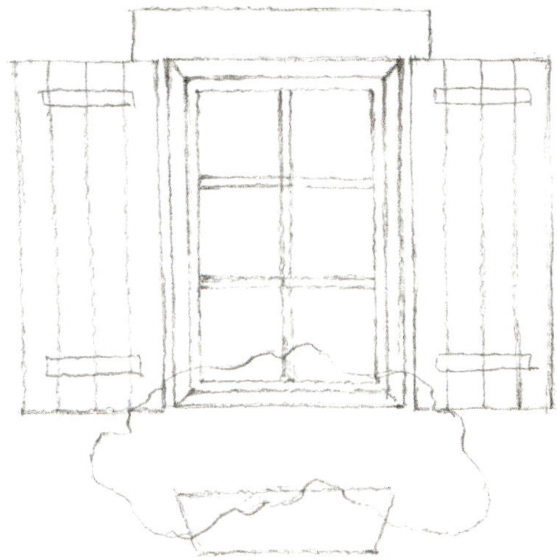

1

2. Use a waterproof black liner to outline the flowers and foliage with wavy, curly and occasionally broken lines. Randomly add small dots, lines and circles at the bottom of the foliage to show blooming flowers and greenery. Draw the shutters' attachments to the window as small rectangles. Using slightly uneven, broken lines, outline the window, shutters, frame and flower box. Draw small dots, comma-like lines and circles around the window. Erase the pencil drawing.

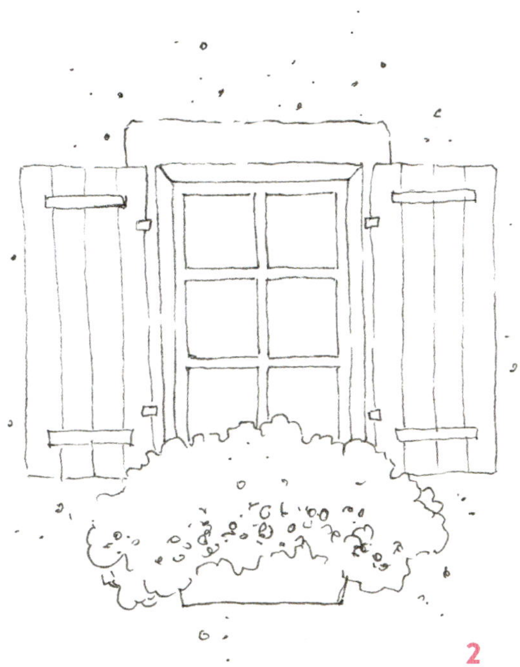

2

3. Mix Yellow Ochre with water to get a light ochre color, then paint the window frame. With broad strokes, paint the background around the window in a spontaneous shape with the same color. Wait for the paint to dry. Mix Permanent Red Light with water to get a light red. Paint the shutters, avoiding the attachments. Add a couple of drops of Permanent Red Light to the light red to make the color darker. With small strokes, paint the upper part of the flowers, leaving some white paper. Dilute Burnt Sienna slightly with water and use it to paint the flower box. After the paint dries, dilute Sap Green slightly with water and use it to paint the foliage below the flowers with small strokes.

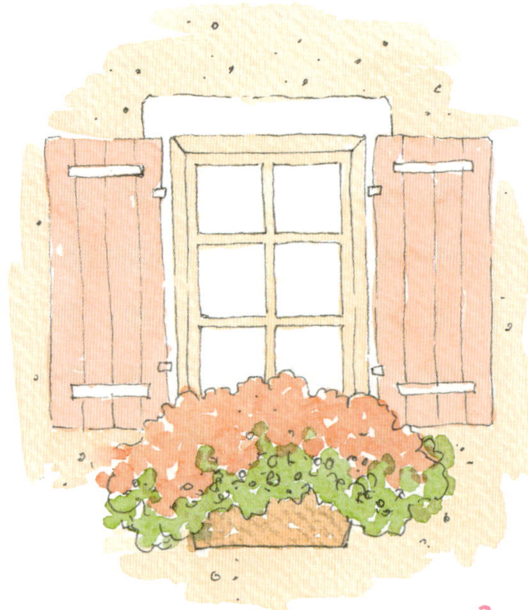

3

4. Mix equal parts Ultramarine Deep and Burnt Sienna and dilute with water to get a light gray color. Paint the window glass. With the same color, paint small, thin shadow strokes around the window frame. Use a medium tone of Burnt Sienna to paint along the window frame's contour and add shadows to the flower box. With a darker shade of Permanent Red Light, paint the lower part of the flowers with small strokes, leaving spots of the previous layer visible. Dilute this color slightly with water and then paint the shutters' wooden panels, leaving vertical lines of the previous layer visible at the panel joints. Use a dark shade of Sap Green to make small, spontaneous strokes on the foliage below the flowers. Amazing!

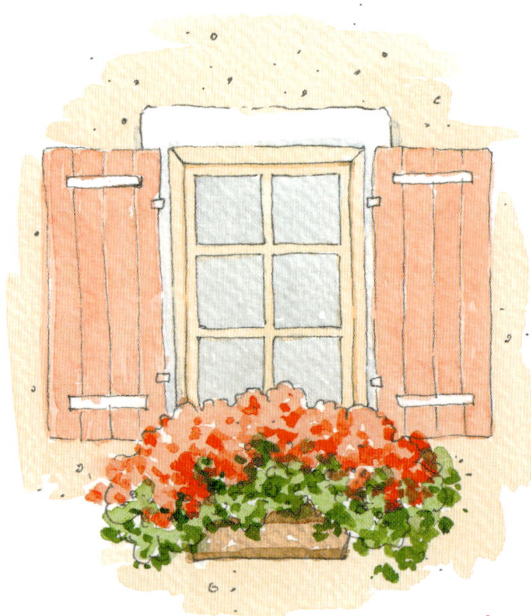

4

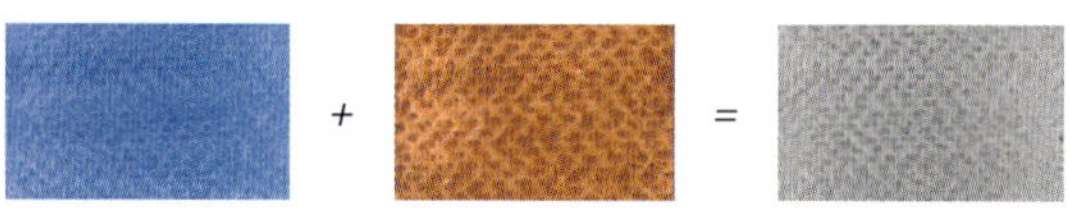

ultramarine deep + burnt sienna

5. Add a bit more paint to the gray color from the previous step and paint curved lines on the window glass from the top downward and to the sides. Fill the area between these lines in the middle to show curtains. With a dark shade of Permanent Red Light, paint thin lines on the shutter panels next to the light lines left earlier. It's okay if you slightly cover them as well. Add shadow lines under the shutters' attachments with the same color. Use various shades of red to randomly paint vertical strokes on different parts of the shutter panels. Great! This will help add texture and volume.

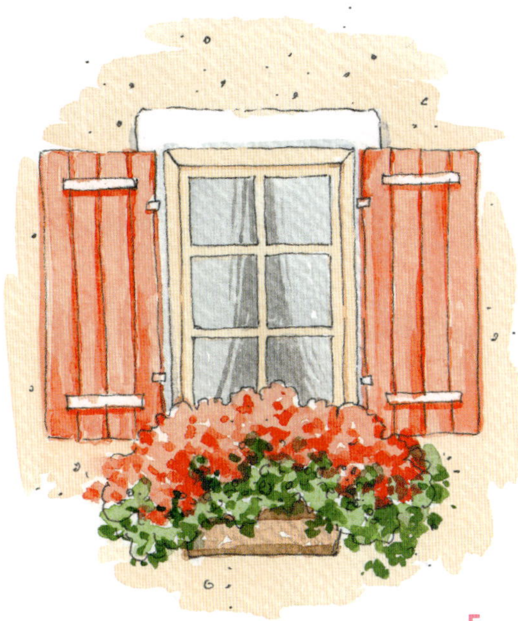

5

6. With the black liner, add shadows to the corners of the window frame, the bottom and top of the shutters and the bottom of the flower box. Inside the frame, where the glass is, add bolder outlines on the top and left sides. Using a white gel pen and moving quickly with your hand, draw two diagonal hatches on each pane of glass. Add white lines at the joints of the shutter panels and also at the bottom and top of these panels. Randomly add small dots to the upper part of the flowers. Draw a few dots spontaneously on the background as well.

Great job! Our sketch is ready!

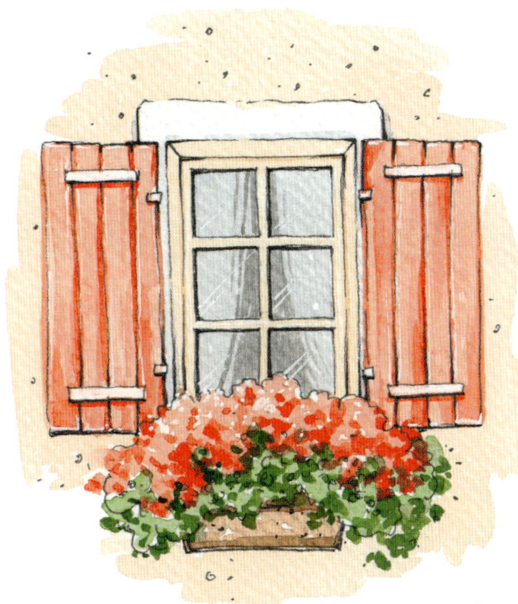

6

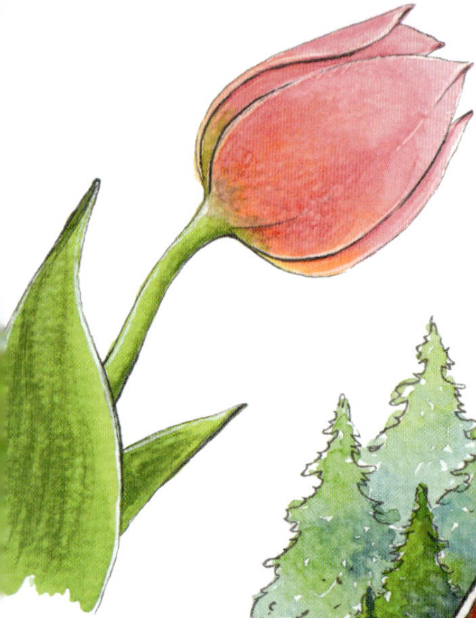
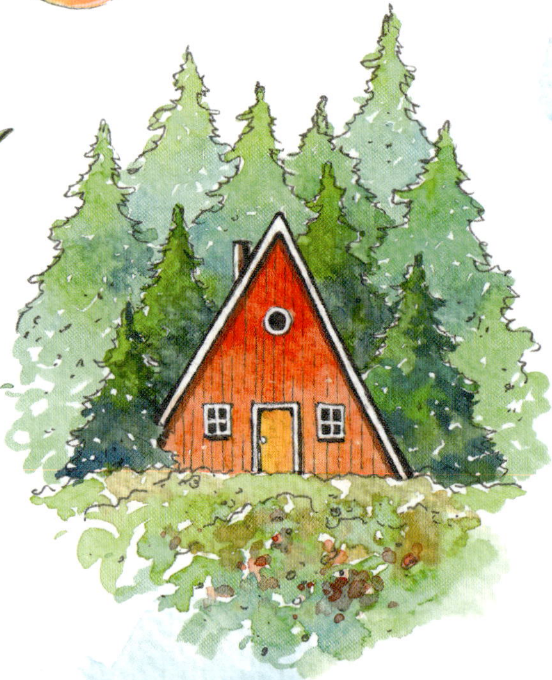
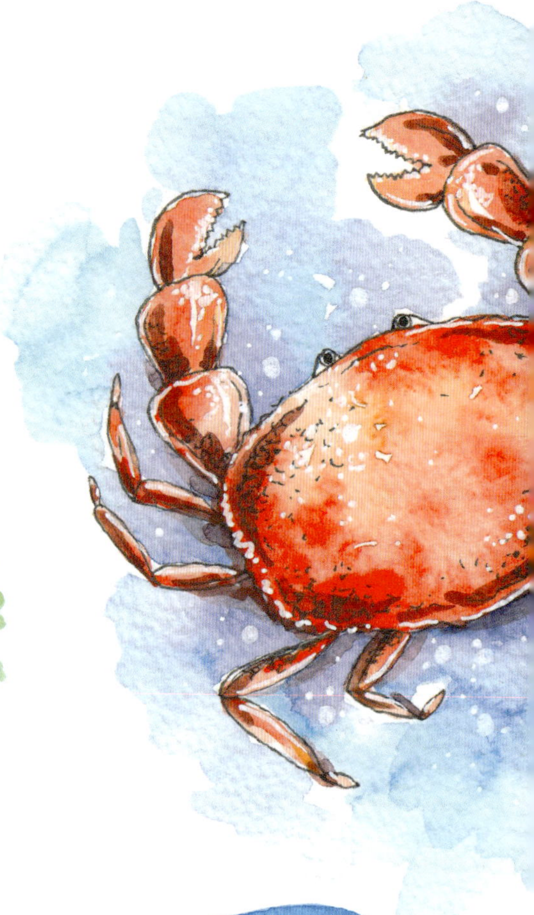
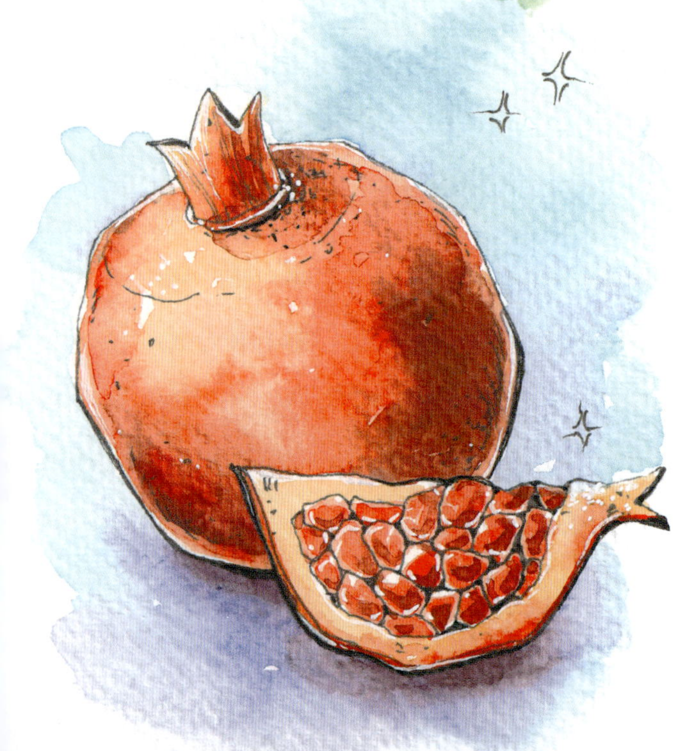
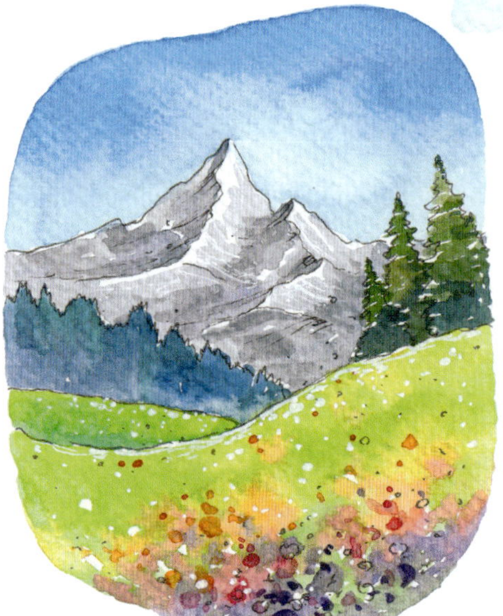

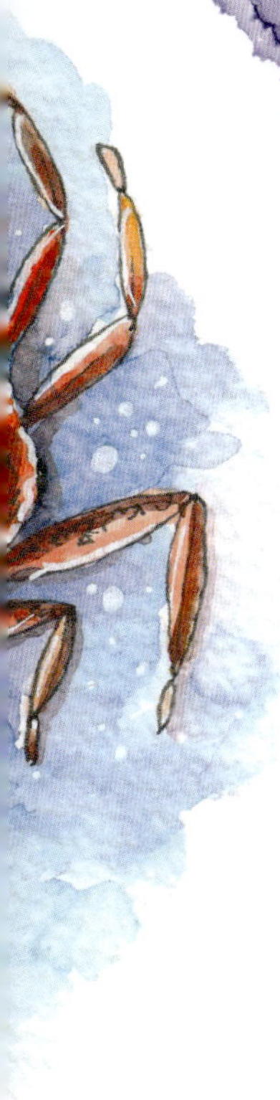

Gradients and Zigzag Lines

In this chapter, we'll continue to explore the world of watercolor magic by studying the art of creating smooth transitions from darker to lighter shades, unveiling the limitless possibilities of color gradients. We will also continue to use glazing and flat wash techniques that will make your sketches come alive in Tulip Tango (page 64) and Forest Cabin Charm (page 76). You will learn how to create soft edges that delicately show the tenderness of color and the nuances of light and shadow in Glowing Lantern Light (page 72), giving your works a picturesque and complete look. Furthermore, you will practice new types of lines and hatches, such as zigzag lines in Garden on the Go (page 84) and various background hatches, empowering you to express the dynamics and emotions in your watercolor sketches. Immerse yourself in the creative process, where each lesson opens new horizons and awakens inspiration!

Lesson 10. Tulip Tango

Experience a spring mood by painting this delicate and exquisite pink tulip. In this lesson, we will explore various shades of pink, playing with depth and intensity. You will practice the art of creating soft color transitions on the bud and leaves, and learn how to detail each petal to give your tulip realism and a three-dimensional look. So, let's begin!

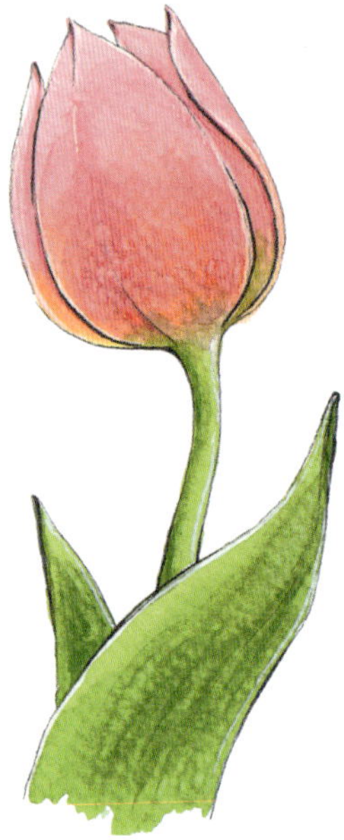

Paint Colors

Quinacridone Rose

Permanent Lemon Yellow

Sap Green

1. Use a pencil to draw an egg-shaped oval with a slight tilt to the left at the top of the paper. From the bottom of the oval, draw two identical stem lines with a slight bend to the right. Create two leaves with smooth, curved lines, making the leaf on the left smaller.

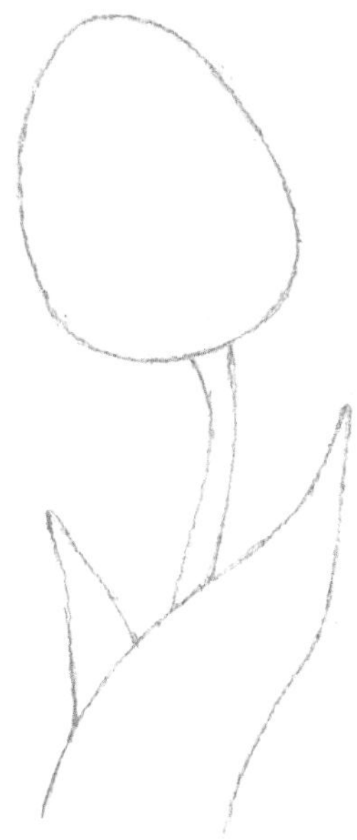

1

2. Great! Let's draw petals on the bud. On the oval, draw a large teardrop shape with a sharp tip pointing upward. Add petals on the right and left of the large petal with smooth, curved lines. Then, to the far right, make a side petal overlapping the first right petal with a smooth, curved line. Add pointed ends to the side and back petals. On the large petal, make a vein with a thin, curved line. Also, draw a vein roughly in the center of the large leaf.

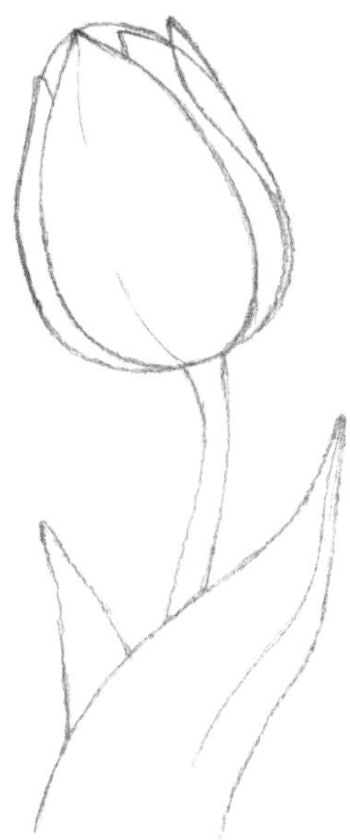

2

3. Use a black waterproof liner to outline the tulip leaves and petals with a thin, smooth line. Outline the stem with smooth lines and connect them with the lines of the bud. Draw light, curved lines with sharp endings for the veins on the petals and leaves. Perfect! Erase the pencil.

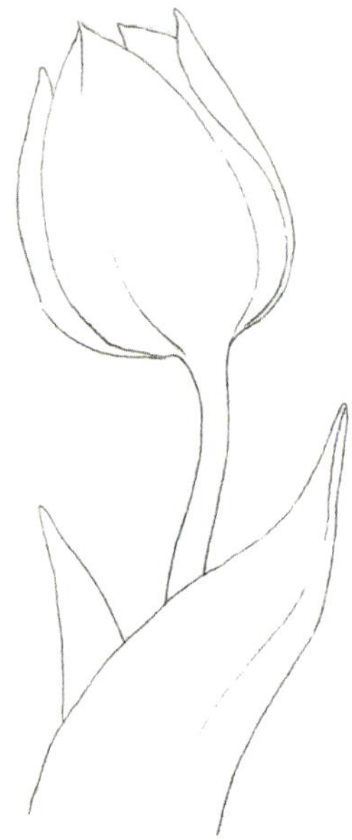

3

4. Prepare all colors on the palette in advance: Quinacridone Rose, Permanent Lemon Yellow and Sap Green. Mix each color separately with water to get light shades. We're going to color the bud and the stem in one go to create a soft transition between these colors. Starting from the top of the flower, paint a light pink flat wash down to the lower part of the bud and then immediately below it. Without waiting for it to dry, add your light yellow mix. Let the pink and the yellow mix directly on the paper. Wash the brush, pick up the light green and apply it to the stem, also allowing it to slightly mix with the yellow paint while everything is still wet. Paint the stem green to the end. The colors on the bud and on the base of the stem should flow into each other. Paint the leaves green, making the edges lighter by mixing in even more water.

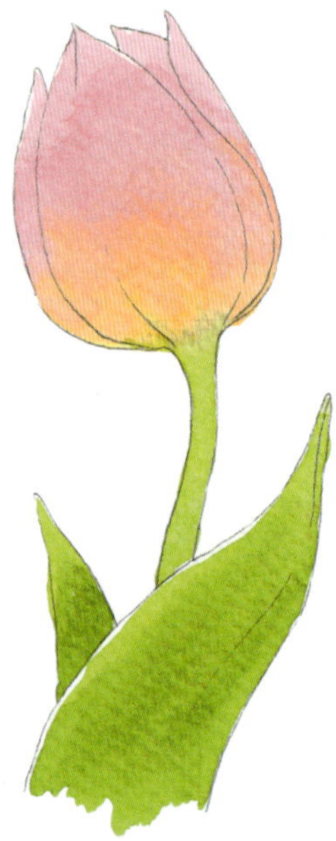

4

5. Let's create a three-dimensional effect with some soft edges. After the watercolor is completely dry, mix a darker shade of pink and apply it on the large petal, closer to the broad lower part. Rinse the brush, and with the now damp brush, blur the edges of the second layer to make them soft. Once the large petal is dry, paint the inner petal on the right, also making a soft edge at the top and a smooth transition to green at the bottom. Similarly, paint the left petal, adding Permanent Lemon Yellow at the bottom. On the far-right petal, paint the right side and make a soft edge to the left. With Sap Green, paint a line along the left side of the stem and also soften the right edge. On the leaves, apply long, curved strokes following the shape of the leaves and blur the edges with a damp brush. Add one green stroke at the tips of the leaves and pink at the tips of the petals. Wait for everything to be completely dry.

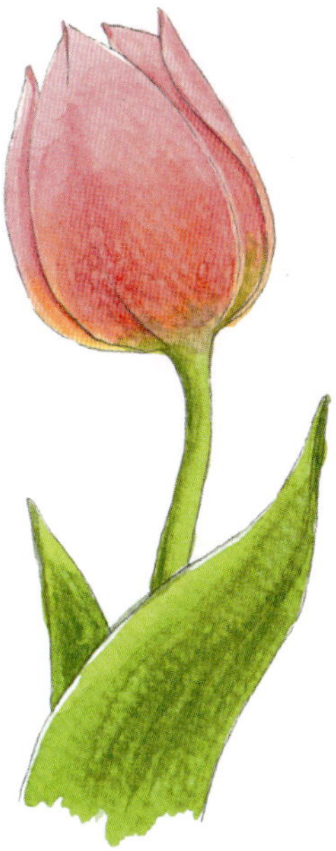

5

6. Amazing! Now, let's do the final step! Use the black waterproof liner to add soft shading lines along the outer contours of the petals. Add a single short hatch to the top tips of the petals. Darken the connection of the bud and the stem on the left, as well as at the bottom of the stem on both sides. On the leaves, add a bold line along the contour. With a white gel pen, add stripes along the inner contour of the leaves, on the right side of the stem and on some edges on the petals.

Great! Our sketch is ready!

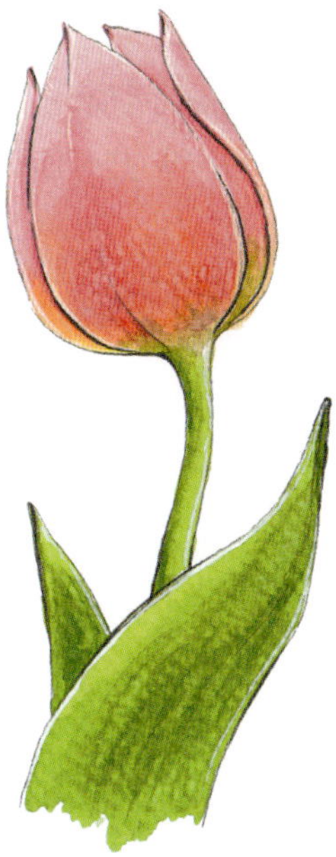

6

Lesson 11. Scarlet Pomegranate Gems

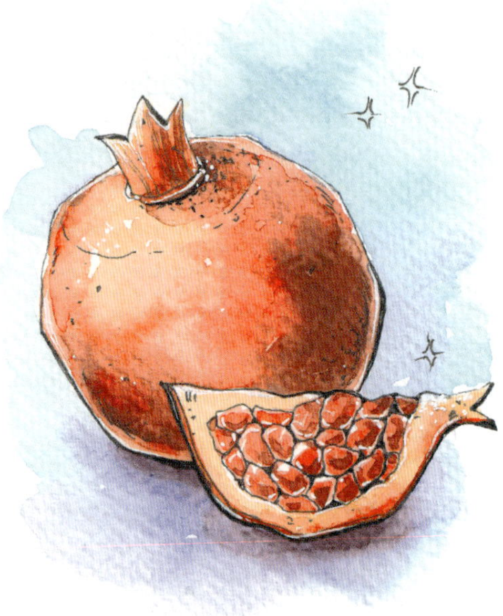

Let's continue with a new lesson, where each stroke brings to life a vivid red pomegranate! This fruit, filled with vibrant color, will be a perfect subject to explore the depth and richness of watercolor paints. You will learn to depict its shiny peel and translucent seeds that seem to sparkle under the sunlight like pure gems. Discover how to create realistic shadows and light with various watercolor techniques, such as gradients and smooth color transitions. Let's start and expand the boundaries of your artistic skills!

Paint Colors

Yellow Ochre

Permanent Red Light

Dioxazine Purple

Cerulean Blue

1. With a pencil, draw a large circle slightly to the left of the center of the paper. At the upper left part of the circle, draw a crown-like shape with three nibs tilted to the left. At the bottom right, draw a semicircle. On the right of it, make the tail. Then make the large circle contour more sharp. At the top of the large circle, draw an oval with large, interrupted strokes. On the semicircle, use a wavy line to mark the boundary of the pomegranate seeds.

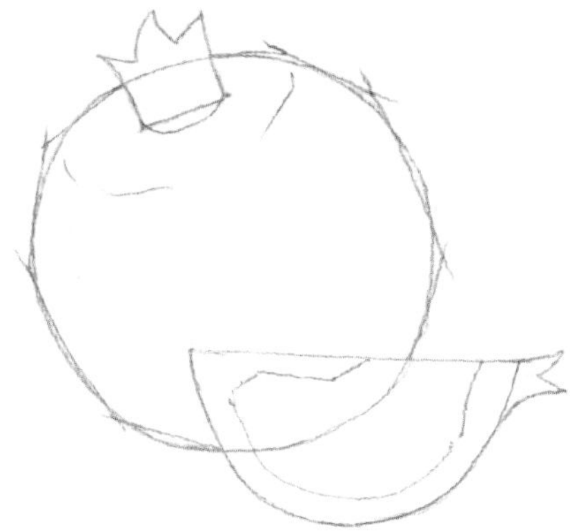

1

2. Using a black waterproof liner, make slightly more crooked lines to outline the pomegranate and the piece of the pomegranate, making some areas darker. Draw the pomegranate seeds as curved, irregular oval shapes slightly overlapping each other and color in the spaces between them black. Add dots, doodles and small hatches in the shadow areas on the whole pomegranate, as well as on the piece of pomegranate. On the background, draw a few small stars with semicircular hatches. Amazing! Let's erase the pencil.

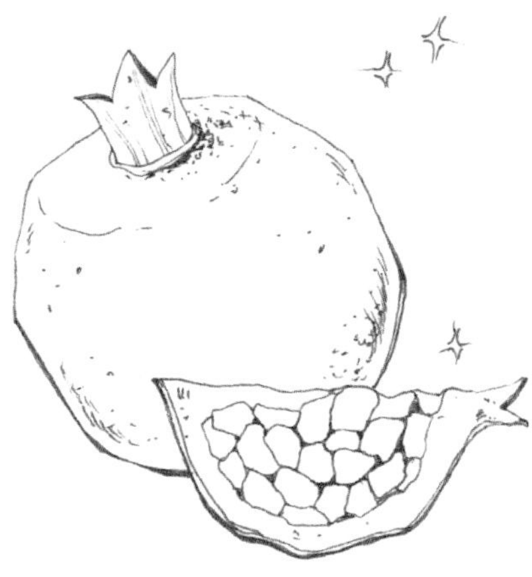

2

3. Prepare Yellow Ochre and Permanent Red Light on your palette. Also mix Permanent Red Light with a small amount of Dioxazine Purple to create a dark red. Add water to the Yellow Ochre and paint the upper part of the pomegranate, gradually transitioning to red, then darker red, leaving the lower contour of the pomegranate lighter. Try to make smooth transitions, but don't worry if they blend chaotically—it will still look beautiful! Use Yellow Ochre and Permanent Red Light to paint the tail of the whole pomegranate. With a light Yellow Ochre, paint the rind of the pomegranate slice, occasionally adding dark red to its lower contour. Paint the pomegranate seeds with Permanent Red Light mixed with water, leaving spaces of white paper.

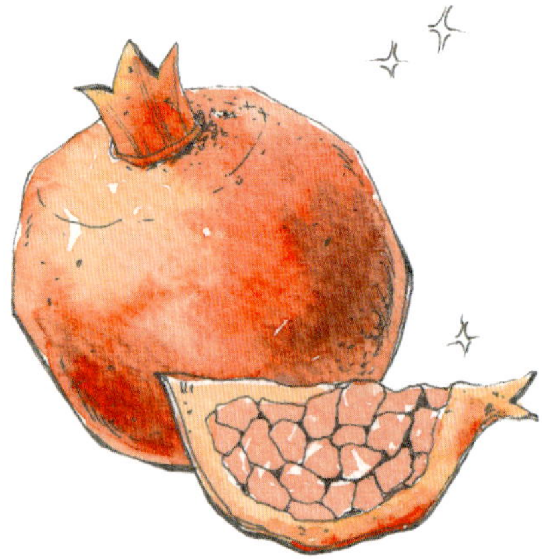

3

permanent red light + dioxazine purple

4. After the paper dries, apply Dioxazine Purple and Cerulean Blue around the pomegranate, diluting and blurring them with water. Make the blue lighter at the top and the purple darker under the pomegranate. This will give the image more contrast. With a dark red mixed from Permanent Red Light and Dioxazine Purple, add a second layer around the contour of the whole pomegranate and blur the edges into the middle of the pomegranate with a damp brush. Also add shadows to the tail and below it on the right side. With Permanent Red Light, loosely paint a second layer over the pomegranate seeds and paint the lower contour of the pomegranate piece as well.

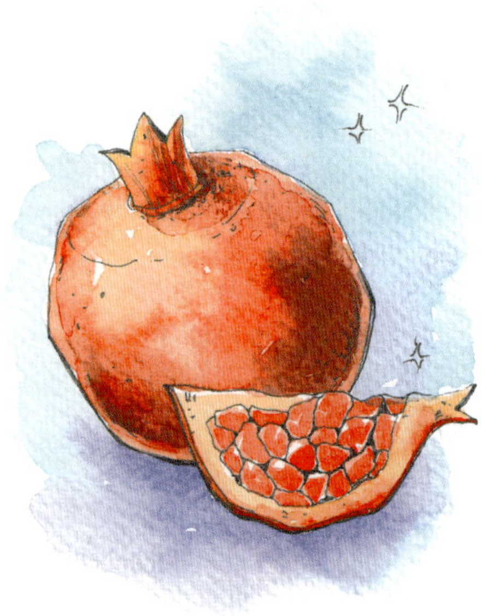

4

5. After the paper dries, apply small strokes of dark red for a third layer on the pomegranate seeds, also leaving previous layers and white spaces visible. That is how glazing works, and it helps make a vibrant, three-dimensional effect. Mix several drops of Permanent Red Light with Dioxazine Purple to make dark lilac. Use this color to add shadows under the pomegranate, and blur with water and a damp brush to create a soft edge. Let's wait for the paper to dry.

permanent red light + dioxazine purple

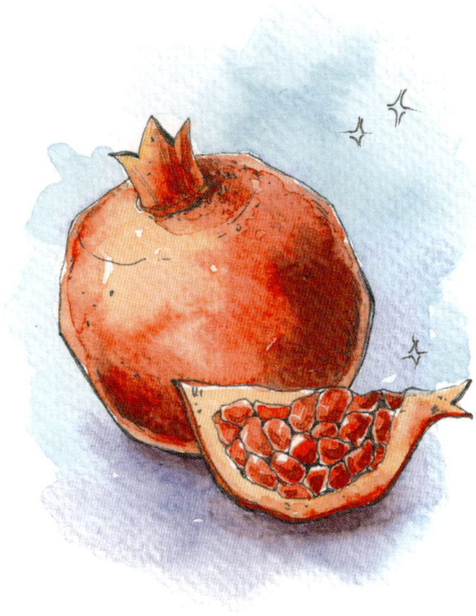

5

6. With the black liner, add shadows under the pomegranate tail with small dots. Also make the outlines on the contour of the pomegranate and the piece of pomegranate bolder on the lower parts. With a white gel pen, add white lines along the inner contour of the pomegranate. This will create reflections and give the fruit a shine. Add white lines on top of and below the tail. And, of course, make a few random dots in different parts of the pomegranate. Add short hatches along the contours of the seeds, on the rind and along the lower contour.

Fantastic! Our sketch is ready!

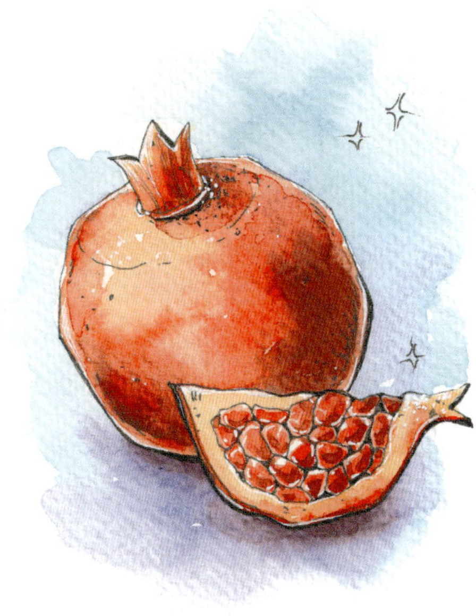

6

Lesson 12. Glowing Lantern Light

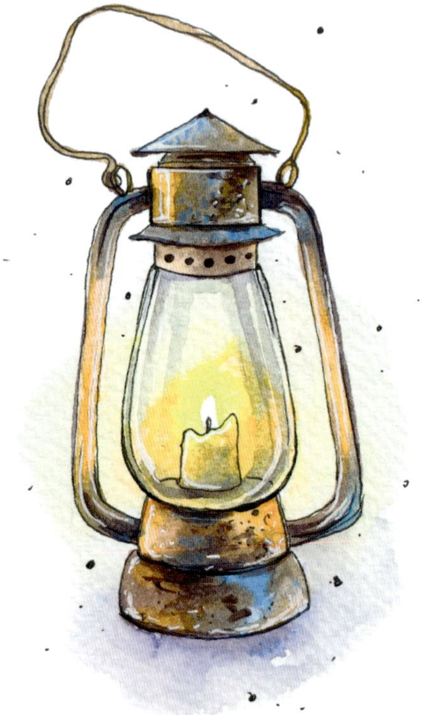

Immerse yourself in the ambience of a cozy evening with this step-by-step watercolor sketching lesson, where we will draw a vintage metal lantern. In this lesson, you will learn how to depict complex textures such as aged metal and glass using graphic hatches and watercolor washes. You'll also learn how to create a glowing effect and add detail to each part of the lantern. Grab your paints and brushes, and let's get started!

Paint Colors

- Permanent Lemon Yellow
- Azo Orange
- Cerulean Blue
- Burnt Sienna
- Ultramarine Deep
- Dioxazine Purple

1. Use a pencil to draw a vertical line in the center of the paper. This is the lantern's central axis. Above the center of the paper, draw a rectangle. Slightly below the center of the rectangle, draw a small trapezoid with a rounded bottom. Above the rectangle, draw a triangle. Connect the triangle and the rectangle with slanted lines. Slightly below the center of the rectangle draw a small trapezoid with a rounded bottom. Above the rectangle, draw a triangle. Connect the triangle and the rectangle with slanted lines. From the rectangle draw the lantern's bulb in a droplet shape. Below the bulb, draw a trapezoid that widens downward. Draw one more trapezoid below it. Make the bottom edges of the lower trapezoids semi-oval. At the bottom of the bulb draw a semi-oval. Draw a candle inside the bulb. Draw the lantern's handles on the right and left with smooth lines. At the top of the handles, draw two droplets (attachment of the upper handle) and use a wavy line for the top handle of the lantern.

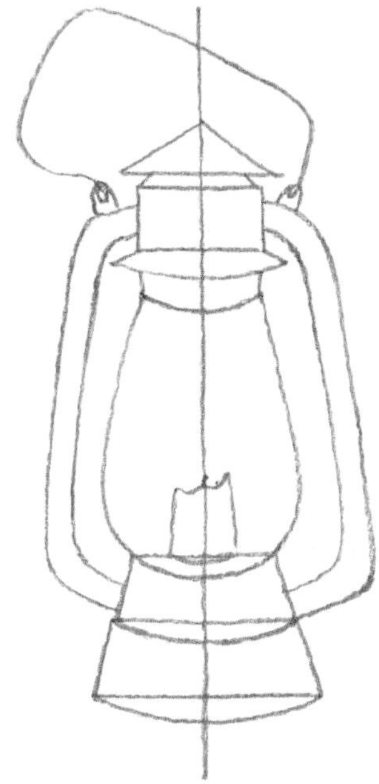

1

2. Use a black waterproof liner to outline the lantern and the candle with a wick inside it. Make the base lines of the lantern bolder. Add thickness to the glass inside the bulb with a thin line. Above the bulb, draw a row of small circles and color them in with the liner. Draw additional interrupted lines at places on the side handles of the lantern along the contour. Add thickness to the upper handle. Place dots, short lines and doodles on the upper and lower parts of the lantern, on the right side. Randomly place dots on the background around the lantern. Erase the pencil.

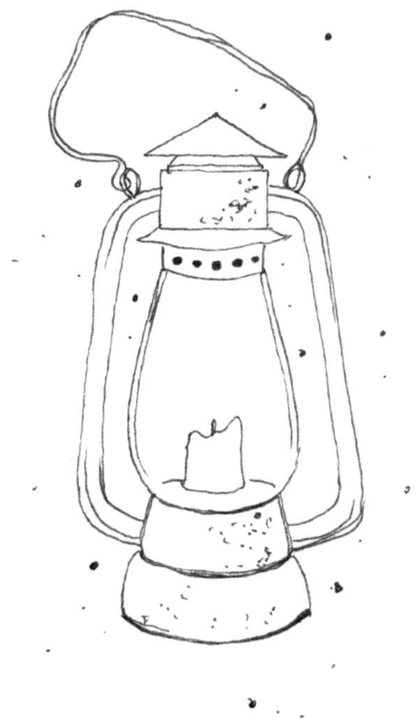

2

3. Prepare Permanent Lemon Yellow and Azo Orange on your palette. Use Permanent Lemon Yellow to paint a small oval around the wick. Leave the inner part of the oval white. Paint the area around the oval inside the bulb, loosely adding Azo Orange on the sides. Also paint the candle, but leave the wick white. With a damp brush, create a smooth, blended area extending to the lantern and the background. Use Azo Orange on the side parts of the lantern to emphasize volume and the glow. Paint the remaining metal parts of the lantern randomly using Cerulean Blue and Burnt Sienna. Try to make smooth transitions between colors. Paint the thin upper handle with Burnt Sienna.

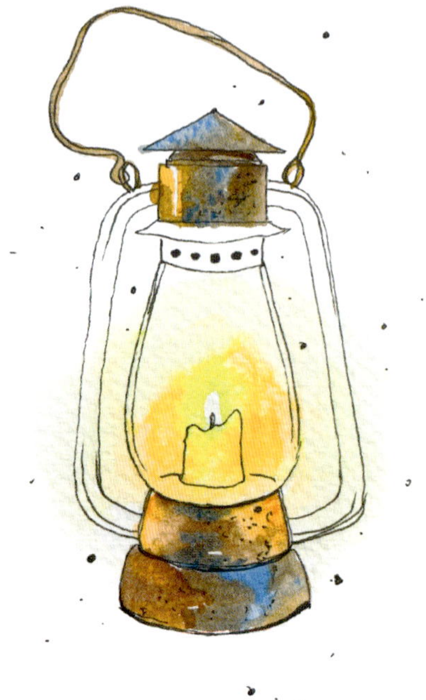

3

4. When the paint is dry, paint the side handles of the lantern. Apply Azo Orange and Burnt Sienna in the middle parts of the handles, next to the glow. Use Cerulean Blue and Burnt Sienna at the top and bottom of the handles, also trying to make smooth transitions between them. Similarly, paint the remaining part of the lantern's top with these colors. It's totally okay if your transitions between colors are not smooth; you are just learning! And I do believe you will do better with practice.

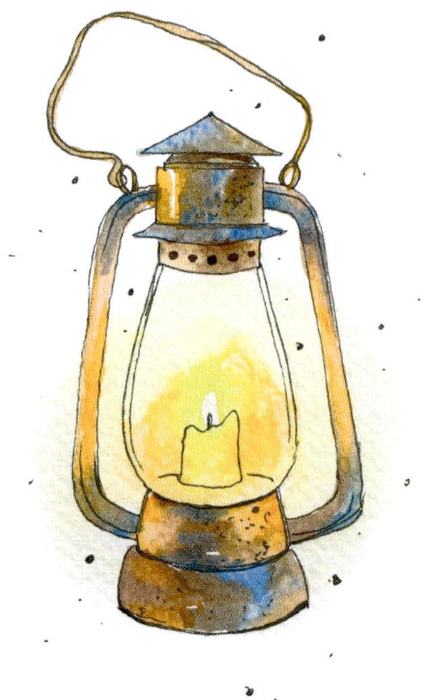

4

5. Using equal parts Ultramarine Deep and Burnt Sienna diluted with water, apply shadows and reflections on the glass in lines following the shape of the bulb. Paint the thickness of the glass on the left side and the candle at the bottom. Mix Dioxazine Purple and Burnt Sienna to create a dark purple-brown color, then add small dark strokes to the top metal part of the lantern and the handles at the joints. Also add semi-oval lines to the base of the lantern and a shadow stroke under the candle. Place small, separate, detached strokes in the shadowy part on the lantern where there are liner hatches. With Dioxazine Purple and Cerulean Blue, create a shadow under the lantern and smooth the edges with a damp brush. Mix Dioxazine Purple with water to lighten it and add lines to the glass bulb.

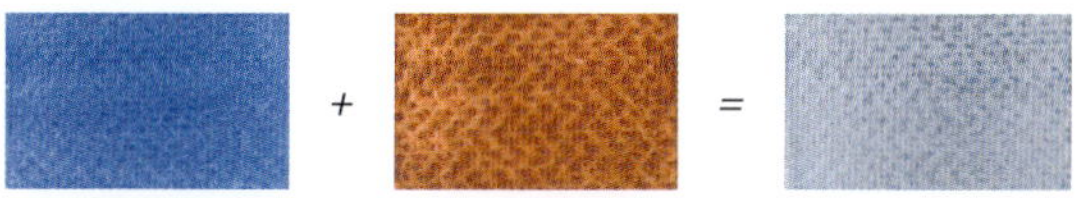

ultramarine deep + burnt sienna

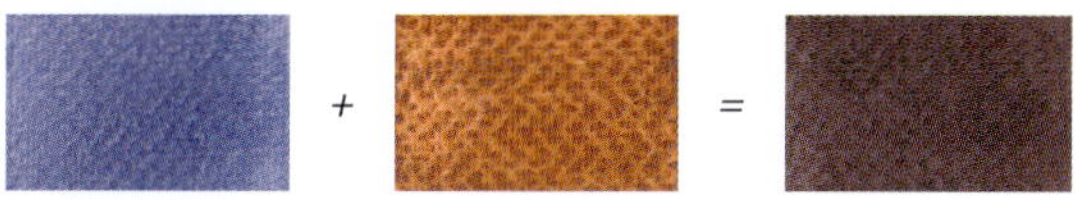

dioxazine purple + burnt sienna

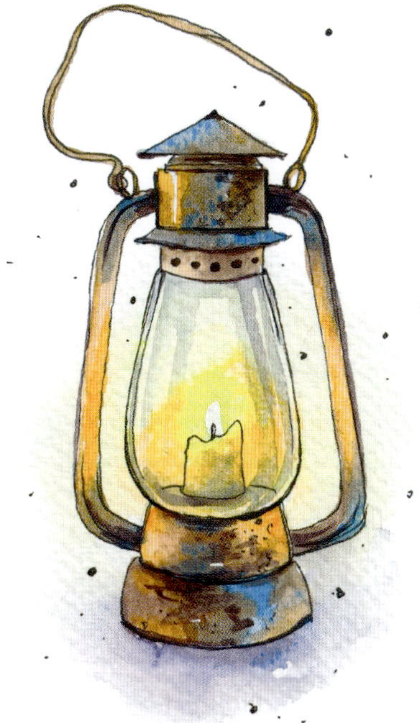

5

6. With a black waterproof liner, make the bottom and some of the top lines of the glass bulb bolder. With a white gel pen, draw lines to show the shiny surface of the metal on the handles, top and base, as well as the glass bulb. If you painted the flame, don't worry! Just redraw it with white pen. Add lines around the candle's contour. Draw small dots and short hatches on the upper and lower parts of the lantern to show the vintage style of the metal.

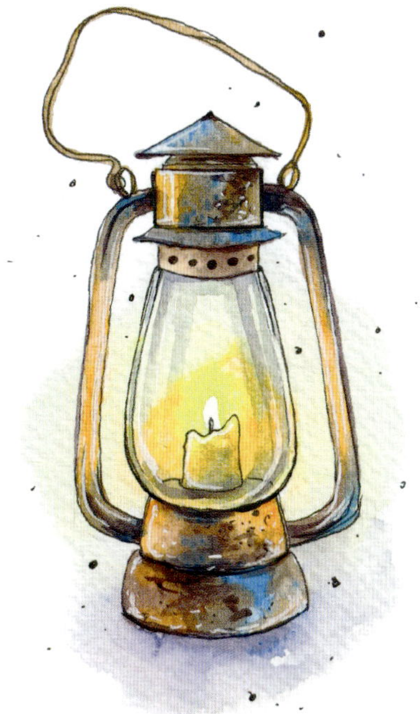

6

Great job! Our sketch is ready!

Lesson 13. Forest Cabin Charm

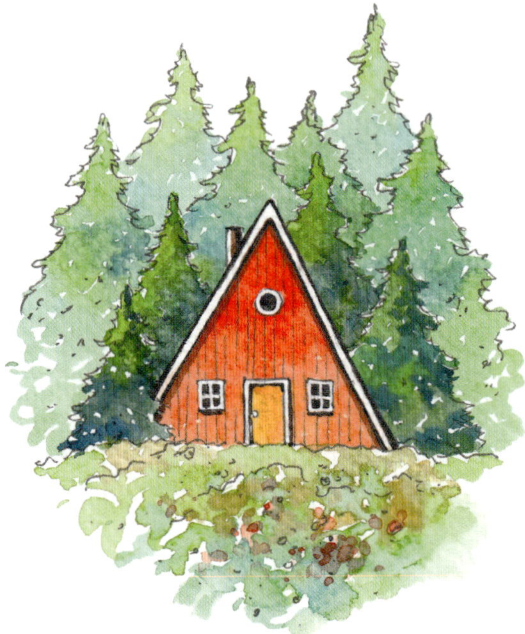

Feel the atmosphere of tranquility and solitude with this bright red cabin in the forest! In this lesson, we will put into practice all the previous knowledge of working with a liner and add zigzag lines and hatches to depict lush fir trees. You'll learn how to show space perspective using watercolor washes, color play and smooth gradients. Create your own charming and cozy little corner with this lesson! So, let's begin!

Paint Colors

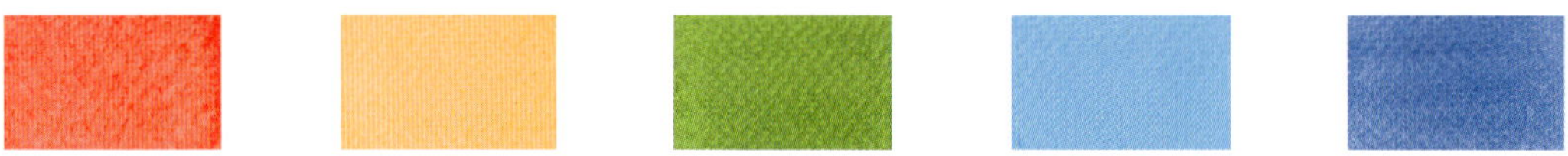

Permanent Red Light | Yellow Ochre | Sap Green | Cerulean Blue | Ultramarine Deep

1. Use a pencil to draw a medium-size triangle below the middle area of the page. This will be a cabin. Draw a narrow rectangular chimney at the top left and a door at the bottom center of the cabin. At the base of the cabin, draw a long, slightly curved line. To the right draw a small, narrow triangle so that the cabin overlaps it. Similarly, draw an even smaller triangle to the left, slightly overlapping the cabin. Just above the cabin, draw a zigzag line with large and small peaks. Draw additional rows of zigzag lines with varying angles and heights, and cross the lines in some places.

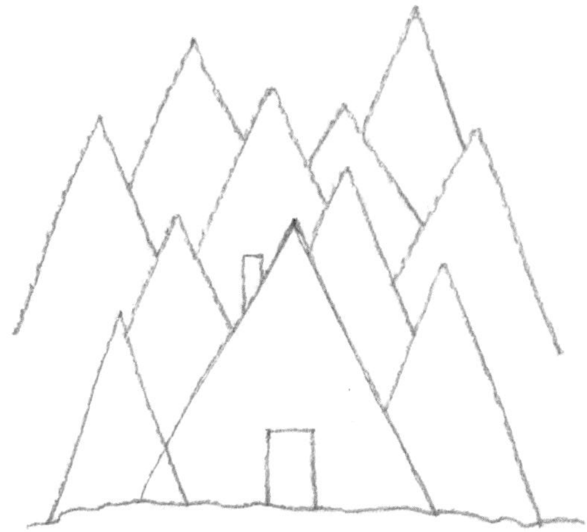

1

2. Use a black waterproof liner to outline the roof of the cabin and the chimney, adding a little dimension to the roof with a duplicate line. At the top of the cabin, draw a round window, color it with black liner and add a frame. Outline the door, then add a frame with a duplicate line and draw a round handle. Draw windows on the right and left sides of the door as squares and color four panes on each with the liner, then add frames as well. With thin lines draw narrow stripes on the cabin, avoiding the windows and door, to show wooden siding. At the bottom of the cabin, use wavy lines to draw the grass lawn. Then draw the fir trees with a slight zigzag and wavy line with interruptions. Randomly draw small dots, dashes and doodles under and around the cabin and on the trees. Perfect! Erase the pencil.

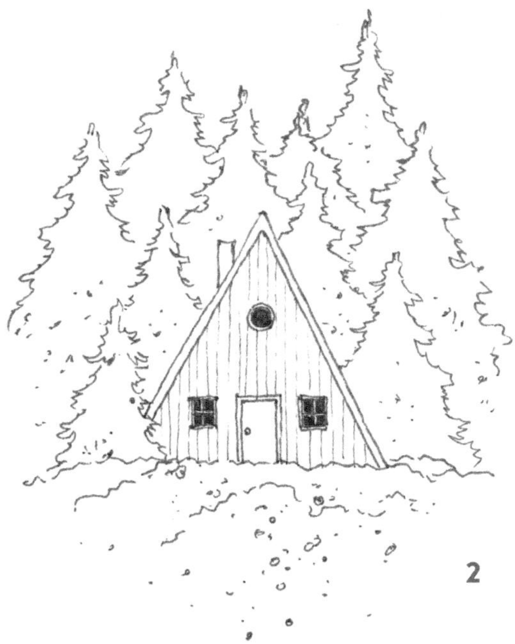

2

3. Paint the cabin, starting from the top with Permanent Red Light and gradually transitioning to Yellow Ochre toward the bottom, leaving the windows and door unpainted. Wash your brush, then dilute Sap Green and Cerulean Blue separately with water to get light shades. Starting with the distant fir trees, paint their tops with light green, then smoothly make the transition to light blue toward their bottoms. After the fir trees dry, move to the next row of trees and also apply a loose wash from green to blue, but use slightly darker shades. After this row of trees dries, mix Sap Green and Ultramarine Deep to get a darker color and paint the next row of trees, from green-blue to the new darker color, leaving only the trees on the right and left of the cabin unpainted.

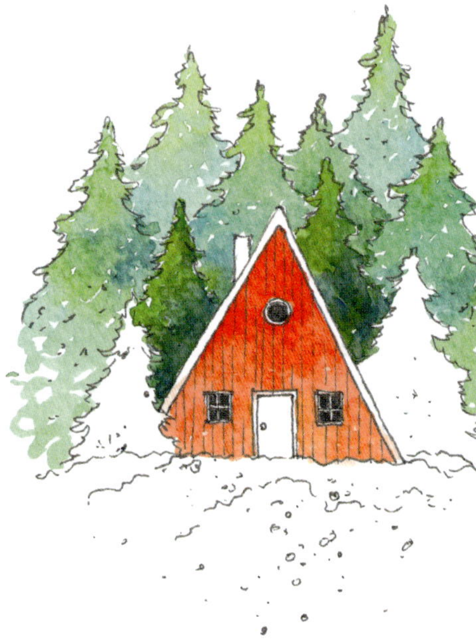

3

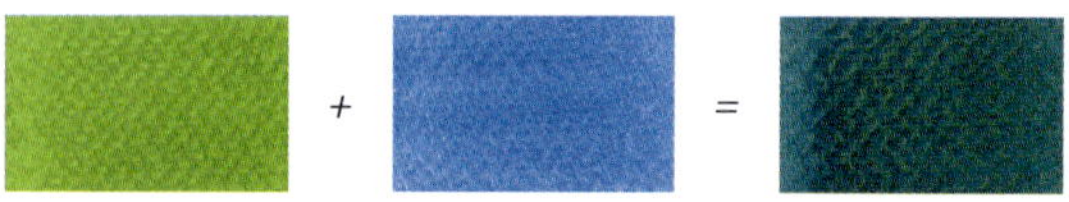

sap green + ultramarine deep

4. After the watercolor dries, paint the remaining trees using darker shades of green and blue than the previous rows, also leaving some white paper spots. Paint the door with Yellow Ochre. Mix Yellow Ochre and Sap Green and add some water to lighten the shade. Start painting the lawn from the top with light green (Sap Green diluted with water) and green-ochre, slightly blurring the wash on the sides, and gradually add a few Cerulean Blue strokes toward the bottom to make flowers. Leave small spots of white paper.

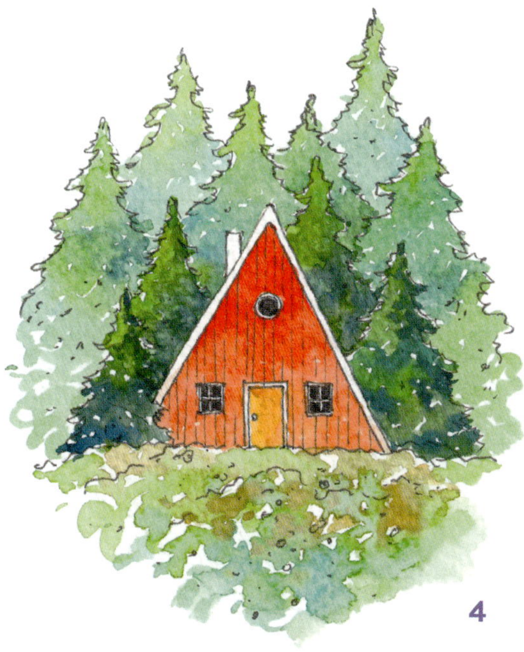

4

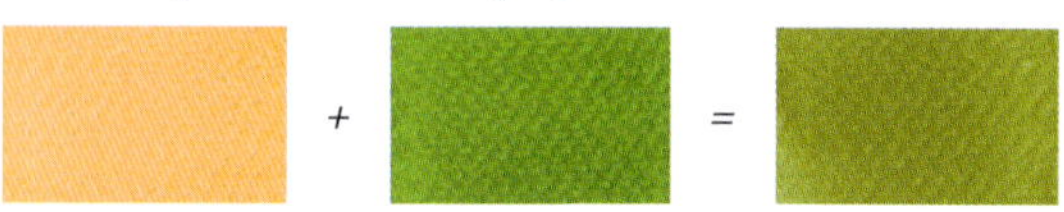

yellow ochre + sap green

5. When the paper is dry, randomly add small Permanent Red Light strokes and dots next to the Cerulean Blue ones on the lawn. Mix Permanent Red Light and Sap Green in equal proportions to get a dark brown shade. Use this color to draw a thin line of shadow under the roof along the contour and on the right side of the chimney. Great! Again, this is how glazing can add more dimension to a sketch!

permanent red light + sap green

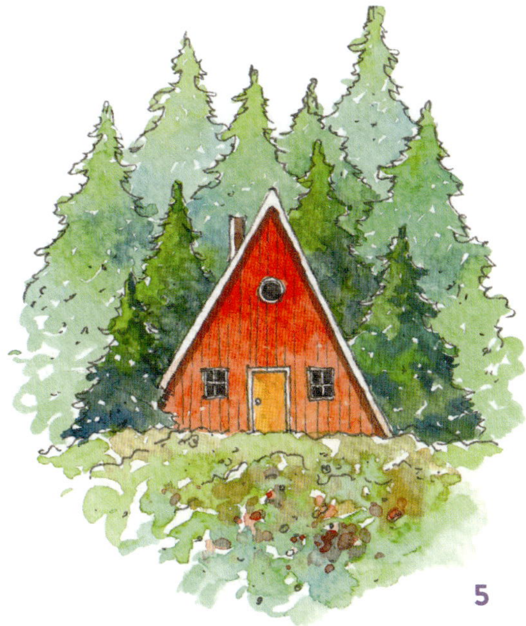

5

6. Let's do the last step when the paper is dry. With a white gel pen, draw a white contour on the roof, the window frames and the door if you've accidentally painted over them. Use a black liner to thicken the outer contour of the roof.

Fantastic! Our sketch is ready!

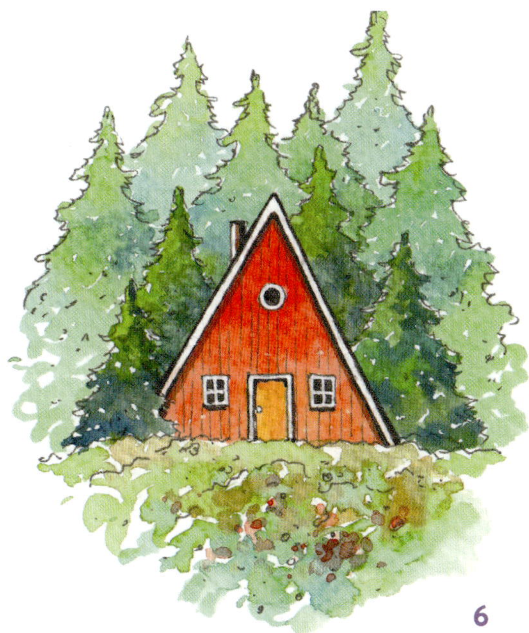

6

Lesson 14. Marine Crab Carnival

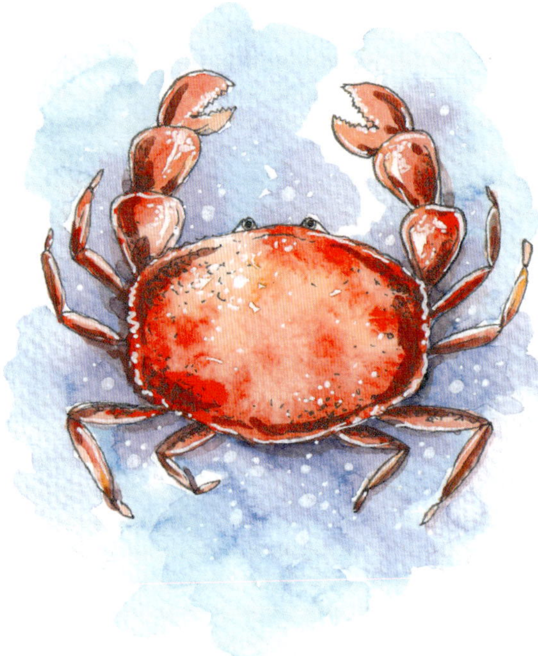

Dive into the colorful world of the underwater kingdom! In this lesson, we'll draw and paint a vibrant sea crab, practicing the technique of beautiful color washes, enhanced with vivid strokes on its claws. You'll learn how to bring to the paper a celebration of color and movement, making each stroke rich and full of inspiration. Let's begin!

Paint Colors

Permanent Red Light

Yellow Ochre

Cerulean Blue

Dioxazine Purple

1. Use a pencil to draw a vertical line in the center of the paper. On either side of the central line, at equal distances, draw two short lines. Connect these lines with curved arches to form the crab's shell. Draw eyes as two small circles on top of the shell. On the lower and side parts of the shell, draw eight legs (four on each side) in the form of elongated, flattened ovals connected to each other. You can make them crooked and playful in shape; feel free to experiment! From the upper corners of the shell, draw the claws in the shape of overlapping curved teardrops. At the tips of these teardrops, draw edges in the shape of a V.

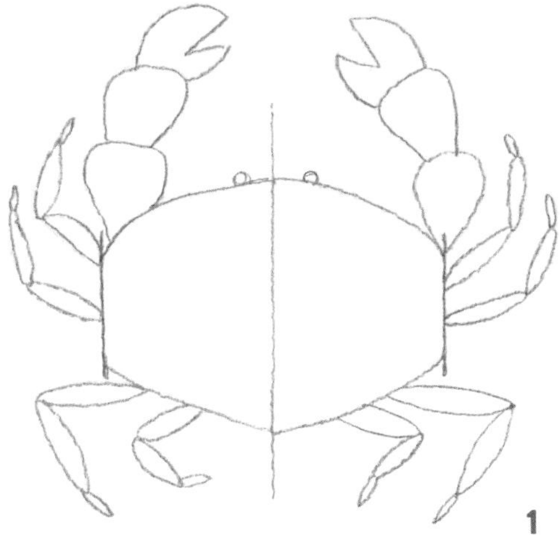

1

2. With a black waterproof liner, outline the shell of the crab using wavy, slightly interrupted lines. Also add wavy lines inside the contour of the shell. Outline the legs and add uneven lines inside them. Outline the eyes and add connecting lines from the eyes to the shell. Outline the claws and add thin, grainy lines inside them. Inside the claws, make the edges zigzag. Add doodles, dots and short hatches to the lower right and upper left parts of the shell, the first segments of the lower legs and on the right and left sides of the claws. Erase the pencil marks.

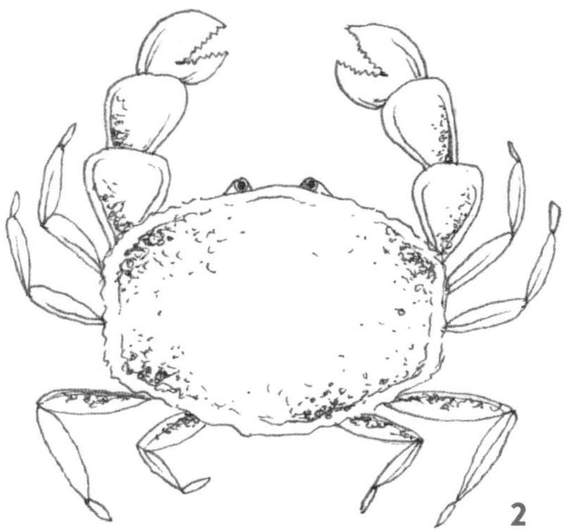

2

3. Prepare Permanent Red Light and Yellow Ochre on your palette and separately mix Permanent Red Light with water to create a light red shade. Let's begin this vibrant wash with the shell. Paint the center with light red and Yellow Ochre, with smooth transitions from one color to another, slightly blurring them with water directly on the paper. Paint the edges of the shell with a darker shade of Permanent Red Light. Feel free to leave some white paper spots and keep playing with colors! Then randomly paint the claws and legs with the same colors, occasionally leaving white paper.

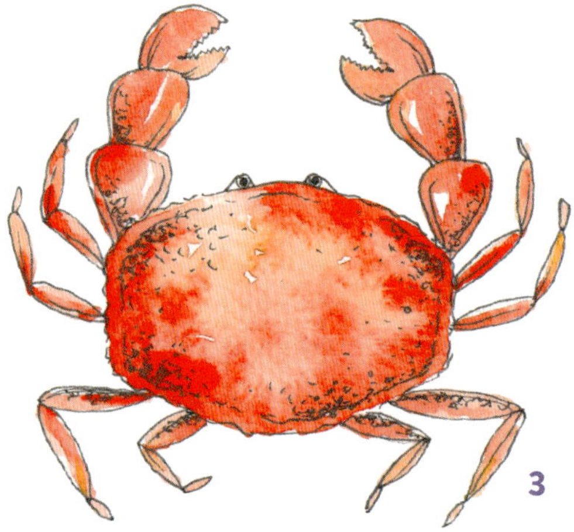

3

4. When the paper is dry, dilute Cerulean Blue and Dioxazine Purple separately with water to make light shades. Paint the background around the crab with large, random strokes, creating smooth transitions from blue to purple. Make any shape of the background you like and leave some white paper. Wait for the paper to dry completely.

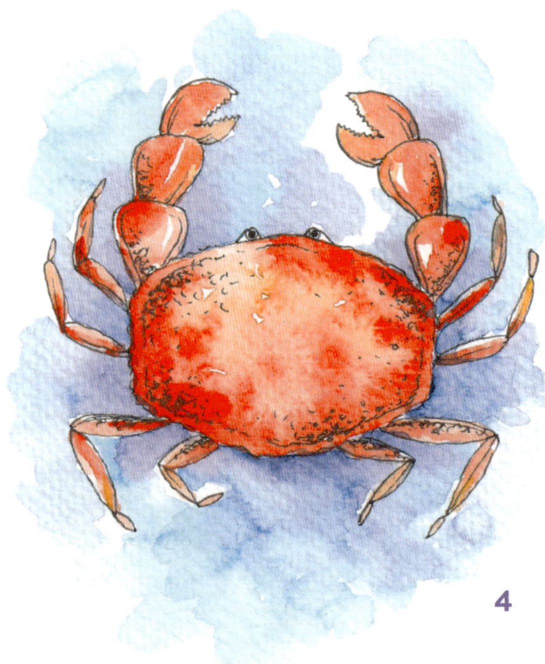

4

5. Mix Permanent Red Light and Dioxazine Purple on your palette in equal proportions. Use this color to draw shadows on the shell, legs and claws near the edges, applying strokes in a loose manner without blending. Dilute this color with water and add shadows under the crab on the background, slightly blurring randomly with water. Amazing! Now let's wait for the paper to dry.

permanent red light + dioxazine purple

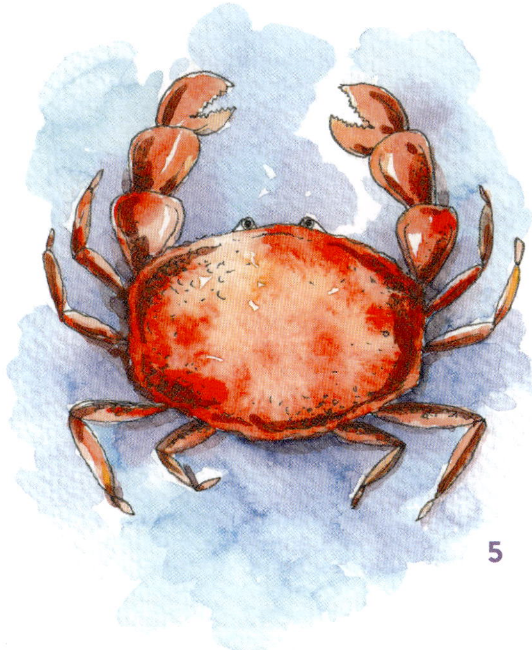

5

6. Use a white gel pen to draw small dots on the claws, shell and legs. Also draw long lines on the edges of the claws, shell and legs, and add zigzag lines on the sides of the shell to emphasize texture. Additionally, randomly add dots and circles of various sizes to the background. Go ahead and make the highlights as you like!

Perfect! Our sketch is ready!

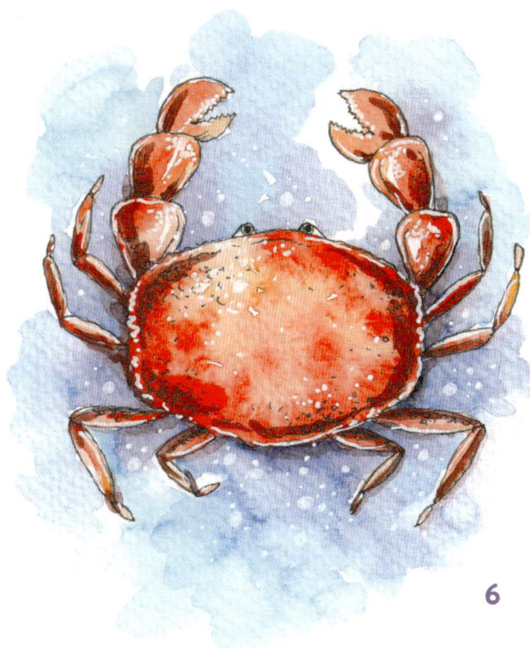

6

Lesson 15.
Garden on the Go

In this lesson, you'll paint a picturesque garden cart filled with flowers and pumpkins. This scene is perfect for practicing rich color transitions, from warm oranges to refreshing yellow-greens and mysterious purples. You'll also learn how to combine colors to create a voluminous effect on greenery and pumpkins, giving your artwork liveliness and dynamics. Let's start!

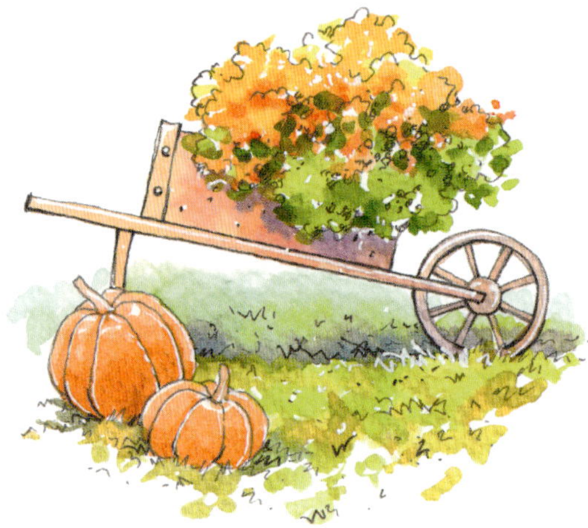

Paint Colors

- Permanent Lemon Yellow
- Azo Orange
- Quinacridone Rose
- Burnt Sienna
- Yellow Ochre
- Dioxazine Purple
- Sap Green
- Cerulean Blue
- Ultramarine Deep

1. Use a pencil to draw a horizontal line below the middle area of the paper. Above it, draw a line slanted to the right and add thickness. This will be the base of the cart. Below the base, draw a line downward on the left and add thickness. In the middle area of the base, draw a rectangle (the basket of the cart) that is also slanted like the base. Add a line on the left side of the rectangle. Above the basket, draw flowers with a wavy line in the shape of a cloud. Great! Next, draw the cart's wheel. On the right side of the base, draw a small circle, then a larger circle. In the lower left part next to the cart, draw two slightly angled circles overlapping each other. These will be the sweet pumpkins.

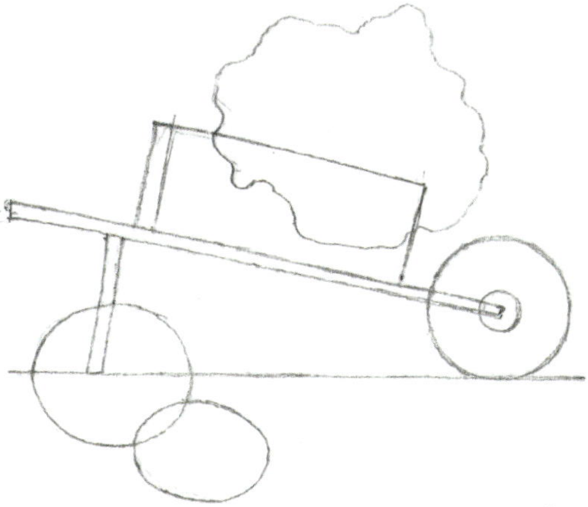

1

2. With the pencil, add wavy lines for the details of the flowers and foliage. On the rectangle on the left side of the basket, draw two small circles (nails). Draw the thickness of the wheel's large circle and diagonal lines inside for the spokes. Draw grass below the cart with short zigzag lines. Add a bit more grass under the wheel and under the pumpkins. Draw oval-like segments and stems on top of the pumpkins with curved lines.

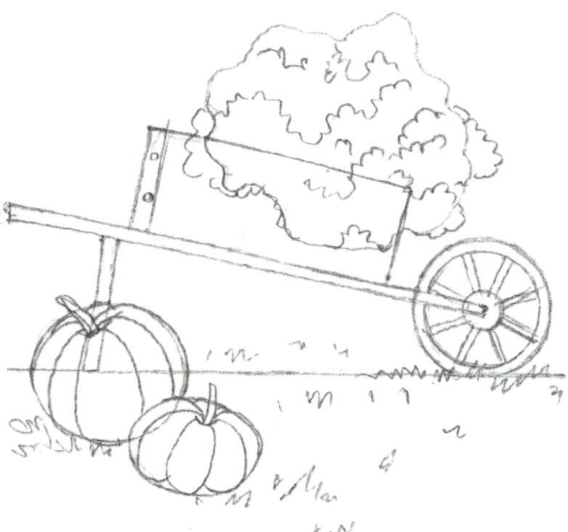

2

3. Use a black waterproof liner to outline the flowers and foliage with a wavy, interrupted line, adding random dots, small doodles and circles in the lower part of the greenery. Also outline the grass with a zigzag line, slightly overlapping the wheel and pumpkins. Outline all details of the cart and pumpkins with a simple line. Erase the pencil.

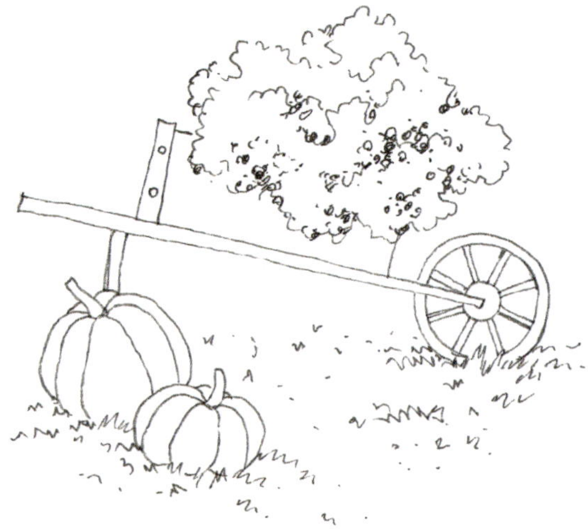

3

4. Add Permanent Lemon Yellow, Azo Orange and Quinacridone Rose to your palette. Start with small, random strokes of Permanent Lemon Yellow on the upper part of the flowers, gradually adding Azo Orange and only slightly mixing the colors. Continue downward with small, random strokes, adding Quinacridone Rose to the Azo Orange. Play with the colors. I'm sure you will do great!

Now mix Azo Orange with water to get a light orange color and paint the upper part of the pumpkins, leaving areas of white paper. Add dark Azo Orange and Burnt Sienna toward the lower part of the pumpkins. Add Yellow Ochre and Dioxazine Purple to the palette. Mix a light ochre color using water and paint the left side of the cart, adding Quinacridone Rose toward the center and Dioxazine Purple under the flowers. Try to create smooth transitions between colors. Paint the wheel with the light ochre and a light shade of purple, also blending them smoothly. Paint the pumpkin stems with light ochre.

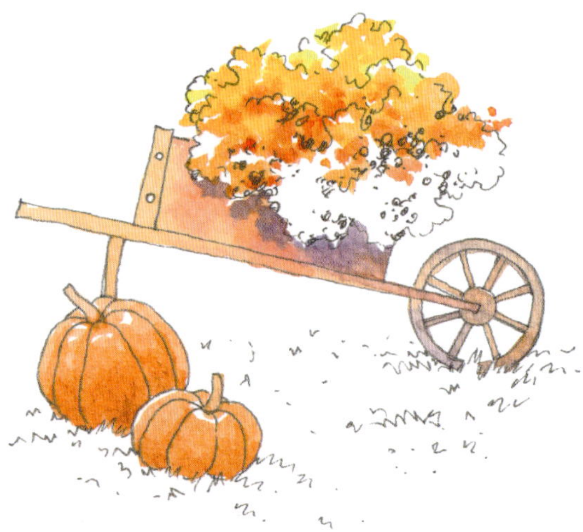

4

5. Mix Permanent Lemon Yellow and Sap Green in equal proportions to get a yellow-green color. Paint the foliage under the flowers with this yellow-green, occasionally leaving white paper spots. While the paper is wet, add small separate Sap Green strokes over the greenery and flowers. Mix Cerulean Blue with water to get a light blue. Begin painting the grass under the cart, gradually adding yellow-green and Ultramarine Deep at the very bottom to create smooth color transitions. Start painting the grass under the wheel and the pumpkins with small yellow-green strokes, occasionally adding Yellow Ochre and light green. Add Sap Green next to the pumpkins. Perfect! Wait for the paper to dry.

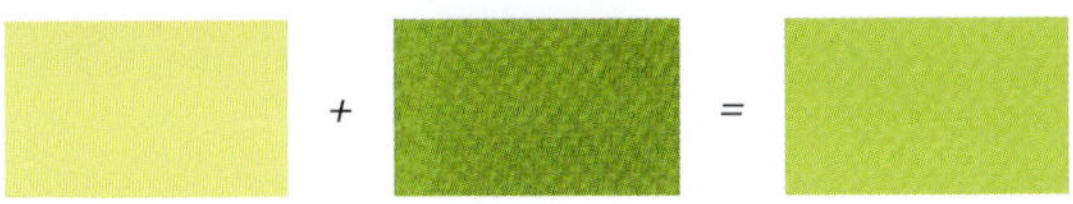

permanent lemon yellow + sap green

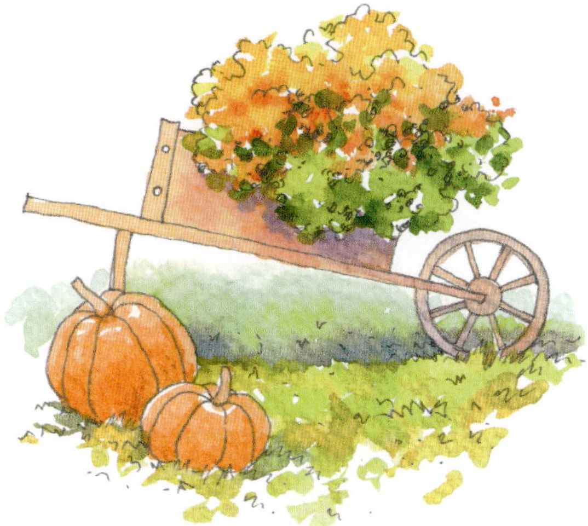

5

6. Use the black liner to make the outlines of the cart and pumpkins bolder in some areas. Add several random dots on the basket. Add small, quick zigzag hatches to the grass to make it more expressive. Add more zigzags under the cart and around the pumpkins. With a white gel pen, draw dots and short lines on the flowers, greenery, cart and grass. Add lines next to the outline on the basket and wheel. Also draw white grass lines under the wheel. Add white lines on the pumpkin segments.

That was great! Our sketch is ready!

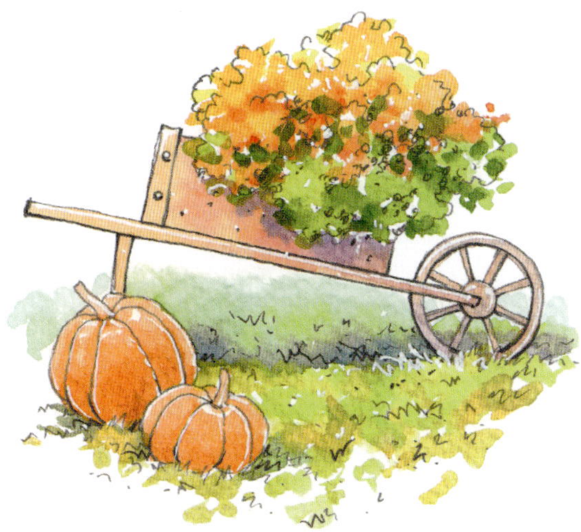

6

Lesson 16. Mountain Harmony

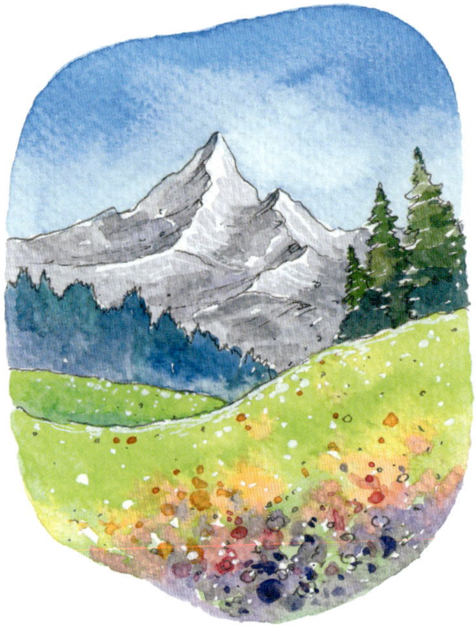

Experience the harmony of nature by painting a mountain landscape with forests and a blooming field. In this lesson, you will learn how nuances of light and shadow work to create the depth and spatial perspective of the fields, lending picturesque charm to your mountains and valleys. Learn to use graphic techniques for trees and watercolors to show a sense of peace and tranquility often found in the heart of natural landscapes.
Let's begin!

Paint Colors

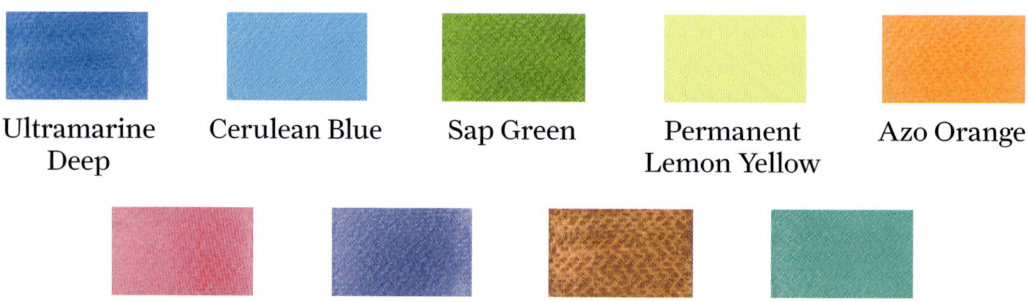

1. With a pencil, draw a curved oval shape in the center of the paper. This will be the overall background of the sketch. Inside the oval, slightly below the center, draw a curved, smooth line. This is the hill in the foreground. To the right, draw three elongated triangles. On the left side of the curved line, draw another curved line, (distant hill) and higher up, with a zigzag line, show a distant forest. Next, smoothly draw the line for the mountains. Make two mountain peaks, one higher than the other. Add winding lines down from the peaks.

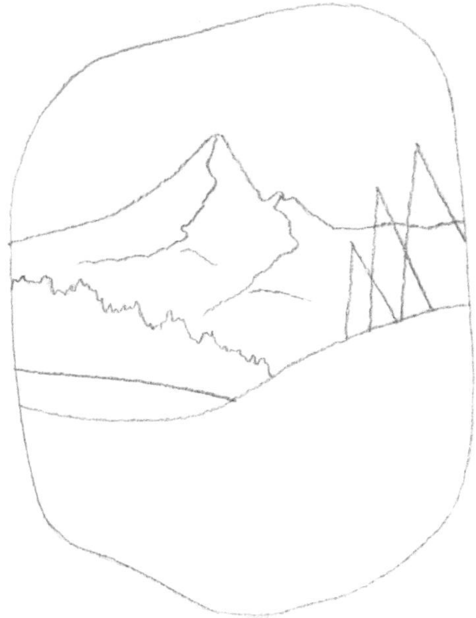

1

2. Use a black waterproof liner to outline the hills with a thin, loose, interrupted line. Draw fir trees on the right and the forest line on the left with zigzag interrupted lines. Outline the mountains with thin, slightly wavy, trembling lines. Trembling, interrupted, loose and crooked lines are perfect for landscapes! Add dots, small circles and doodles randomly at the bottom of the sketch. These will be lovely flowers. Great! And now erase the pencil.

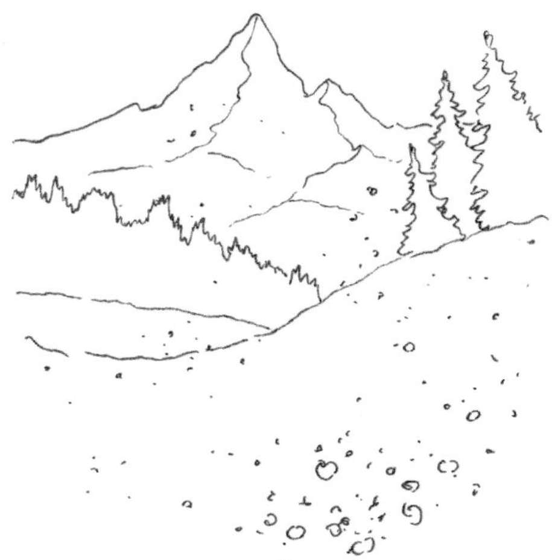

2

3. Use Ultramarine Deep and Cerulean Blue to paint the sky, softly blending with water toward the mountains. Mix Sap Green and Permanent Lemon Yellow in equal proportions to get a yellow-green shade and paint the distant hill. Then smoothly transition to Cerulean Blue at the bottom of the hill. Add Azo Orange, Quinacridone Rose and Dioxazine Purple to the palette. Paint the large hill, starting at the top with yellow-green and Sap Green. From the middle area, add Azo Orange, Quinacridone Rose and Dioxazine Purple strokes, leaving white spots.

sap green + permanent lemon yellow

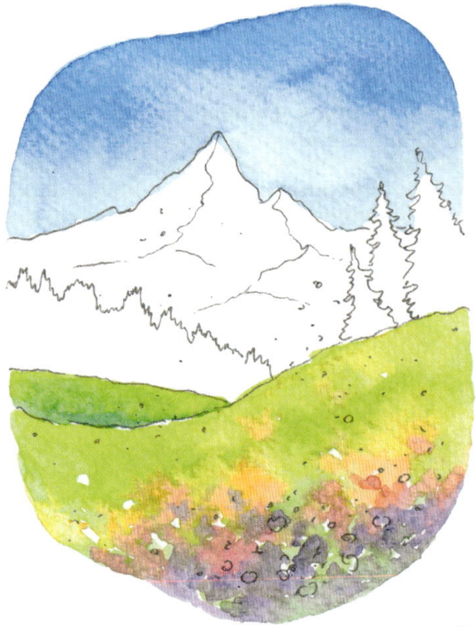

3

4. Mix Ultramarine Deep and Burnt Sienna in equal proportions to get a gray-blue color. Also mix a light gray separately, adding water to the gray-blue mix. Paint the mountains with light gray and gray-blue, leaving white spots, occasionally adding light purple. Wait for it to dry. Mix Phthalo Green with Ultramarine Deep in equal proportions to get a dark blue-turquoise color and paint the distant forest, randomly adding Ultramarine Deep and Phthalo Green. Make the lower part of the forest lighter with a damp brush. Wait for the paint to dry.

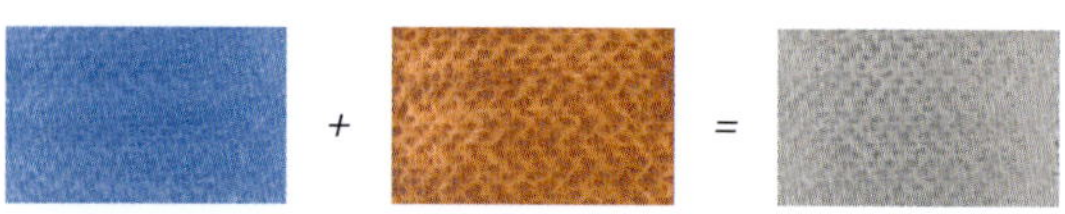

ultramarine deep + burnt sienna

phthalo green + ultramarine deep

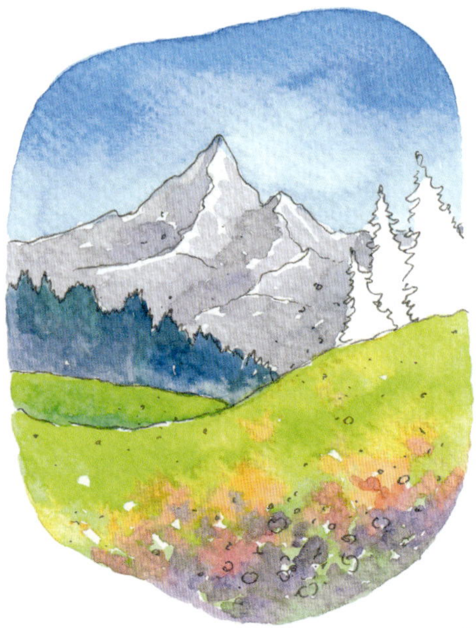

4

5. On the mountains, add a second layer of gray-blue shadow strokes. Also with bright Azo Orange, Quinacridone Rose and Dioxazine Purple, add small, separate strokes of various sizes to the flowers on the hill at the bottom. After the mountains dry, mix Sap Green and Ultramarine Deep in equal proportions to get a dark green. Paint the fir trees with horizontal thin strokes of Sap Green, Phthalo Green and dark green, leaving white paper spaces. So many colors! But I'm sure you are doing great! Just keep practicing.

sap green + ultramarine deep

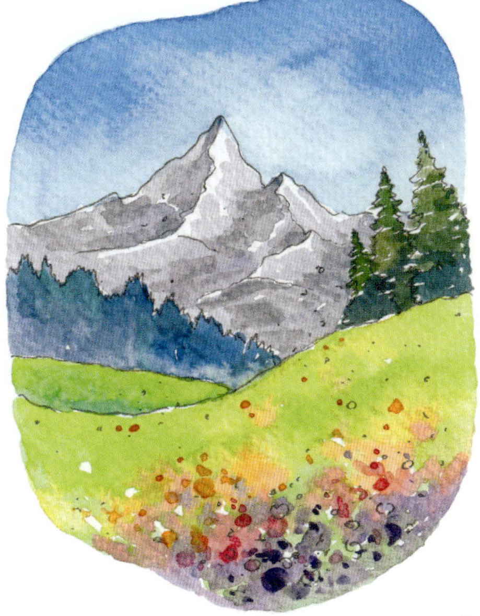

5

6. When the paper is dry, use the black liner to add thin, barely visible lines going down and to the left side of the mountains. With a white gel pen, add thin lines in the opposite direction, on the right side of the mountains. Draw an uneven white line under the contour line on the foreground hill. Randomly add dots of various sizes to both hills.

Feel proud of yourself! Such great work! Our sketch is ready!

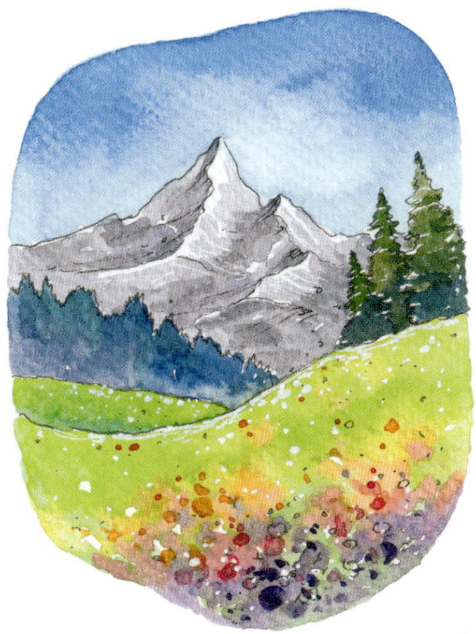

6

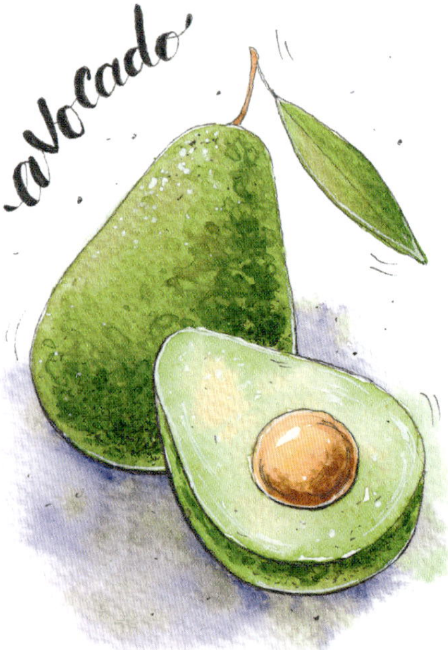
avocado

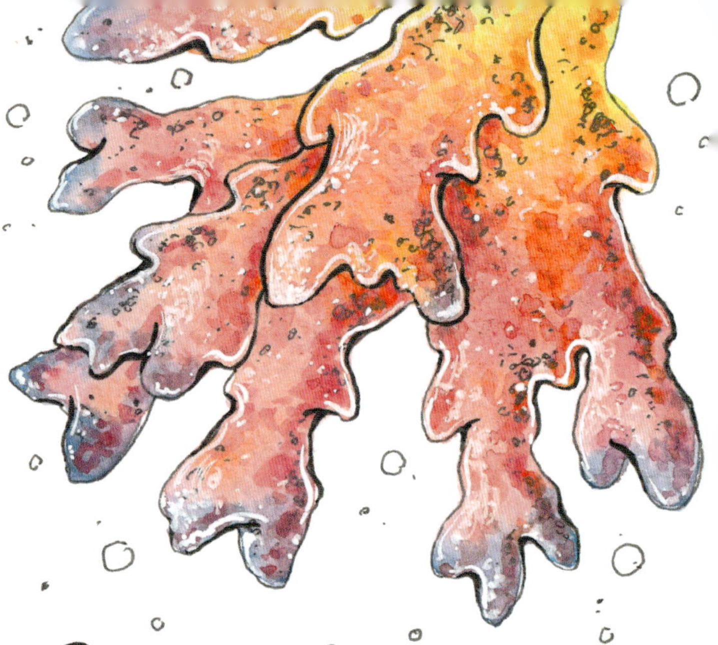

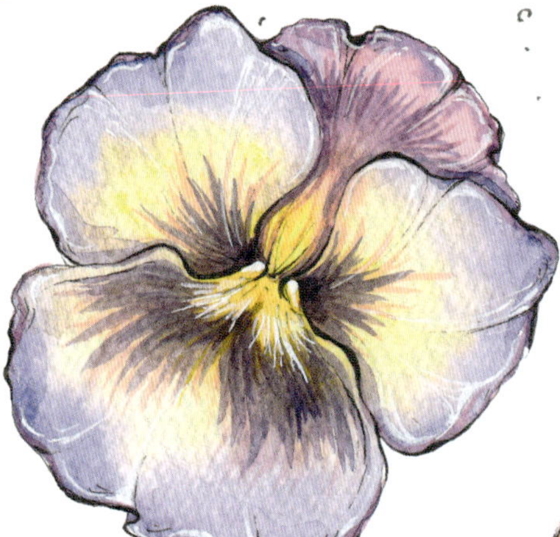

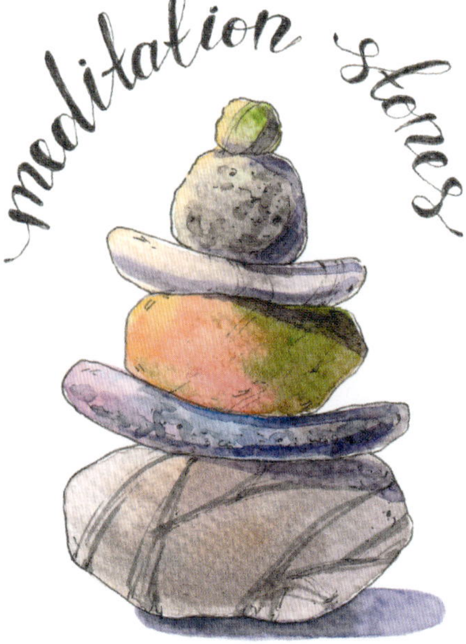
meditation stones

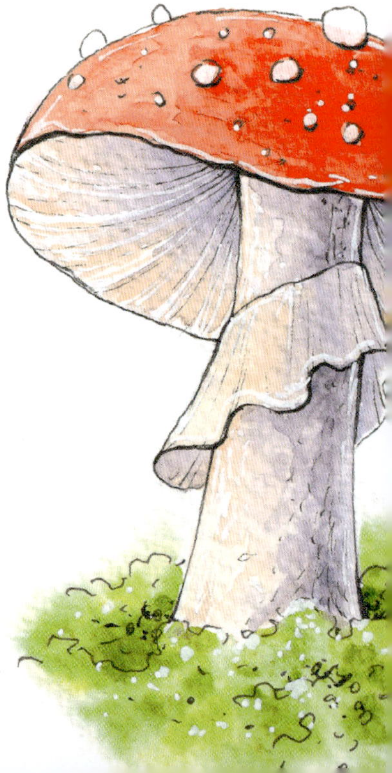

Wet-on-Wet and Lettering

In this chapter, you will discover a new and powerful watercolor technique—wet-on-wet. This technique will open up a horizon of new creative possibilities for you! Explore how diverse colors flow into each other in Reef Rhapsody (page 102) and Viola Floral Fusion (page 106), creating unique washes and textures. You will learn how to let go and enjoy the process as you watch your painting transform into something magical right before your eyes. Plus, it's a lot of fun! Additionally, in this chapter, you will also dive into the basics of lettering in Avocado Amigos (page 94) and Calming Meditation Stones (page 110), learning how to add beautiful letters to your watercolor sketches, making them even more expressive and personalized. This skill will add beauty to your art projects and expand your understanding of watercolor sketching.

Lesson 17. Avocado Amigos

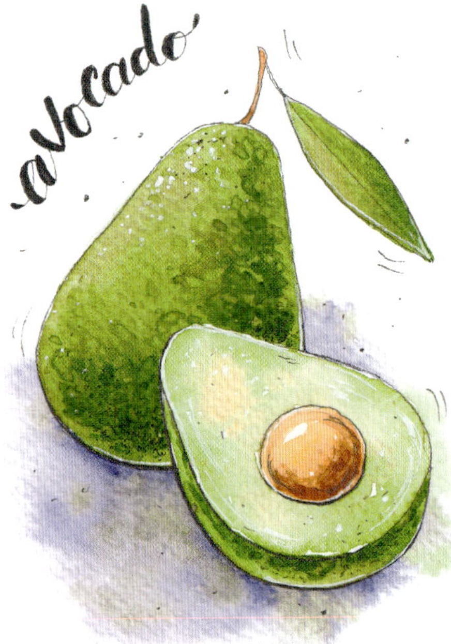

The ever-versatile avocado! In this lesson, you will learn how to show the natural textures of its peel and rich green shades of this nutritious fruit. You will discover how to create realistic dimensions and soft shadows using the wet-on-wet technique to make your avocado look as appetizing as possible. Additionally, this lesson will introduce you to lettering. Let's begin!

Paint Colors

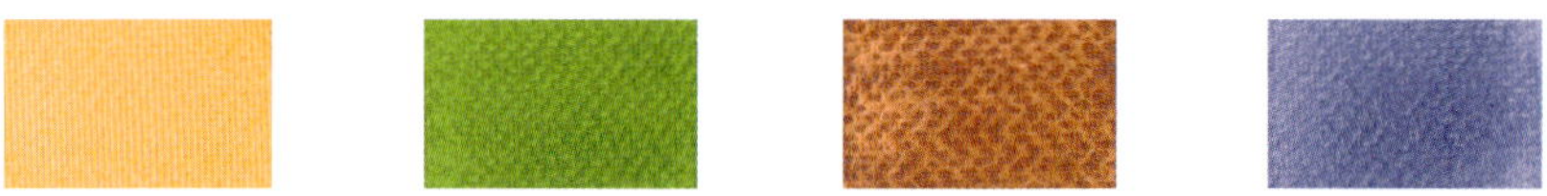

Yellow Ochre | Sap Green | Burnt Sienna | Dioxazine Purple

1. Use a pencil to draw a slanted-left teardrop shape below the center of the paper. This will be an avocado half. In its center, draw a smaller, more rounded oval (the pit). Add a curved line at the bottom of the teardrop to show the skin of the half. Above and slightly to the left of the avocado half, draw a slanted-right teardrop behind the half. This will be the whole avocado. At the top of it, draw a short line for a stem. On the stem, draw an avocado leaf with smooth, semi-oval lines. On the top left, draw a curved line and write the word "avocado" in handwritten cursive.

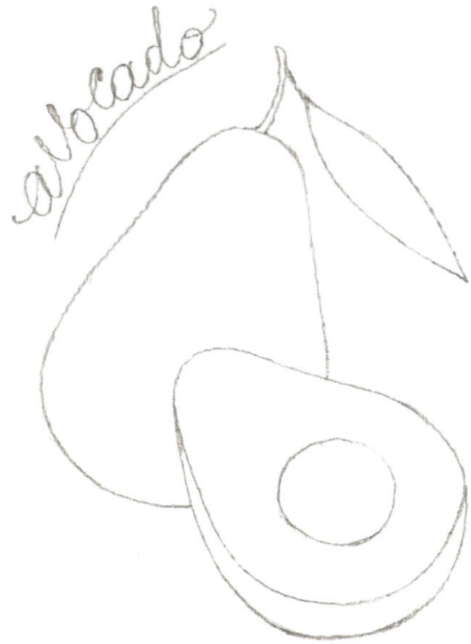

1

2. With a waterproof black liner, outline the avocados and leaf. Add short, curved lines close to the contour on the pit. Add dots and small strokes on the edges of the whole avocado, at the bottom of the peel of the half and slightly on the pulp of the avocado. Add dots and short strokes to the background around the avocado. Outline the lettering and add thickness to the letters on their vertical lines. Erase the pencil.

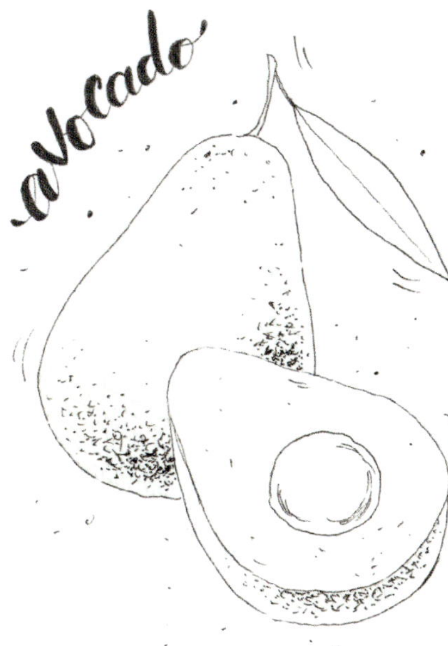

2

3. Mix Yellow Ochre and Sap Green in equal parts to get an ochre-green. Also prepare Sap Green separately on the palette. Paint the leaf and the peel of the half avocado with ochre-green and Sap Green, making smooth transitions between these colors. Try to make the bottom part of the peel lighter using ochre-green. Now let's get acquainted with a new technique, wet-on-wet. Prewet the whole avocado with clean water. While the paper is wet, apply ochre-green from the top left, gradually adding Sap Green toward the center. These colors will blend because the paper is wet, and that is exactly what we need! Use only Sap Green at the bottom of the avocado. Perfect! Watch the watercolor flow and enjoy the unexpected textures! Collect the extra water from the avocado with the brush or a napkin.

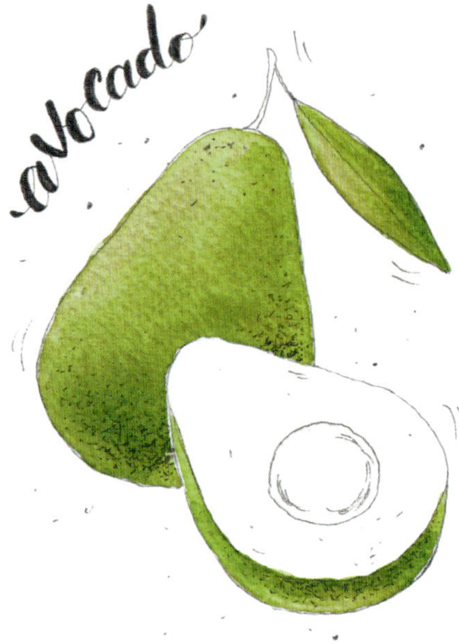

3

yellow ochre + sap green

4. Use Yellow Ochre and Burnt Sienna to paint the pit with a smooth transition between the colors and leave a white paper spot—a highlight on the upper left area. Paint the stem with Burnt Sienna. After the whole avocado dries, apply Sap Green in small, separate strokes as a second layer on the shadow part of the avocado. With a wet brush, blend these dark strokes into the first layer, toward the middle area of the avocado. Similarly, add shadow strokes to the upper part of the peel of the half avocado. Wait for everything to be completely dry.

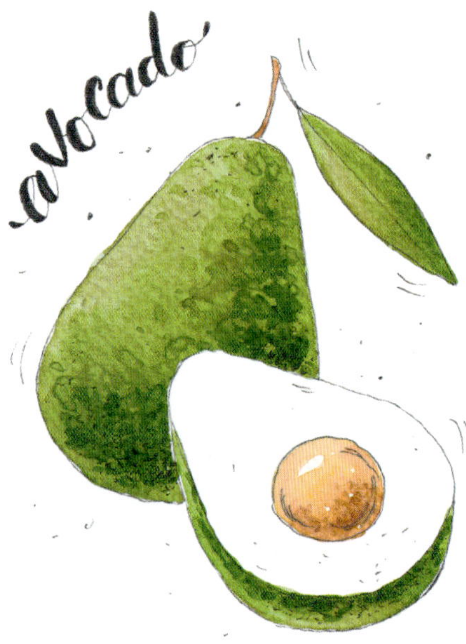

4

5. Separately mix Yellow Ochre and Sap Green with water to get light shades. Paint the pulp of the avocado with these colors, allowing the watercolors to make smooth transitions between them. After the paper dries, apply Burnt Sienna with curved strokes to add a shadow to the lower right side of the pit. Mix Dioxazine Purple with water to get a light purple. Also prepare Dioxazine Purple separately. Let's create a cast shadow using the wet-on-wet technique! Prewet the paper under and slightly around the avocado, apply light purple and closer to the avocado apply Dioxazine Purple. While the paper is still wet, add a few strokes of light green. Trust the process. The beauty of watercolor is in how it blends and surprises you! If there is some extra water, collect it with the brush or a napkin and soften the edges of the shadow with the damp brush.

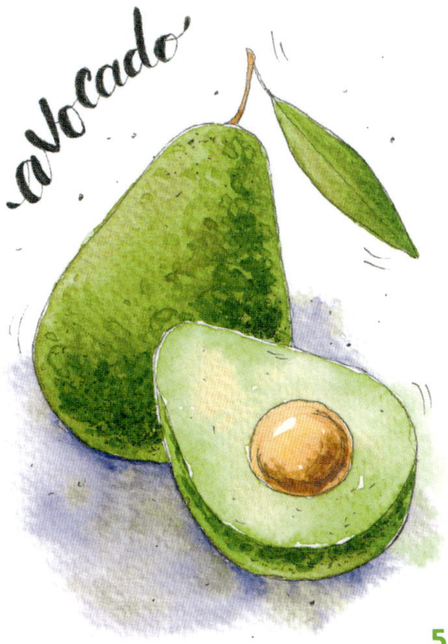

5

6. Use the black liner to darken the lower outlines of the whole and half avocado. Use a white gel pen to draw lines at the bottom of the whole and half avocados along the outlines. Also draw lines on the half, on the leaf and near the contour on the pit. Put dots on the top of the whole avocado and on the half avocado.

Amazing! Our sketch is ready!

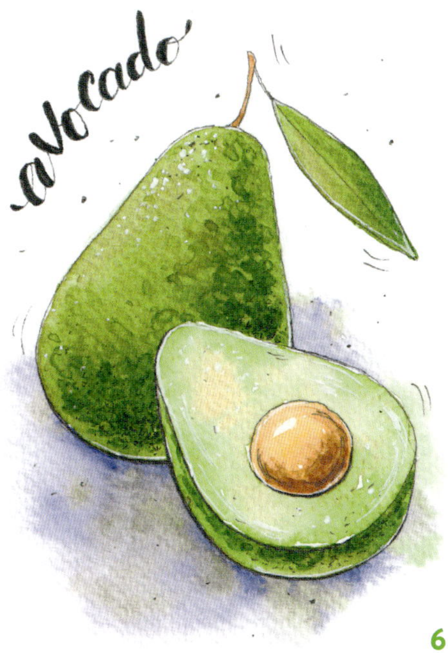

6

Lesson 18. Ruby Amanita Mushroom

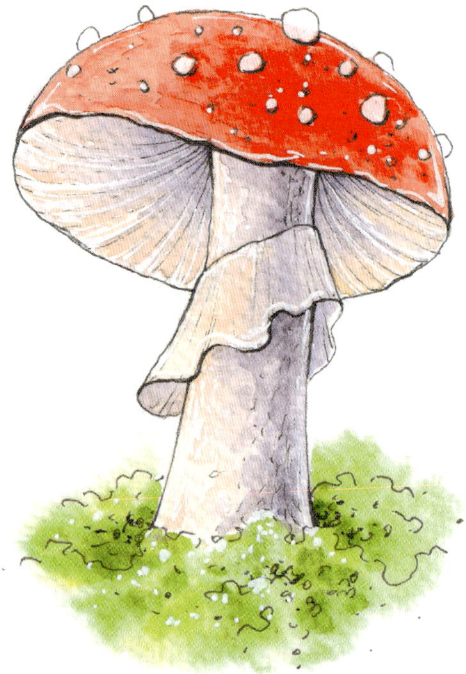

Get inspired by the magic of the forest! The bright ruby amanita mushroom is perfect for exploring light and shadow. You will also learn about different graphic techniques to draw the stem and cap of the mushroom. We'll use the wet-on-wet technique to create realistic-looking moss, and practice using accent colors and contrasts to add a magical mood to your sketch. Let's get started!

Paint Colors

Permanent Red Light	Yellow Ochre	Dioxazine Purple	Sap Green	Permanent Lemon Yellow

1. Use a pencil to draw a slightly curved vertical line in the center of the paper. Add a similar line next to it; this will be the mushroom's stem. At the top of these lines draw a slanted, uneven oval. Draw a semicircle from edge to edge on top of the oval; this is the cap of the mushroom. On the stem draw a semi-oval line and a wavy line downward. Connect these lines to the stem on both sides. This is the ring of the mushroom. At the bottom of the stem draw short, wavy lines. Randomly draw small circles of different sizes on the cap to show scales.

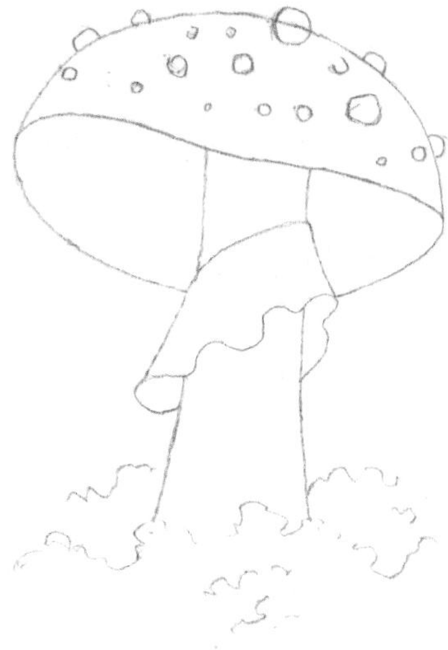

1

2. Use a waterproof black liner to outline the mushroom. Add quick hatches to the ring on the stem. Inside the cap draw smooth, thin and occasionally uneven lines directed toward the center of the cap. On the stem, draw vertical short lines and dots on the right side. Add small dots and doodles on the mushroom cap. Also, add dots and doodles under the mushroom and near the bottom of the stem to show moss. There's no right or wrong here. Experiment and let your hand move freely! Erase the pencil lines.

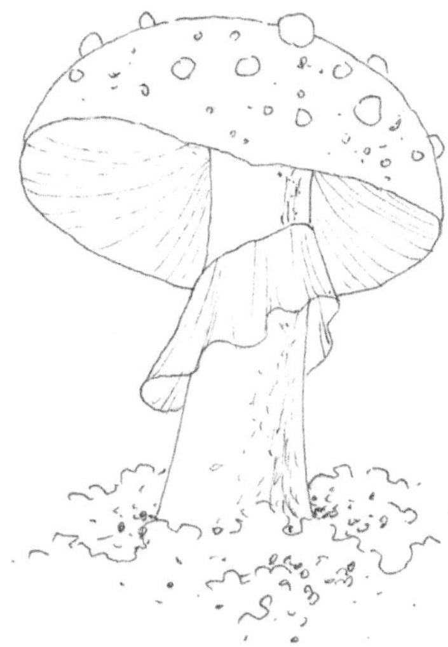

2

3. Mix Permanent Red Light with a bit of water and apply it to the cap with a simple wash. Feel free to cover the circles! Mix Yellow Ochre and Dioxazine Purple separately with water to get light ochre and light purple. Paint the stem with these colors, creating smooth transitions. Add a bit more light ochre on the left and light purple on the right. Prepare Sap Green and Permanent Lemon Yellow separately on the palette. Add water to the Sap Green to get light green. Prewet the paper around the bottom of the mushroom, and while it's still wet, randomly apply light green and Permanent Lemon Yellow. Add Sap Green closer to the stem. If there is some extra water, collect it with the brush or a napkin. Wait for everything to dry completely.

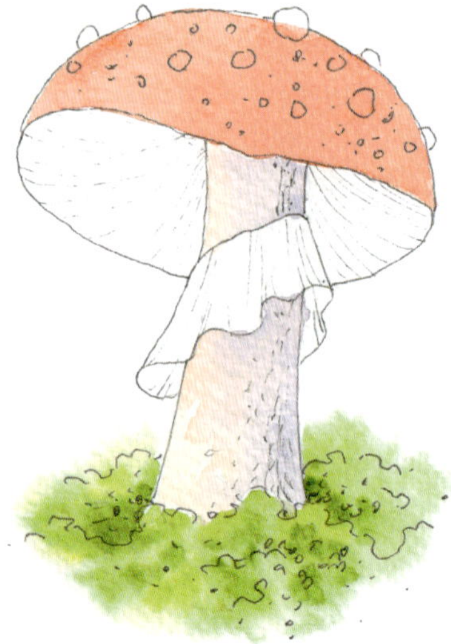

3

4. Apply Permanent Red Light with small strokes on the right part of the cap, not reaching the right edge. Soften it with a damp brush toward the left and right sides. Use the light ochre and light purple to paint under the mushroom cap as well as on the ring. Add more light ochre around the edges and light purple toward the middle. Then make a second layer of light purple and use short, vertical strokes on the right side of the stem, and then soften them with a damp brush toward the left. Paint under the ring with light purple. Great! Now, let's wait again for the paper to dry.

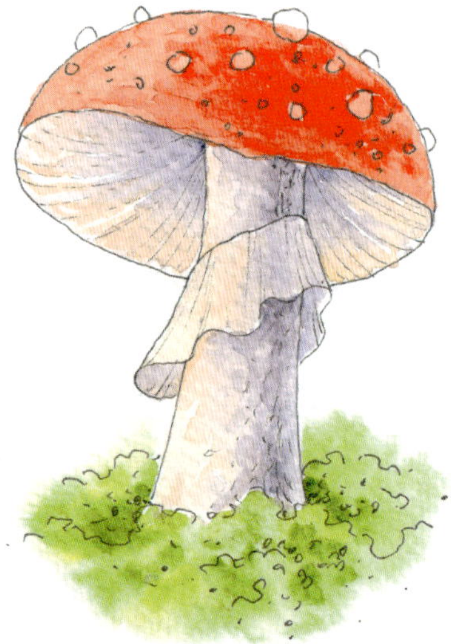

4

5. Use the black liner to make the nearest line of the cap and the wavy line of the ring bolder. Add darker lines on the stem, moss and under the cap. Use a white gel pen to color in the scales. Draw lines around the contour of the cap. Add smooth, curved and randomly detached lines under the cap, directed toward the center. Draw a line next to the contour of the ring and on both sides of the stem. Place dots and doodles on the left side of the stem and randomly on the moss.

Well done! Our sketch is ready!

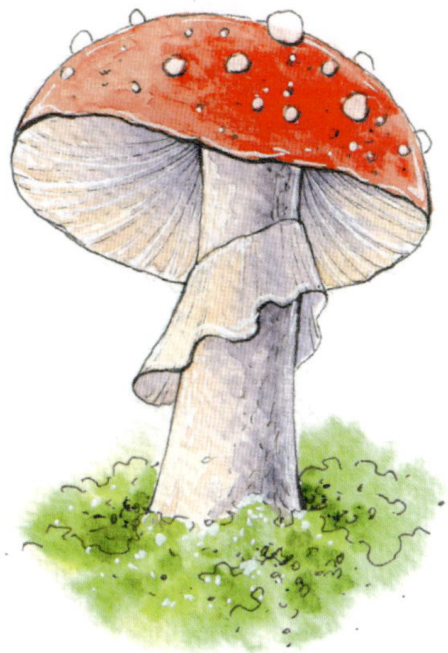

5

Lesson 19. Reef Rhapsody

Dive into the underwater world in this watercolor painting of a coral reef. In this lesson, you will explore complex structures of reefs and a rich palette of underwater colors. You will continue to practice layering and the wet-on-wet technique to create texture, playing with paint flows and gradients. This lesson is perfect for those looking to expand their artistic horizons and get inspired by the melody of the sea. Let's begin!

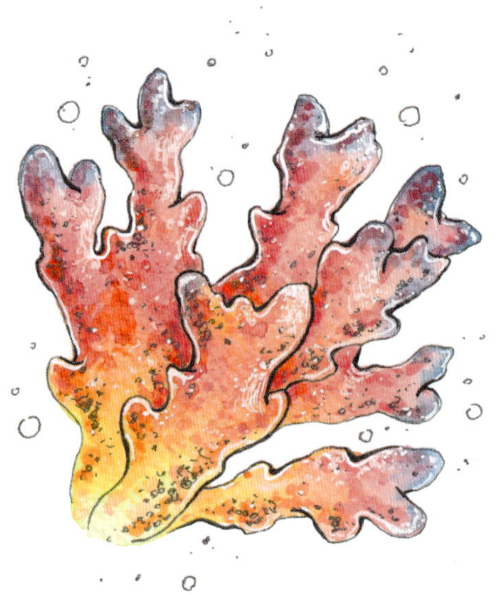

Paint Colors

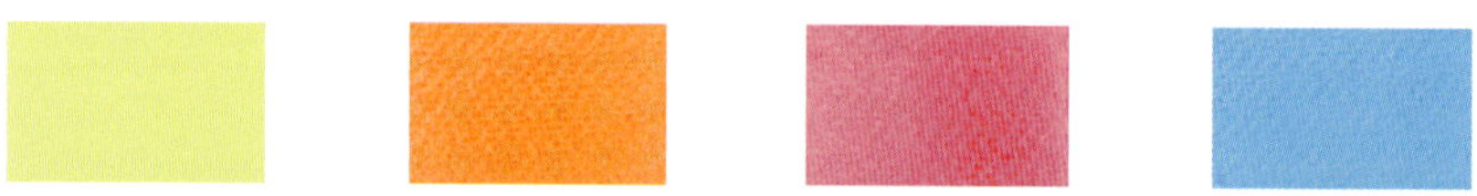

Permanent Lemon Yellow	Azo Orange	Quinacridone Rose	Cerulean Blue

1. Use a pencil to draw an elongated drop in the lower left part of the paper. To the right add two more drops, one larger and one smaller. Draw another drop at the bottom right. Behind these drops draw a wavy line with four peaks. Inside all these shapes draw lines resembling branches, with central veins and small branches going in various directions from these drops and shapes. Great! Now, we have a simplified form of corals. You can do it a bit differently in shape; feel free to play with forms!

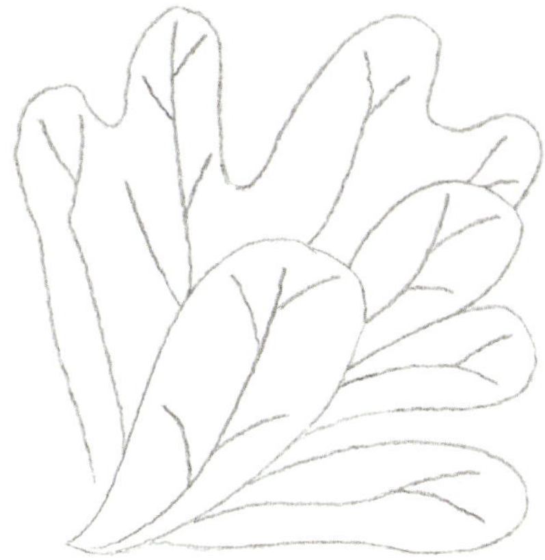

1

2. Use a waterproof black liner to outline the corals with a curvy line, giving them uneven wavy edges while using the internal branches as a guide. Randomly draw small dots and doodles on the corals, closer to their edges on the right or left, to show shadows and dimension. Add bubbles around the corals on the background as circles of various sizes and dots. Erase the pencil marks.

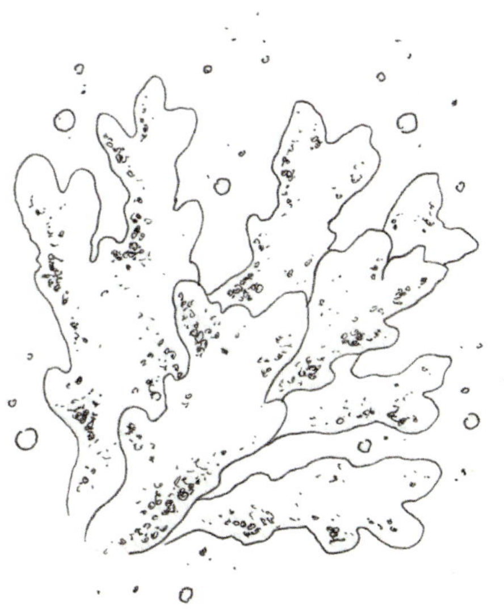

2

3. Prepare Permanent Lemon Yellow, Azo Orange, Quinacridone Rose and Cerulean Blue on your palette. Prewet the corals with clean water, trying not to go beyond the outlines. Starting from the bottom, add Permanent Lemon Yellow, then above it use Azo Orange, then make a smooth transition to Quinacridone Rose and at the top edges add Cerulean Blue. Relax and observe the process! Allow the colors to blend and flow beautifully into each other. If there is some extra water, collect it with the brush or a napkin. Wait for everything to dry completely.

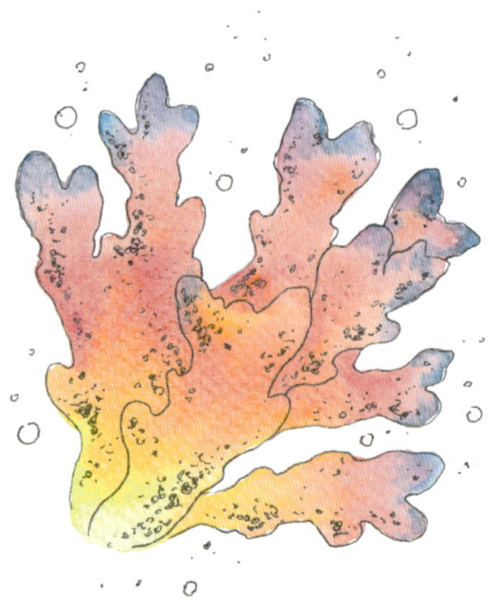

3

4. Randomly apply Azo Orange and Quinacridone Rose with short, small and separate strokes closer to the contours of the corals. Use more orange toward the bottom and more pink at the top. Add more pink strokes on the corals that are in the back to create a shadow. Amazing! And again, let's wait for the paper to dry.

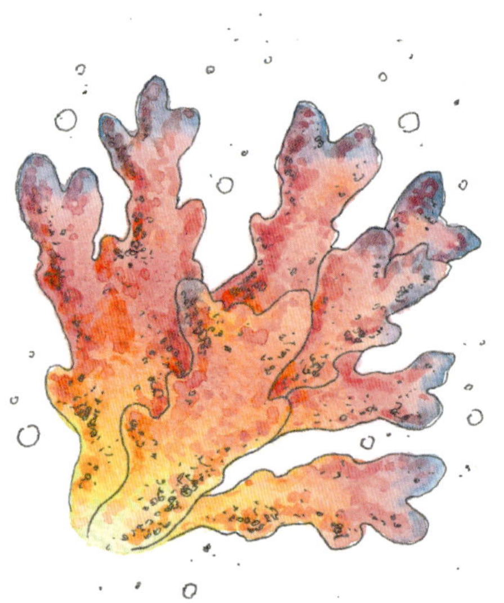

4

5. Use the black liner to make the outlines of the corals bolder in random areas, sometimes overlapping onto the corals themselves in some of the bends. Use a white gel pen to make smooth, wavy lines in some places along the inner contour of the corals. Randomly draw short lines, dots and doodles on the corals a bit more on the right side to emphasize dimension and texture.

Wonderful! Our sketch is ready!

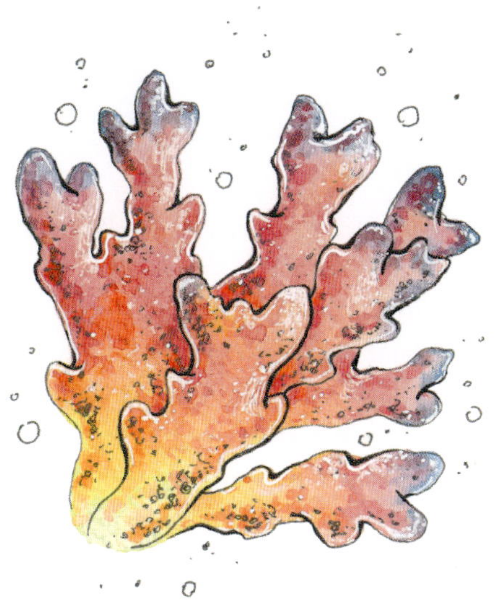

5

Lesson 20. Viola Floral Fusion

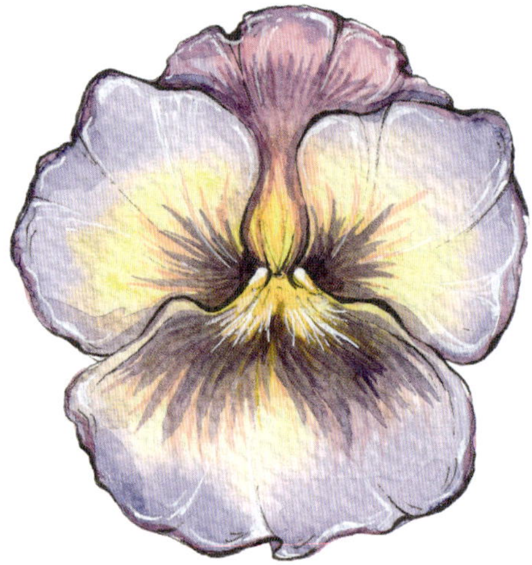

Discover the delicacy, beauty and kaleidoscope of colors of a viola flower. In this lesson, you will learn how to paint the finest folds on the petals, practice the intricacies of drawing thin details and recreate a bright, vivid flower. You'll find out how using the wet-on-wet technique and layers of watercolor can achieve an effect of lightness and the transparency of the petals. Let the paints swirl in a dance of vibrant hues! Prepare your brushes and paints, and let's begin!

Paint Colors

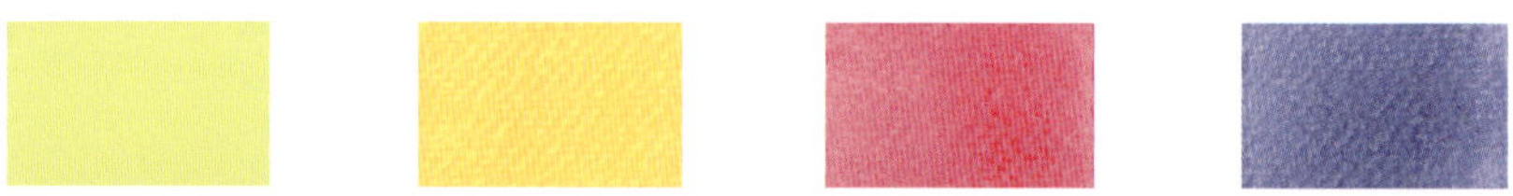

Permanent Lemon Yellow	Azo Yellow Medium	Quinacridone Rose	Dioxazine Purple

1. Use a pencil to draw a slightly wavy line just below the center of the paper to create a large, wide drop shape. This will be a large viola petal. Draw two smaller drops above on either side, slightly tucked under the large petal. At the top also draw a curved line. This will be the upper petal. In the center of the flower, draw two small drops pointing downward and to the sides.

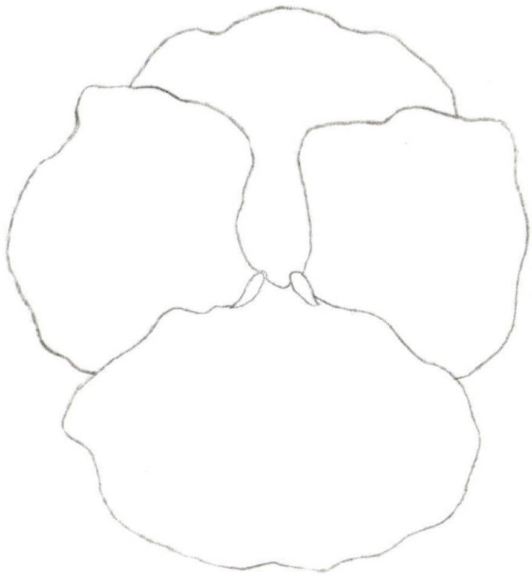

1

2. Use a waterproof black liner to outline the petals with curvy lines. At some points on the edges of the petals, make slightly more curled outlines. These will be small folds. Add quick hatches toward the center of the flower on the bends of the folds. Also add two short, curved dashes on the edges of the petals to emphasize the folds. Outline the drops in the center of the flower with an interrupted line. Add random, thin hatches on the petals from the center of the flower, as well as from the edges to the center. Erase the pencil.

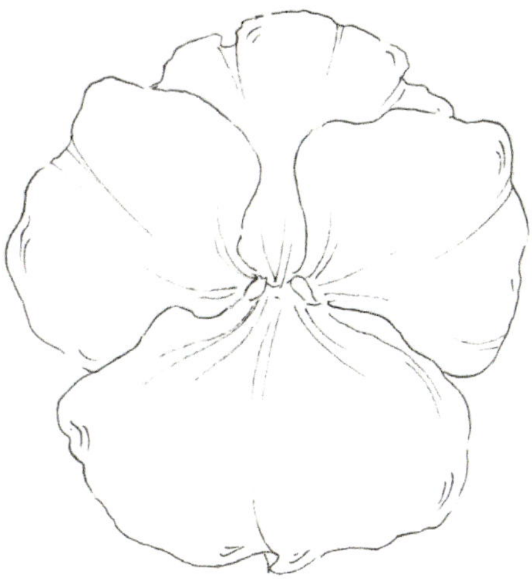

2

3. Prepare Permanent Lemon Yellow, Azo Yellow Medium, Quinacridone Rose and Dioxazine Purple on the palette. Prewet the entire flower with clean water and apply Permanent Lemon Yellow in the middle, slightly stretching it in line strokes from the center to the petals. Add a bit more to the lower petal and less to the upper petals. You are doing great! Make small strokes of Dioxazine Purple around the edges of the petals, except for the top one. Try not to mix the colors; just let them flow into each other naturally. If there is some extra water, collect it with the brush or a napkin. Add Azo Yellow Medium with a few long strokes from the center to the lower large petal. Add Quinacridone Rose and Dioxazine Purple to the upper petal. Wait for everything to dry completely.

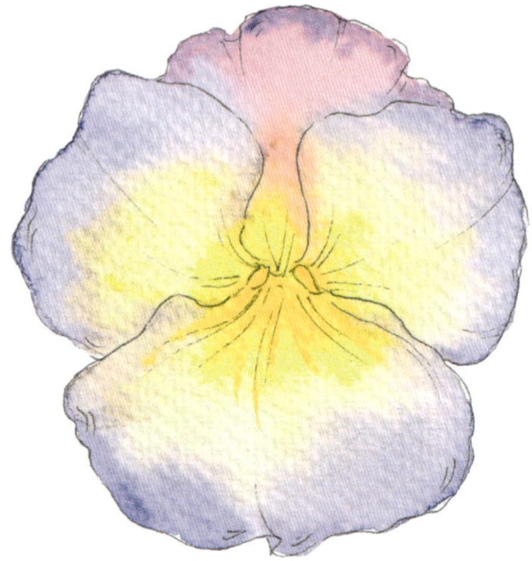

3

4. Mix Quinacridone Rose and Dioxazine Purple in equal proportions and dilute a bit with water to get a lilac color. Use it to make curved strokes following the shape of the petals, starting from the middle area. Paint longer strokes on the upper petal and shorter strokes on the lower and side petals, leaving the first layer slightly visible. Along the edges of the petals, add short, loose strokes with the same color. Perfect! Glazing is magic! Let's wait for the paper to dry.

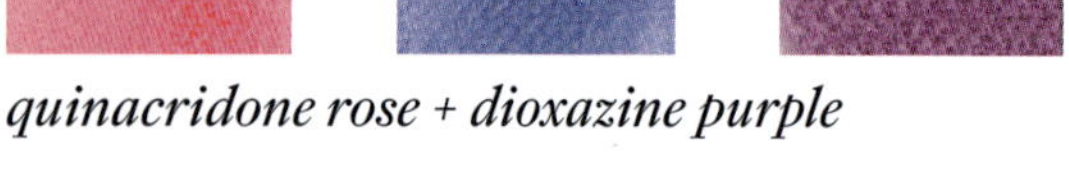

quinacridone rose + dioxazine purple

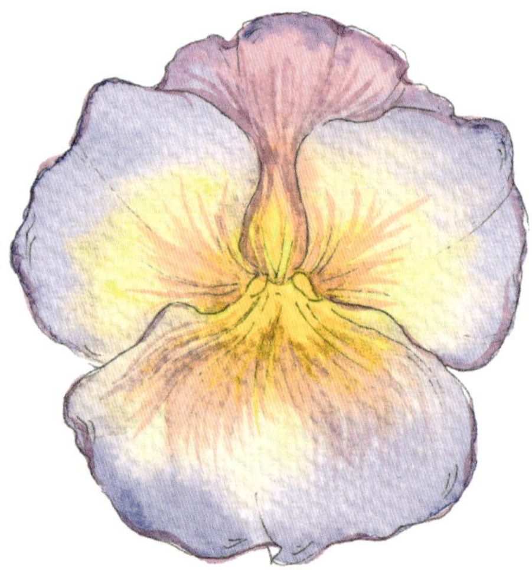

4

5. Mix Dioxazine Purple with water to get a light purple. Make short, loose strokes with light purple and Dioxazine Purple along the contours of all petals, leaving the previous layers slightly visible. Using both light purple and Dioxazine Purple, paint the inner surface of the folds. Add a second layer of shorter thin strokes from the center on the side and lower petals. On the upper petal, near the edge, paint short, thin strokes as well. Make shadow lines from the lower petal to the side petals and from the side petals to the upper one.

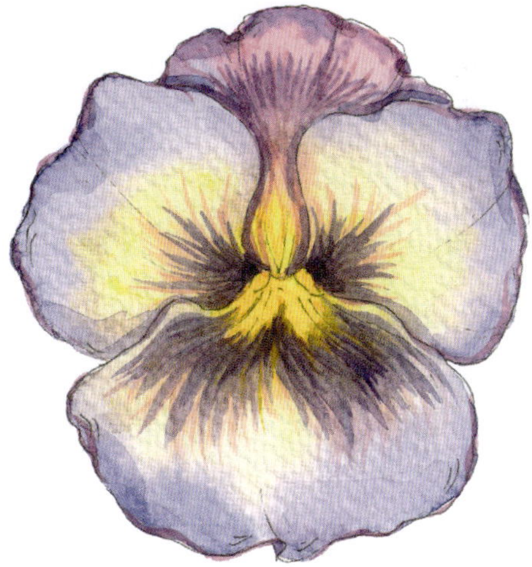

5

6. Use the black liner to softly and smoothly make some of the contour lines of the petals bolder. Use a white gel pen to draw soft, smooth lines near the petals' inner contour. Add quick, curved hatches from the edges of the petals toward the center of the flower and on the folds to create dimension. Draw curved, short strokes and two ovals above them on the large petal, closer to the center.

Great work! Our sketch is ready!

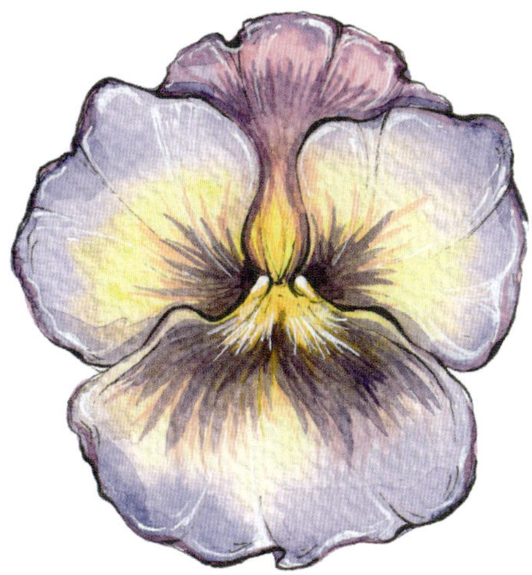

6

Lesson 21. Calming Meditation Stones

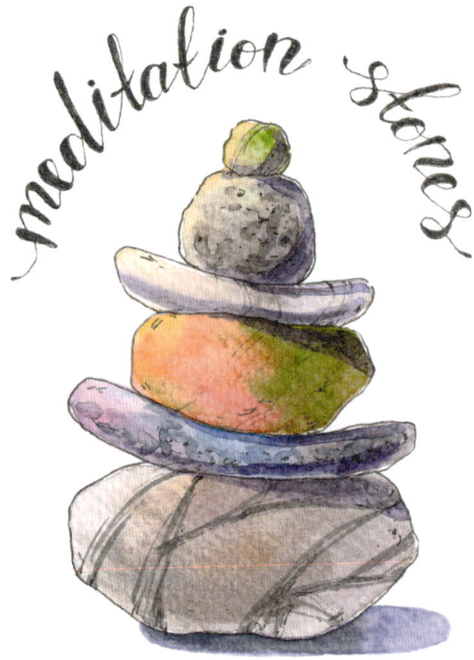

Explore the tranquility and minimalism of meditation stones in this lesson. You will learn how to create relaxing compositions that perfectly depict harmony and balance. Practice how to accentuate textures and shadows on each stone to give them realism and depth. With the wet-on-wet technique, you'll experience the meditative effect of flowing colors. Let's get started!

Paint Colors

- Sap Green
- Yellow Ochre
- Dioxazine Purple
- Burnt Sienna
- Ultramarine Deep
- Azo Orange
- Quinacridone Rose
- Cerulean Blue

1. Use a pencil to draw a slightly curved oval in the lower part of the paper. This will be the bottom stone. Above it, draw a flattened oval with edges curving upward. On this oval draw another smaller, thicker and more curved oval. On top of it, draw a smaller, flattened oval with the edges curving upward. Then, place a smaller, rounder stone on top and, finally, the smallest round stone on top of that. Draw a semi-oval line to place lettering above the stones. Write "meditation stones," or any words you want, in handwritten cursive along this line.

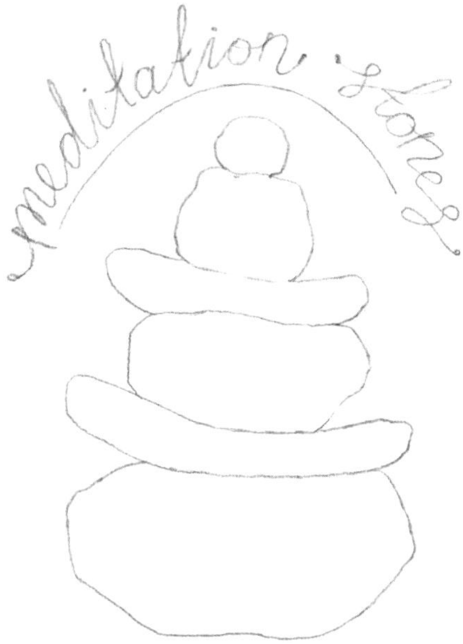

1

2. Use a waterproof black liner to outline the stones with a smooth, slightly uneven line. Randomly draw thin, curved and short lines on some of the stones to create a pattern. On the remaining stones, draw small dots, lines and doodles for texture. Outline the lettering and make the vertical lines of the letters bolder by coloring them black. Erase all the pencil marks.

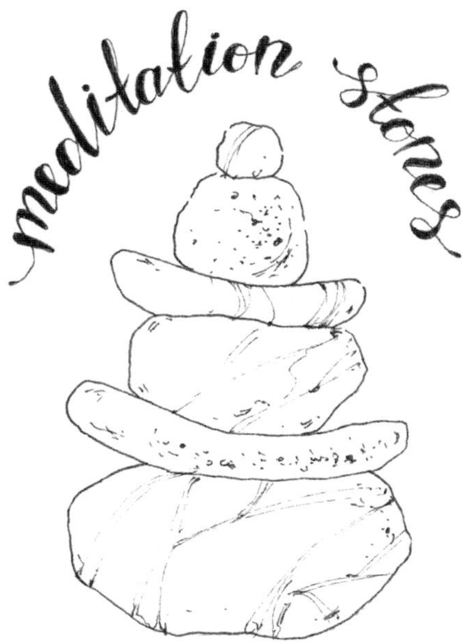

2

3. Prepare Sap Green, Yellow Ochre, Dioxazine Purple and Burnt Sienna on your palette. Mix Burnt Sienna and Ultramarine Deep in equal proportions to get a gray color. Prewet the top stone with clean water and paint it with Yellow Ochre and Sap Green, letting the colors blend naturally. Prewet the next stone and paint it with Yellow Ochre, gray and Dioxazine Purple, letting the colors smoothly blend and making the stone lighter on the left and darker on the right. Then prewet the third stone and paint it with Yellow Ochre and Dioxazine Purple, using more ochre on the left and more purple on the right. Your sketch is your playground. Enjoy the experiments!

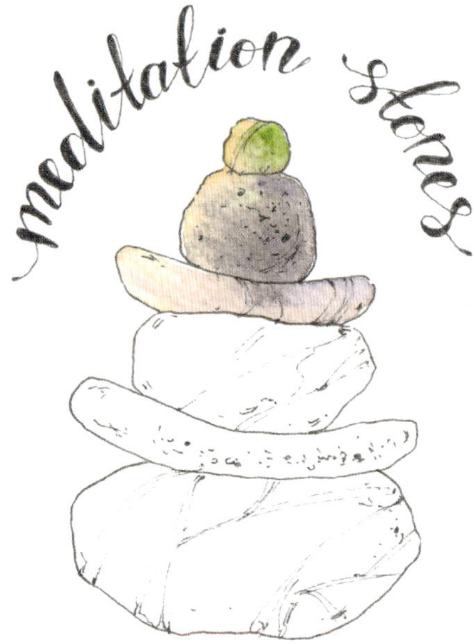

3

burnt sienna + ultramarine deep

4. Prepare additional Yellow Ochre, Azo Orange, Quinacridone Rose, Sap Green and Cerulean Blue on the palette. Prewet the next stone with clean water and paint it with Yellow Ochre, Azo Orange and Quinacridone Rose on the left and middle, and add Sap Green on the right. Let the colors flow into each other without mixing them too much on the paper. Prewet the next stone with clean water, then paint it with Quinacridone Rose and Cerulean Blue on the left and middle, and gray and Dioxazine Purple on the right. Paint the last stone with gray, Dioxazine Purple and Burnt Sienna. Great! Wait for the paper to dry completely.

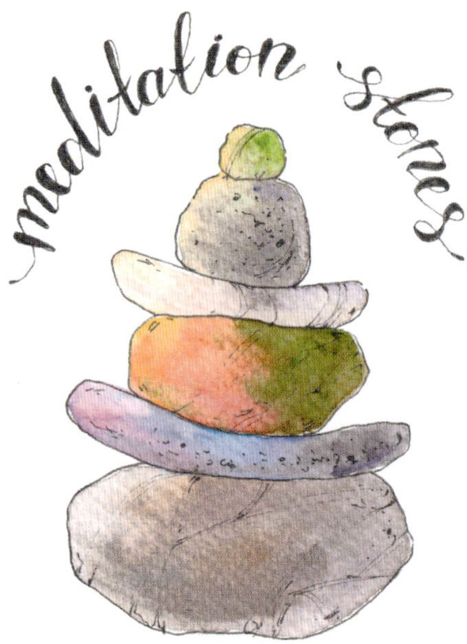

4

5. On the second stone from the top, add small, random, separate strokes and dots with gray to show the rough texture. On the second stone from the bottom, also randomly paint small separate dots of Cerulean Blue and Dioxazine Purple. On the lowest stone, paint interrupted lines of different thicknesses with gray. You are doing great! Wait for the paper to dry again. Paint shadows on the stones on the right side with a simple flat wash of Dioxazine Purple. Paint an oval cast shadow under the lowest stone with gray and Dioxazine Purple.

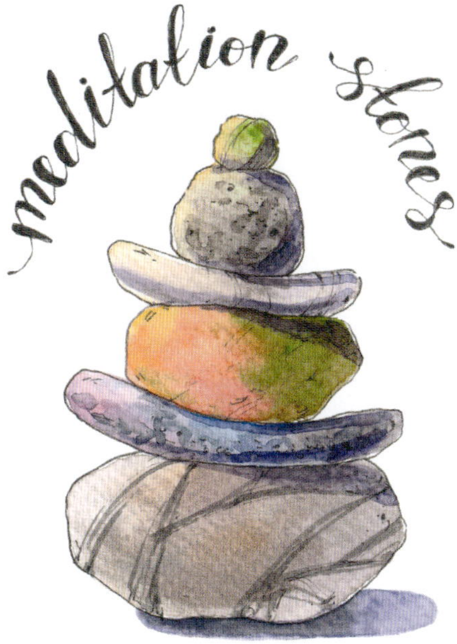

5

6. Use the black liner to softly and smoothly make some of the contour lines of the stones bolder. Use a white gel pen to draw lines inside the contours of the stones to emphasize their shape, shine and dimension. Add dots and short lines to enhance the rough texture on some stones. On the third and fifth stones from the top, add white lines to make the pattern brighter.

You are doing great! Our sketch is ready!

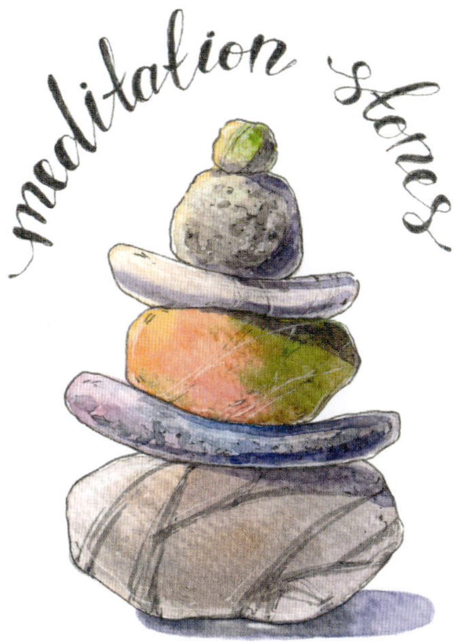

6

Lesson 22. Topiary Tweets

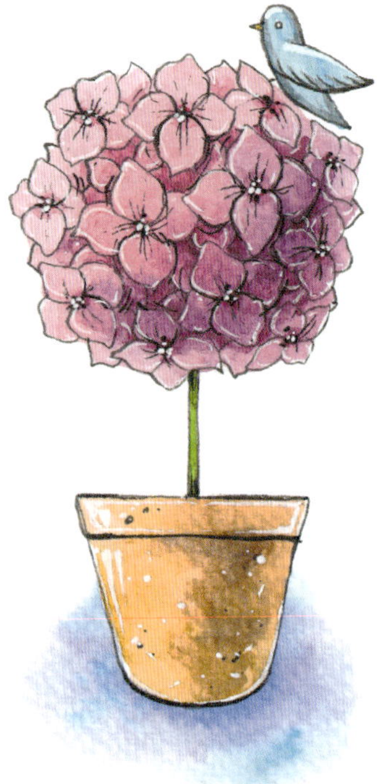

Discover the beauty of nature with this topiary and a cheerful little bird. This lesson will teach you how to depict various pink shades and the fine details of a feathered friend, adding a sense of lightness and liveliness to your work. We'll explore how to apply colors and shadows properly to achieve the most natural and appealing results. You'll learn how to softly blend colors on the flower and create dimension with watercolors, making your artwork expressive and full of enchanting details. Let's begin!

Paint Colors

Quinacridone Rose

Dioxazine Purple

Cerulean Blue

Sap Green

Yellow Ochre

Burnt Umber

1. Use a pencil to draw a straight vertical line in the center of the paper. At the bottom of it, draw a trapezoid that widens upward, then draw a semi-oval line at the bottom of the trapezoid. This is the pot. At the top of the vertical line, draw a large circle. Inside the circle draw smaller circles randomly in the center and ovals closer to the edges. In the upper right of the large circle, draw a small drop with a sharp tip pointing downward and to the right, and above it, a slightly smaller drop with the tip pointing right. This is the bird.

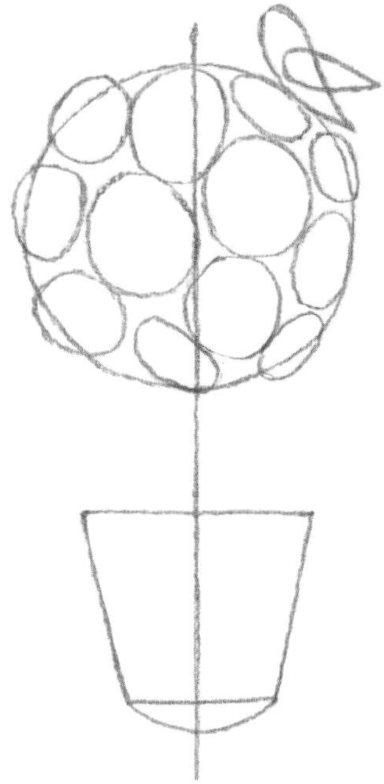

1

2. Put dots in the center of each circle and oval. Draw petals in the shape of droplets from their centers to show flowers, with four petals per flower. Start with the central circles and make the petals larger, then move to the ovals and make the petals smaller. Draw some petals slightly overlapping others.

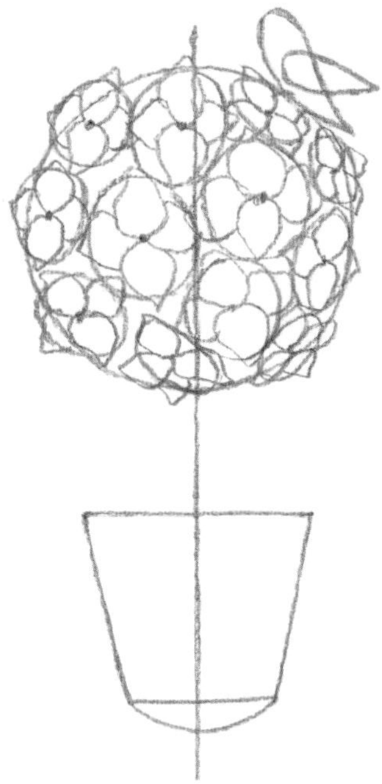

2

3. Use a waterproof black liner to outline the pot. Draw a horizontal line to make the rim, then add several dots and short hatches randomly on the pot. Draw the topiary's trunk with two lines. Randomly fill the space between the flowers with lines and shapes resembling petals. Outline the bird's wing, skipping the line at the top. Add several short hatches in a row at the bottom of the wing. Outline the bird and draw a triangular beak and a circular eye. Great! Let's erase the pencil drawing.

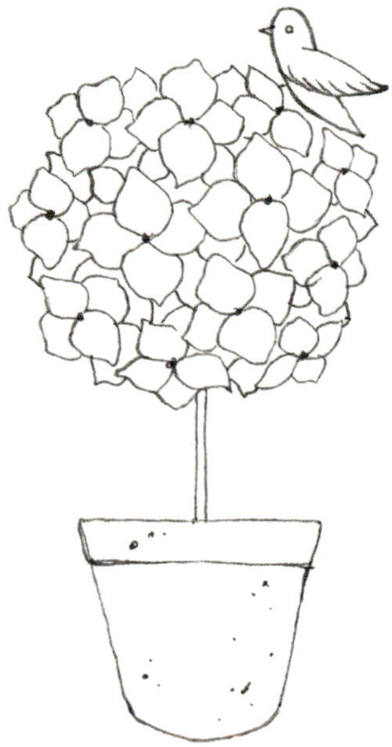

3

4. Prepare Quinacridone Rose and Dioxazine Purple on the palette. Mix a light pink shade separately using Quinacridone Rose and water. Paint the topiary flowers with light pink, adding more Quinacridone Rose toward the middle and a bit of Dioxazine Purple at the lower right. Try to create smooth transitions between the colors, leaving the very right edge light pink. Add Cerulean Blue to the palette. Prewet the paper under the pot with clean water and add Dioxazine Purple and Cerulean Blue next to it. Try to make smooth transitions between the colors without mixing them too much on the paper. Add a bit more Dioxazine Purple under the pot for shading. If some extra water remains, collect it with the brush or a napkin and soften the edges of the shadow with a damp brush. Add water to the Cerulean Blue to get a light blue color and use this to paint the bird, leaving the beak white.

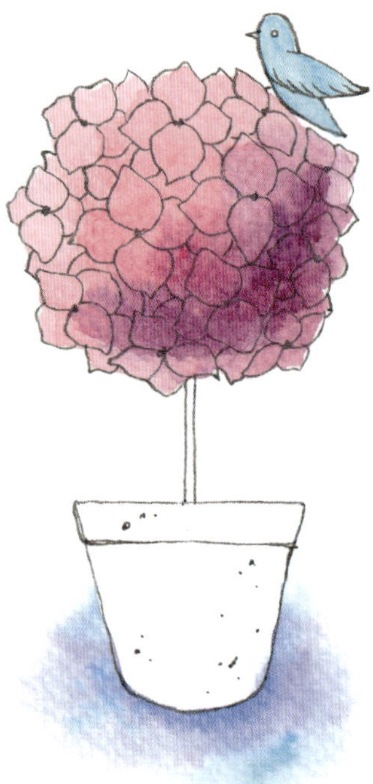

4

5. Paint the topiary's trunk with Sap Green. Add a few drops of Dioxazine Purple to Quinacridone Rose and paint the spaces between the topiary's flowers and several random dots in the centers of the flowers. Add Yellow Ochre and Burnt Umber to the palette. Paint the pot with Yellow Ochre and add small strokes of Burnt Umber near the middle to show the shadow. Try to make smooth transitions between the colors. Paint the bird's beak with Yellow Ochre. Add a few drops of Burnt Umber to Cerulean Blue, and dilute with water to get a light shade of gray-blue and paint around the contour of the bird.

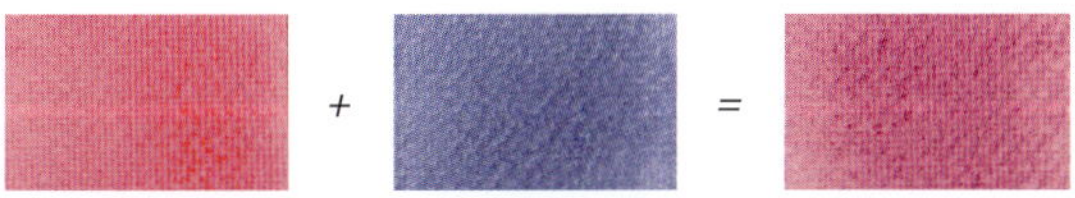

quinacridone rose + dioxazine purple

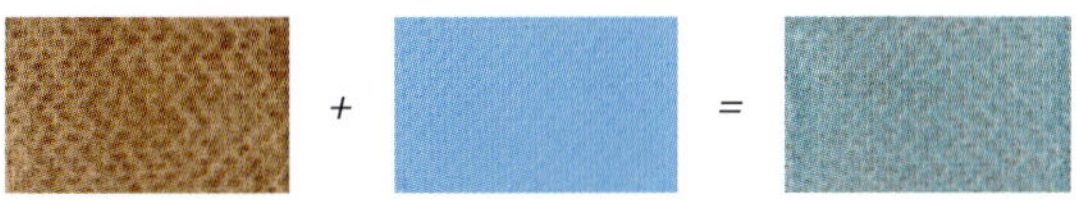

burnt umber + cerulean blue

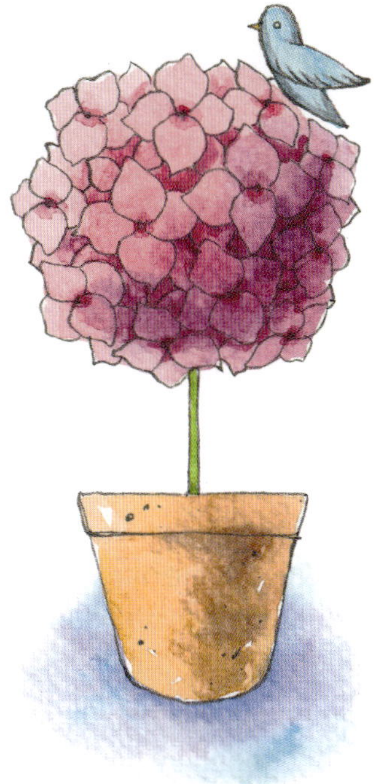

5

6. Use the black liner to make some of the contour lines of the petals bolder. In the centers of the flowers, draw dots and short hatches for veins. Make the lines on the bird's wing darker at the bottom and add shading at the top and bottom of the topiary's stem. Draw some parts of the pot's contour bolder, especially at the bottom. Use a white gel pen to draw free and loose lines at the petals' edges. Place several dots in the centers of the flowers. Add white lines on top of the bird's head and wing. On the pot draw lines next to the contour and also place some random dots.

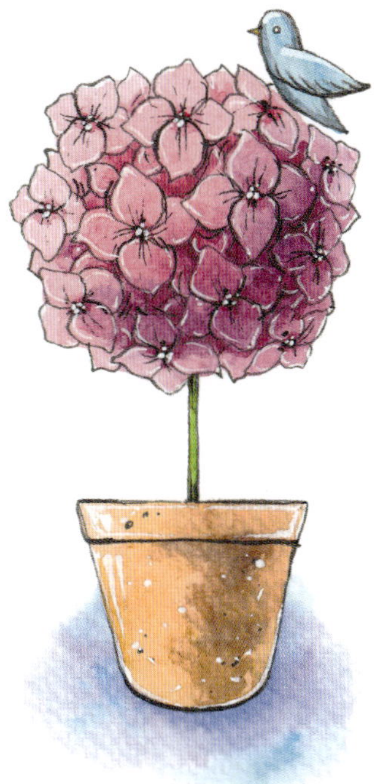

6

Wonderful! Our sketch is ready!

Lesson 23. Antique Key and Ribbon

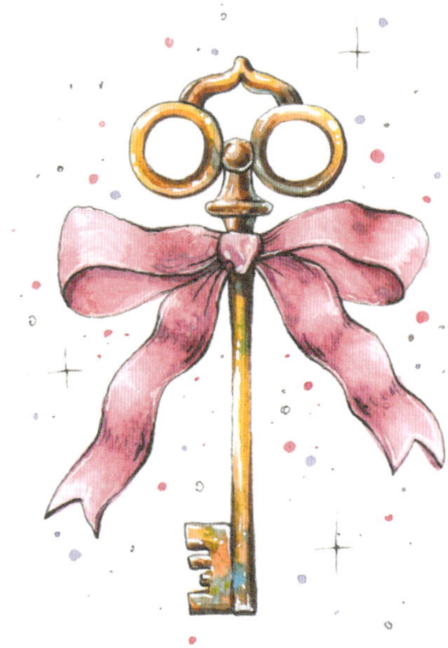

Bring a touch of vintage charm to your artwork! This lesson will unveil the intricacies of drawing antique metal objects and textile accessories. You will learn how to use light and shadows in watercolor to give your key dimension and shine and to lend your ribbon softness and realism, creating a piece of art filled with charm and delicacy. Let's start!

Paint Colors

Quinacridone Rose

Yellow Ochre

Burnt Sienna

Cerulean Blue

Dioxazine Purple

Burnt Umber

1. Use a pencil to draw two vertical lines close to each other in the center of the paper. Connect them at the bottom with a horizontal line and draw a small rectangle with a notched side on the left. At the top of the vertical lines, draw a small oval; this is the center of the bow, a knot. Draw curved loops to the left and right of the knot. Inside each loop, add a curved line to show the ribbon's twist. Also draw a curved line downward on both sides. Add thickness to the lines and draw them with fishtail cut ends. Above the knot draw a more flattened and elongated oval. Slightly higher, draw a small circle. Connect the circle to the oval with curved lines. From this circle, draw two larger circles to the sides and add thickness to them. Connect these two circles at the top with two curved lines, each with a slight point in the middle.

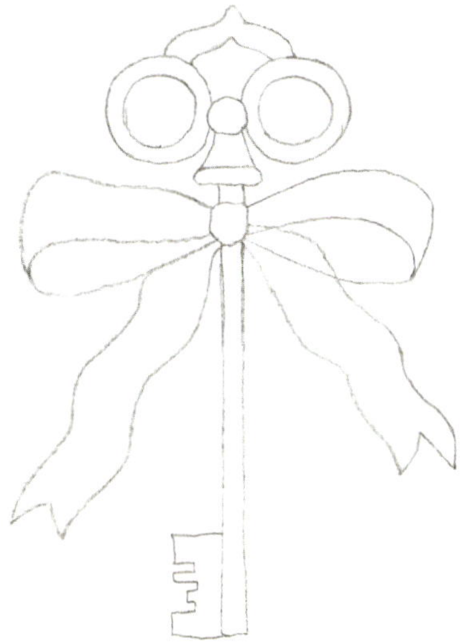

1

2. Use a waterproof black liner to outline the key with a simple line. Outline the bow with a slightly wavy line. Add short lines at the folds of the bow. Randomly draw small dots, circles and stars with sharp ends around the key to create a sparkling effect. Amazing! You are doing great! It is okay if your drawing is a bit different; you can also add your own details to the background if you like. Erase the pencil marks.

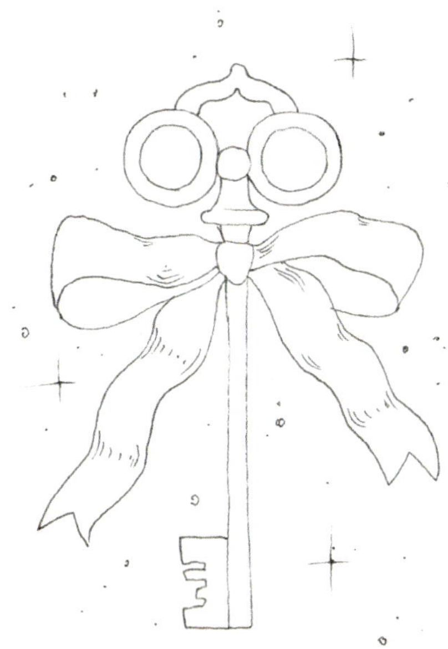

2

3. Prepare Quinacridone Rose on the palette and mix a light pink separately using Quinacridone Rose and water. Prewet the entire bow with clean water and paint it light pink, adding Quinacridone Rose on folds while the paper is still wet. Remove extra water with the brush or a napkin and wait for it to dry completely. Prepare Yellow Ochre, Burnt Sienna and Cerulean Blue on the palette. Paint the key primarily using Yellow Ochre, occasionally adding Burnt Sienna and Cerulean Blue. Trust the process! Let these colors flow into each other and also leave some areas of white paper.

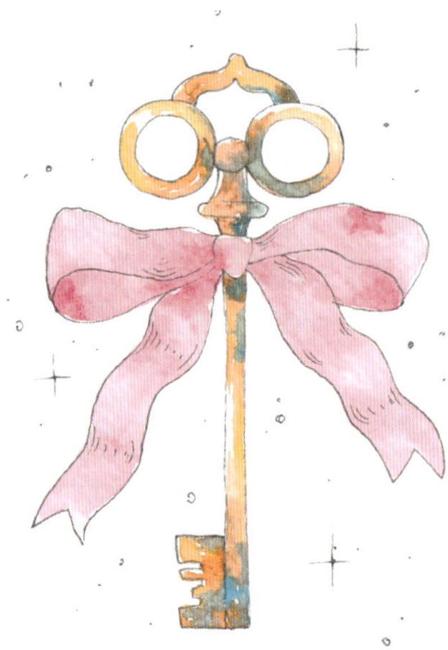

3

4. This step is for glazing and making soft edges! Use Quinacridone Rose to paint the bow at the folds and where the liner lines are, inside the bow and near the knot, to show shadows. Soften the edges of the strokes with a damp brush. Paint small dots and circles of Quinacridone Rose and Dioxazine Purple around the key. Apply shadows with thin lines of Yellow Ochre and Burnt Umber on the key. Create smooth transitions between these colors so they blend together.

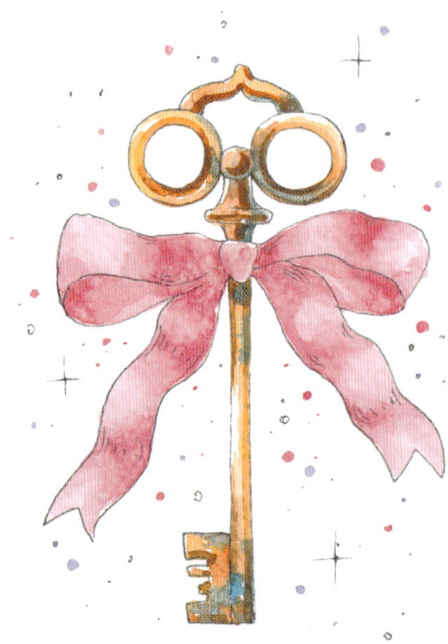

4

5. Mix Quinacridone Rose with a few drops of Dioxazine Purple to get a darker pink. Use this color for the third layer of strokes on the bow at the folds, where we already applied shadows with the second layer. Keep the previous layers slightly visible. Soften the edges with the damp brush as well. Apply short, quick strokes of Yellow Ochre on the key's light areas. Then paint Burnt Umber in the shadow areas, especially at the bottom of the key, near the knot's top and bottom and on the upper elements of the key.

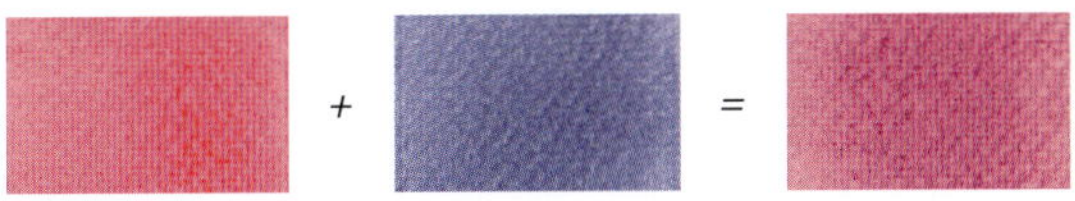

quinacridone rose + dioxazine purple

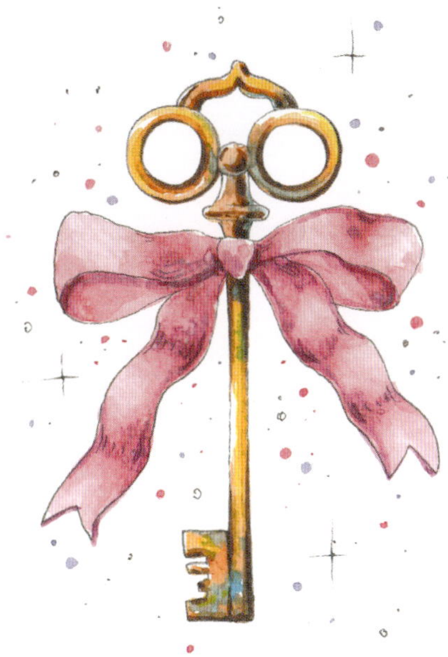

5

6. Use the black liner to make the outline of the key and bow bolder in some shadow areas. Use a white gel pen to add dots and short stripes near the Yellow Ochre and near the spots of white paper on the key. Draw smooth white lines on the lower edges of the bow's loops and knot and on the upper edges of the ribbon strings. Use the white gel pen to make short lines on the upper folds of the ribbon's loops.

Fantastic! Our sketch is ready!

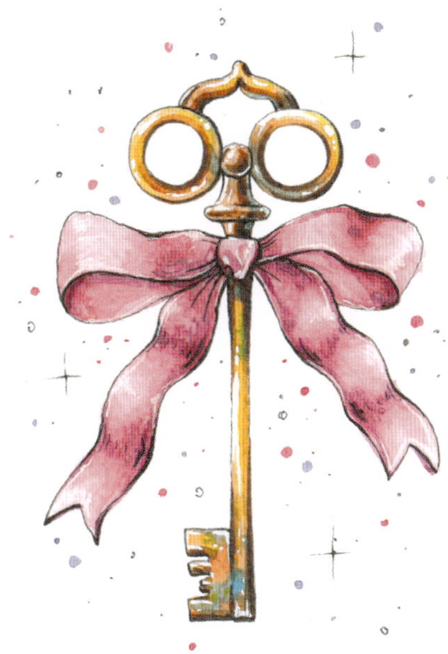

6

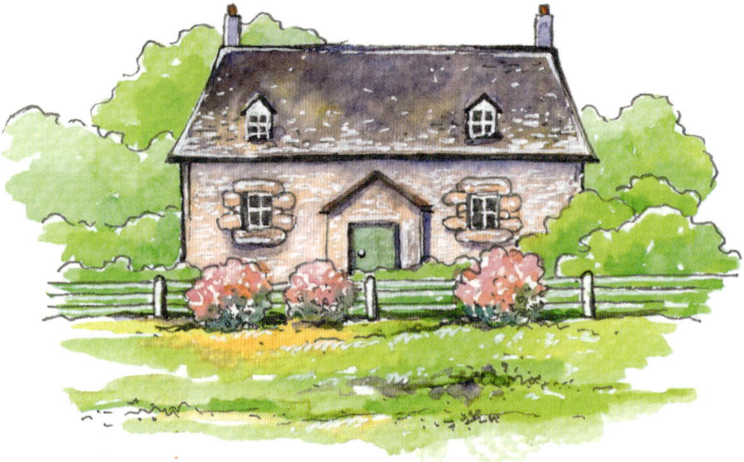

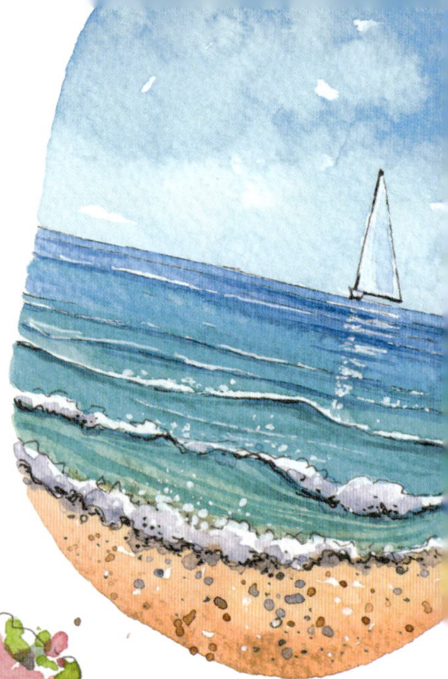

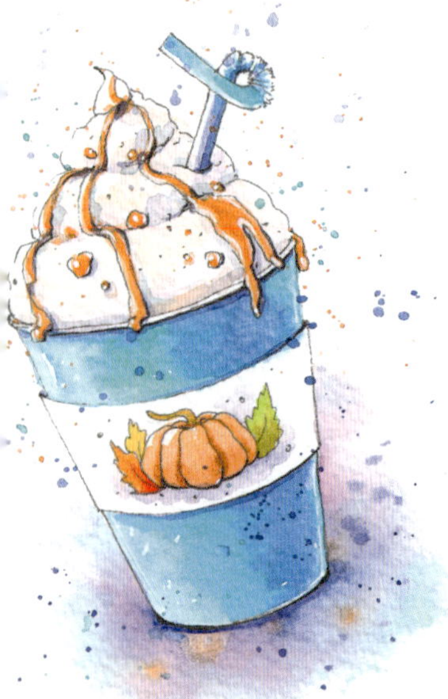

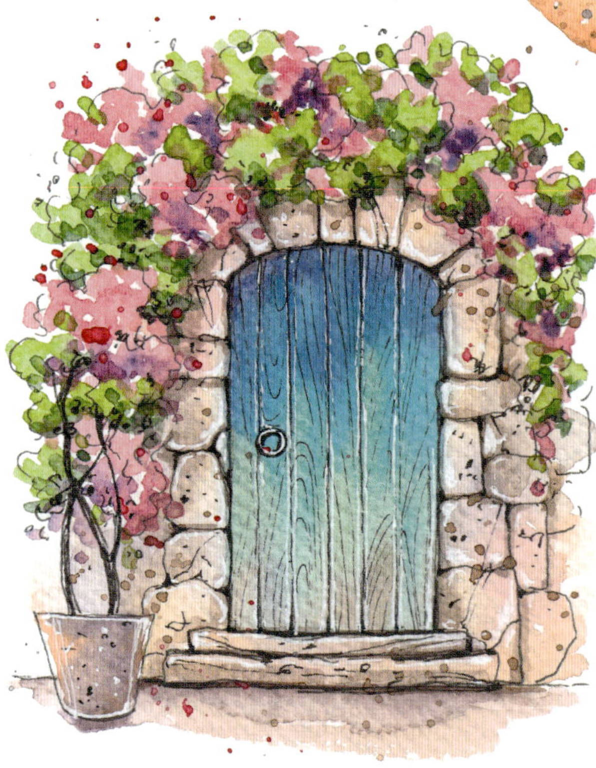

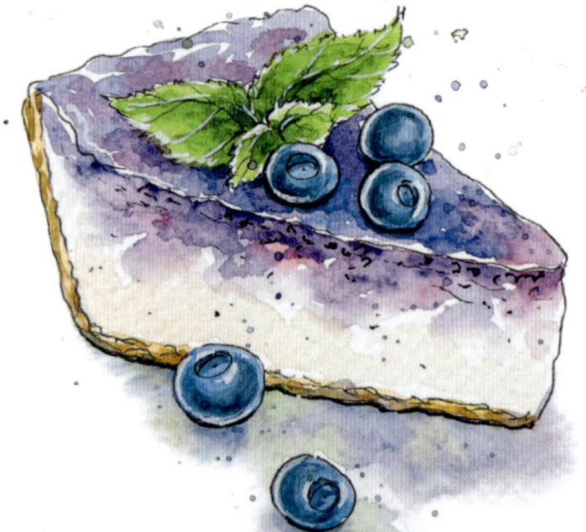

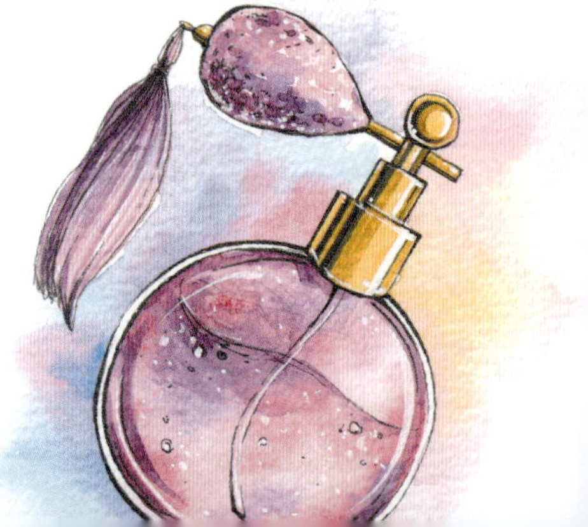

Strokes and Textures

In this fantastic chapter of the book, you will elevate your skills to a new level by integrating all the techniques from previous chapters and adding a variety of new methods to create diverse, vibrant textures and materials. From sea foam in a Seascape Serenade (page 151) to dripping sweet syrup on a Pumpkin Latte (page 128) and the crystal clear glass of our Bottled Beauty Perfume (page 137), you will learn to create these unique effects and more using liner and watercolor. Additionally, we will explore the magical technique of watercolor splatters, which will add energy and vitality to your works. Prepare for an exciting journey through a world of magical, captivating colors!

Lesson 24. Joyful Blooming Cactus

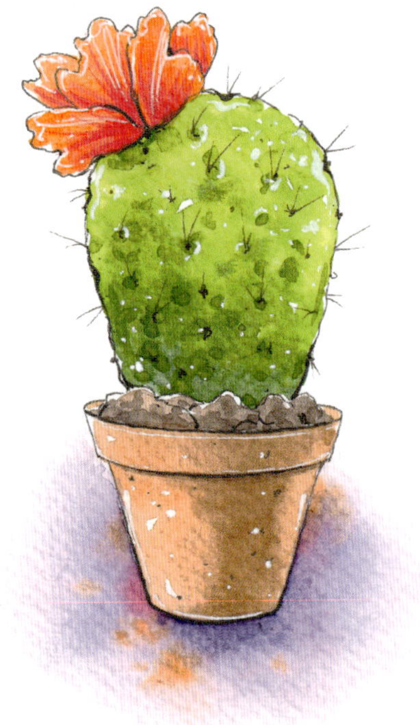

Add a touch of exotic vibes to your watercolor journey! In this lesson, you'll learn how to capture the unique texture of a cactus, its prickly needles and its bright flower. You'll discover how to play with saturated shades of green, orange and pink to create a vibrant natural effect. And of course, we'll practice smooth transitions to create dimension and the wet-on-wet technique for a vibrant cast shadow. Prepare the materials and let's begin!

Paint Colors

Permanent Lemon Yellow

Sap Green

Ultramarine Deep

Azo Orange

Quinacridone Rose

Burnt Umber

Dioxazine Purple

1. Use a pencil to draw a trapezoid widening upward at the bottom of the paper. This is the pot. At the top of the pot, draw a large teardrop shape. This is the cactus. At the top left side of the cactus, draw a tilted oval for the flower. Draw wavy lines for the petals of the flower from a center point on the cactus. Draw a semi-oval at the bottom of the pot from the outer points. At the top of the pot, draw two short lines on its sides. Connect the ends of these lines with semi-oval lines. This is the rim of the pot. Inside the pot, draw wavy, curvy lines to depict the soil. Make the edges of the pot rim rounded over the soil to show its dimension.

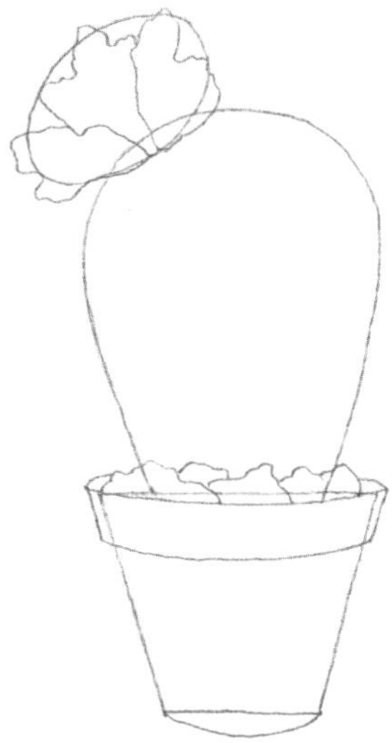

1

2. Use a black waterproof liner to outline the pot. Add tiny dots and doodles to the pot. Outline the soil in the pot with a slightly curly, thin line and do the same for the flower, adding more petals behind it. Outline the cactus with an interrupted and uneven line. Draw dots at approximately equal distances from each other on the cactus. With sharp, short hatches, draw one or two hatches from one point to depict needles. Skip some dots for natural results. Great! Erase the pencil.

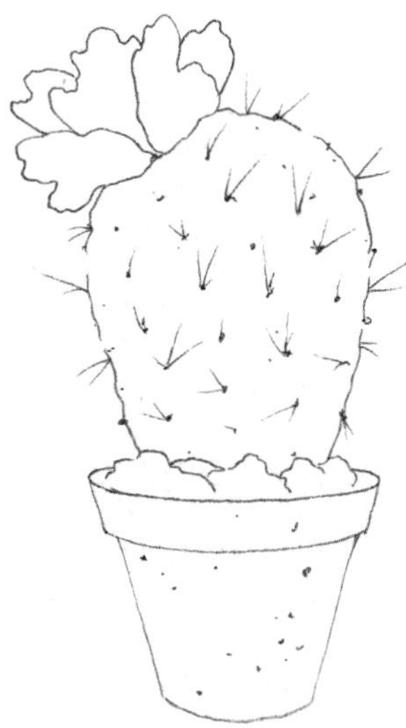

2

3. Prepare Permanent Lemon Yellow, Sap Green and Ultramarine Deep on your palette. Also mix Sap Green and Ultramarine Deep in equal proportions to get a dark green. Paint the cactus, starting with more Permanent Lemon Yellow at the top, then blending it into Sap Green. As you move down, add more Sap Green and dark green. Try to leave some white paper spots. Great! Wait for it to dry completely.

sap green + ultramarine deep

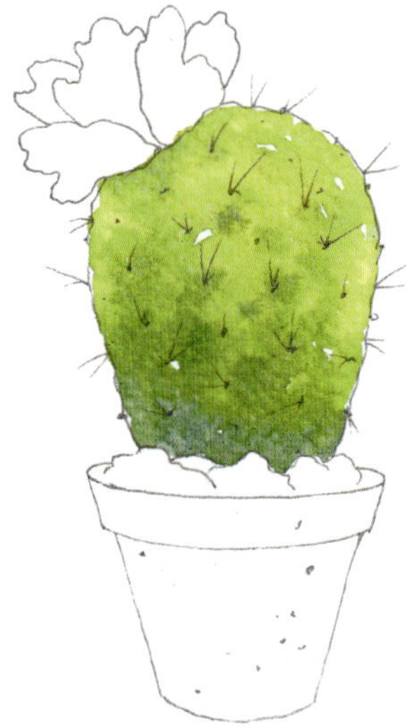

3

4. Paint the flower petals with Azo Orange and Quinacridone Rose, using more Azo Orange at the top and more Quinacridone Rose at the bottom. Create smooth transitions between these colors. Mix a gray-brown using Burnt Umber and a few drops of Ultramarine Deep. Paint the soil with this color, leaving some white paper spots. Dilute Burnt Umber with water to get a light brown. Paint the pot with light brown on the left and right; from the middle to the right, paint with a less diluted Burnt Umber, creating smooth transitions between these colors. Perfect! Wait for the paper to dry.

burnt umber + ultramarine deep

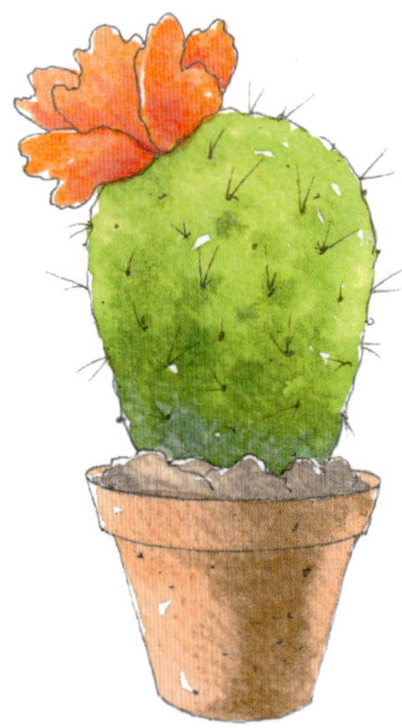

4

5. Paint the center of the flower with Quinacridone Rose and make quick, short strokes on the petals to show the veins. On the cactus, near the dots, randomly draw small dots, strokes and doodles with Sap Green, a bit less at the top and a bit more at the bottom of the cactus. Add a second layer of gray-brown to the soil, leaving previous layers slightly visible. Under the rim of the pot, add a shadow with a thin semi-oval line of gray-brown. Prewet the paper under the pot with clean water. Paint a shadow with Azo Orange, Quinacridone Rose and Dioxazine Purple, creating smooth transitions without mixing the colors too much. Remove extra water with the brush or a napkin and soften the edges with a damp brush. Wait for everything to dry.

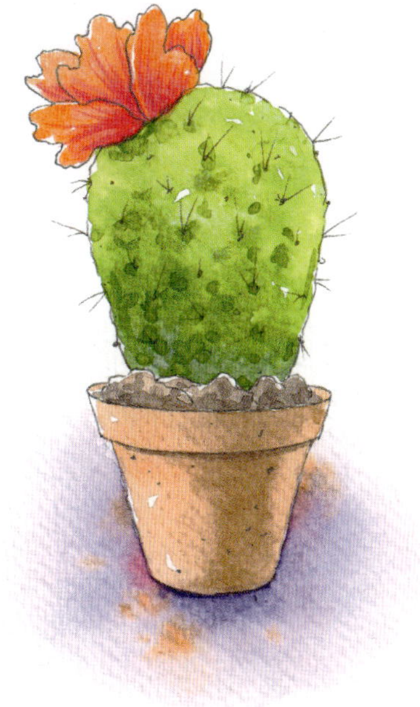

5

6. Use the black waterproof liner to make some outlines bolder, especially under the pot. Then use a white gel pen to make an inner contour and the veins of the flower petals on the cactus. Randomly place dots and doodles on the cactus and a few on the pot. Draw long, thin lines on the rim, on the sides and at the bottom of the pot.

Amazing! Our sketch is ready!

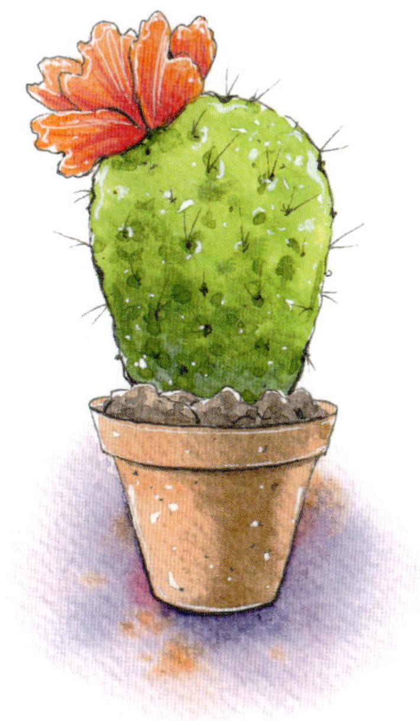

6

Lesson 25. Pumpkin Latte

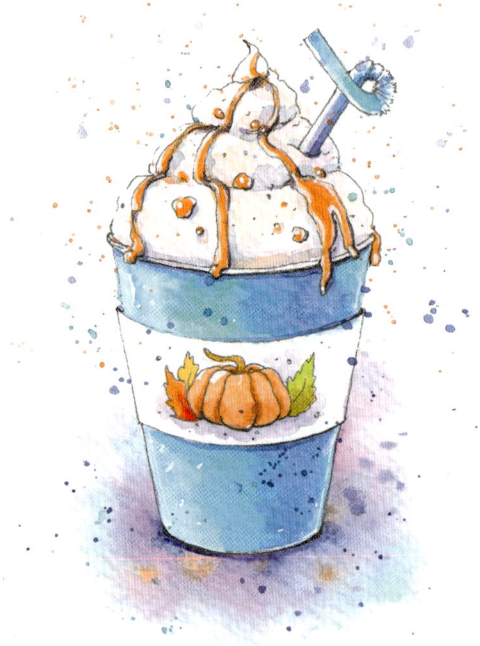

Dive into the autumn coziness of this lesson by drawing a pumpkin latte! Learn how to depict lush whipped cream, dripping sweet syrup and sprinkles, adding realism and a delicious sparkle to your drink. Discover how to use warm and contrasting autumn shades to create a beverage that looks as cozy as a real one smells. You will also explore a new technique: watercolor splatters, which will enliven any of your sketches. Let's begin!

Paint Colors

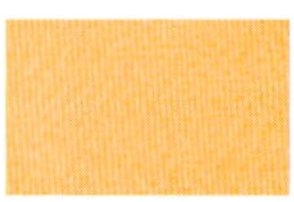

Yellow Ochre

Dioxazine Purple

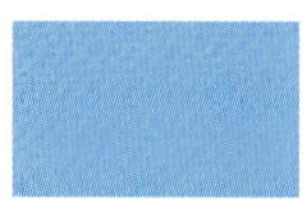

Cerulean Blue

Phthalo Green

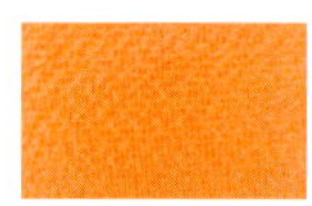

Azo Orange

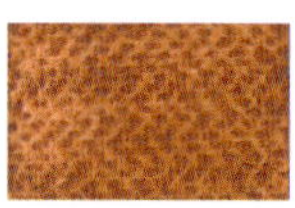

Burnt Sienna

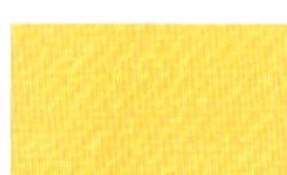

Azo Yellow Medium

Permanent Red Light

Permanent Lemon Yellow

1. Use a pencil to draw a trapezoid, widening upward, slightly below the center of the paper. Draw semi-oval lines at the top and bottom of the trapezoid. This is the cup. Draw a triangle on the trapezoid, and on the right side of the triangle, draw a loopy line. This depicts the whipped cream and straw. It's not necessary to make the lines perfectly straight; feel free to transform them and make them a bit crooked or slanted.

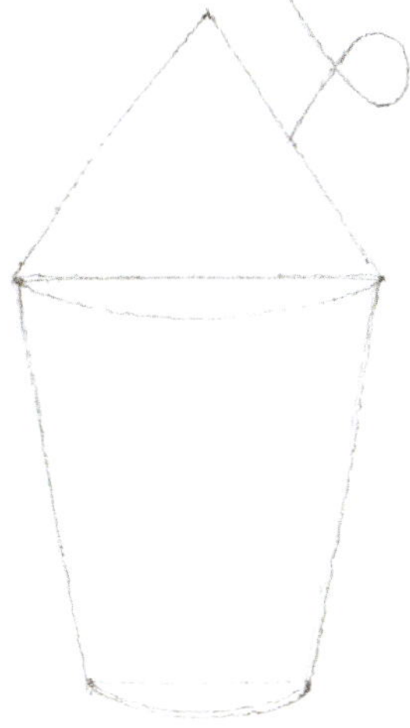

1

2. Draw two semi-oval lines for the cardboard holder, slightly extending beyond the cup's edges, approximately in the center of the cup. Connect these lines with straight ones going downward. In the center of the holder, draw a pumpkin oval, dividing it into segments with oval lines. Draw a curly stem at the top of the pumpkin. To the right and left of the pumpkin, draw a couple of uneven droplets of different sizes. Divide the triangle of whipped cream into four oval-shaped parts with a wavy line. Add a sharp tip to the top part. Draw dotted wavy lines from the tip of the whipped cream to the cup dripping down all four parts of the whipped cream. These will be the direction lines of the syrup. Draw a thickness to the straw with a duplicate line at a small distance.

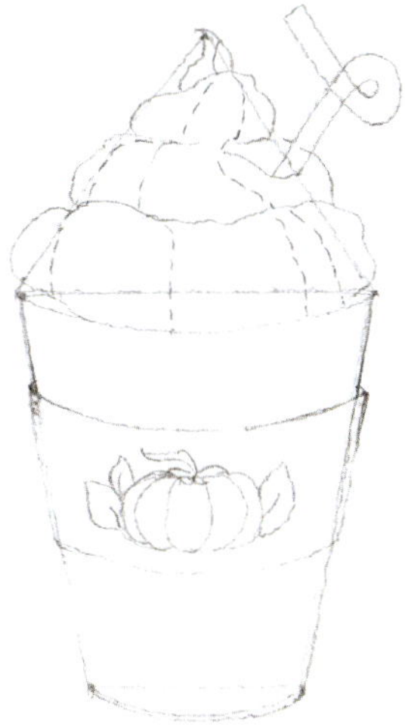

2

3. Use a black waterproof liner to outline the cup and the cardboard holder, but skip the rim of the cup. Outline the pumpkin and draw leaves on the holder from the droplets, adding zigzag edges. Add small dots around the pumpkin. Draw the dripping syrup from the top of the whipped cream with wavy lines along the dotted lines, adding more width in some areas. Outline the rim of the cup with a double line, skipping over the syrup. Outline the whipped cream with a thin, uneven line. Add random irregular circles and dots to the whipped cream. On the bend of the straw, add fold lines and outline the straw, making the top part of the loop in front. Remember, art isn't about perfection. It's about expression. Let your emotions guide your hand.

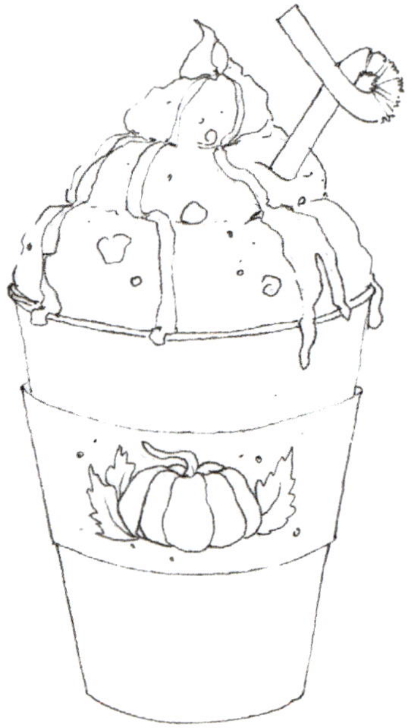

3

4. Mix Yellow Ochre and Dioxazine Purple separately with water to get a very light ochre and a very light purple. Use these colors to randomly paint the whipped cream, leaving spots of white paper. Mix a turquoise color from Cerulean Blue and Phthalo Green in equal parts. Add water to the Cerulean Blue to get a light blue. Use the light blue, turquoise and Dioxazine Purple to paint the upper part of the cup to the holder. Make the coloring with smooth transitions, from lighter on the left to turquoise to Dioxazine Purple and again to lighter on the right edge. Similarly, paint the cup under the holder. Also use these colors to paint the straw.

cerulean blue + phthalo green

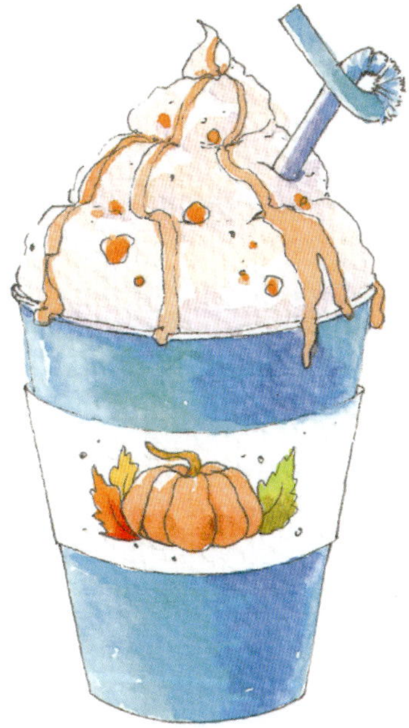

4

Mix Azo Orange with water to get a light orange. Paint the syrup and sprinkles on the whipped cream with the light orange and the Azo Orange. Paint the pumpkin on top with light orange, leaving white paper, and smoothly add Burnt Sienna toward the bottom. Paint the pumpkin stem with Yellow Ochre. Use Azo Yellow Medium, Permanent Red Light and Azo Orange to paint the leaves to the left of the pumpkin. Mix Permanent Lemon Yellow with a few drops of Phthalo Green, and color the leaf on the right with that and some Yellow Ochre. Wait for the painting to dry.

permanent lemon yellow + phthalo green

5. Add a second layer of Azo Orange to the syrup, leaving the previous layer visible along the edges. Also, with light ochre, light purple and light orange, add shadows on the whipped cream at the edges of the rows, under the syrup and near the rim of the cup. Add light purple shadows to the straw, under the rim, under the syrup on the cup, above and below the holder and under the pumpkin. Soften the shadow under the pumpkin with a damp brush. Add lines of shadow to the pumpkin segments with Burnt Sienna. Prewet the area under the cup with clean water. With Dioxazine Purple, Quinacridone Rose and turquoise, paint the shadow. Remove extra water with the brush or a napkin and soften the edges with a damp brush. Before everything dries, pick up Azo Orange and make several splashes on the sketch by hitting the brush ferrule with a finger, another brush or a pencil. Try to get the splashes on the shadow and the upper part of the sketch. Do the same with Dioxazine Purple and turquoise.

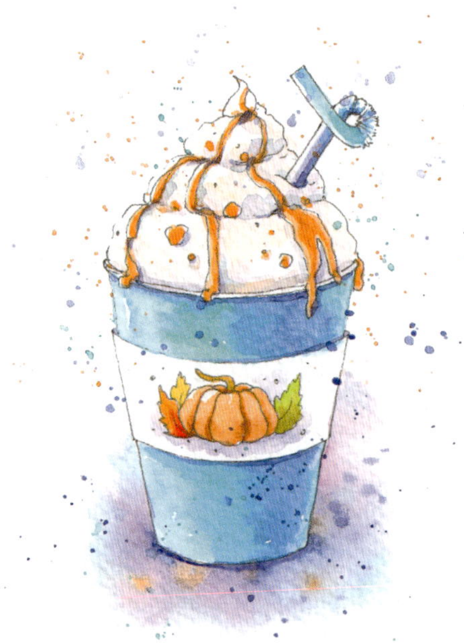

5

6. After the paper is completely dry, use the black liner to make some outlines bolder, especially under the cup, on the rim, in some places on the syrup, at the bottom of the pumpkin and on the holder on the right. Use a white gel pen to add lines and highlights on the left side of some edges of the syrup, especially on the dripping droplets. Add dots to the sprinkles and on the cup on the left side as well. Draw thin lines inside the contour of the cup on the left, on the right and a little at the bottom.

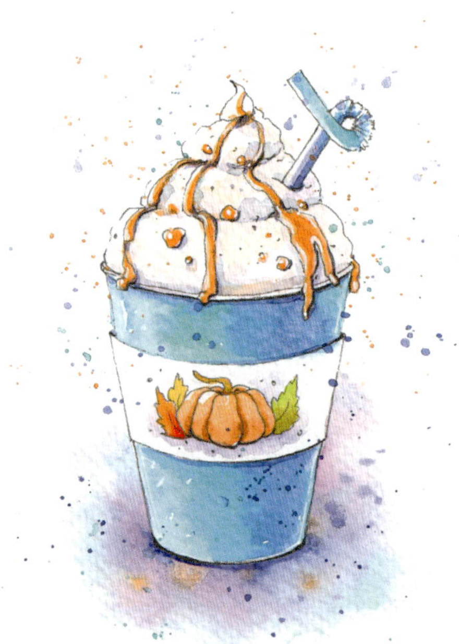

6

Great work! Our sketch is ready!

Lesson 26. Blueberry Dessert Dreams

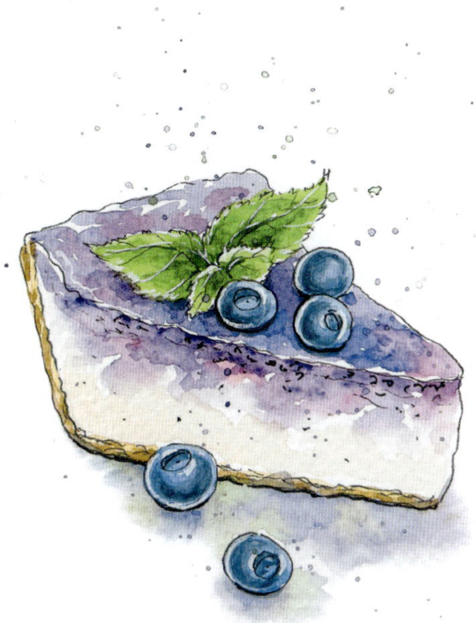

In this lesson, you will explore how to convey luscious textures and the juicy shades of berries and mint leaves, recreating a realistic dessert on paper. You will learn how to highlight the glints on the jam and create the illusion of volume on the berries, making the cheesecake look so rich and tasty. Discover how to create delicious textures of cheese, crust and various realistic details. Get your brushes and paints, and let's get started!

Paint Colors

- Dioxazine Purple
- Quinacridone Rose
- Permanent Lemon Yellow
- Sap Green
- Phthalo Blue
- Yellow Ochre
- Burnt Sienna

1. Use a pencil to draw a slanted line below the center of the paper. Draw two vertical slanted lines, one longer on the left and a shorter one on the right. Connect these lines with a slightly curved line.

Draw another curved, slanted line to the left, from the right point of the first curved line. Connect the top line points to form a curved triangle. This will be the cheesecake. From the center, draw leaves on the cheesecake as curved teardrops of different sizes with sharp tips. Randomly draw berries like circles and ovals on the cheesecake and a couple of berries next to it. Amazing!

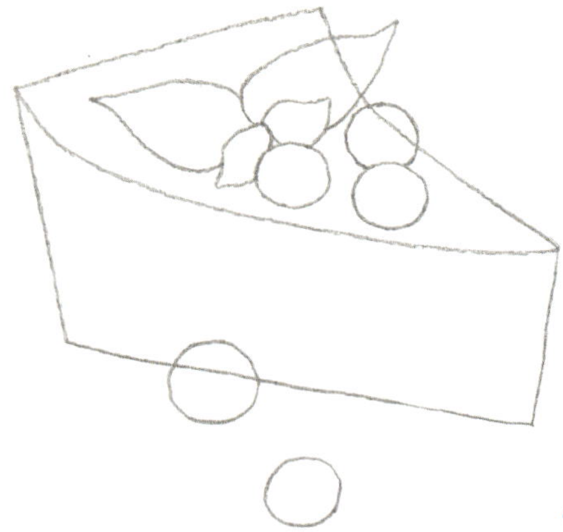

1

2. Use a black waterproof liner to outline the berries. On some blueberries draw tops in the form of ovals and semi-oval lines inside and make dots inside the ovals. Outline the leaves with an uneven zigzag line. Draw veins on the leaves with a thin, smooth line. Outline the cheesecake with a wavy, interrupted line. Add the thickness of the crust at the bottom and the side. Also add a thin, curly line under the top layer of jam. Draw small dots and doodles on the cheese filling. Erase the pencil marks.

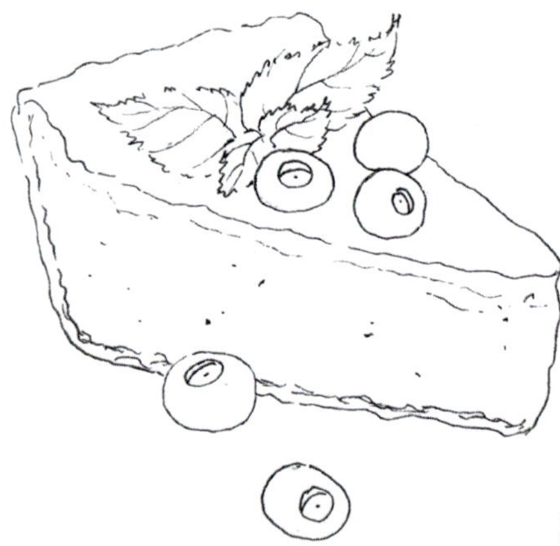

2

3. Paint the top part of the cheese filling with Dioxazine Purple and Quinacridone Rose, leaving white paper and slightly blending the lower edge with a damp brush. Mix Permanent Lemon Yellow and Sap Green in equal parts to get a yellow-green. Gradually color the leaves around their contour with yellow-green, leaving white paper on the edges, and closer to the middle and bottom use Sap Green. Dilute Phthalo Blue with water and paint the berries. Color the crust with Yellow Ochre mixed with water to get a lighter shade. Great! The first layer is done!

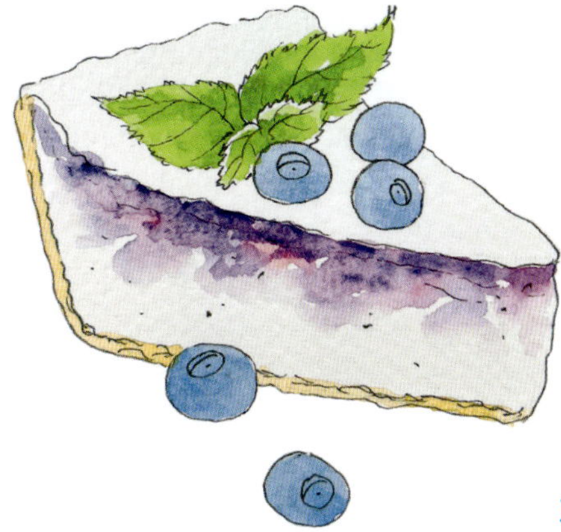

3

sap green + permanent lemon yellow

4. Paint the top of the cheesecake with Dioxazine Purple and Quinacridone Rose, leaving white paper and creating smooth transitions. Add Phthalo Blue under the berries and leaves for shadows. Darken the crust with small strokes of Burnt Sienna, leaving the previous layer visible. Paint the bottom of the cheesecake with very light, almost invisible Yellow Ochre. When the paper is dry, prewet the area under the cheesecake and under the berries with clean water. Color the shadow with Dioxazine Purple and Phthalo Blue, not mixing the paints too much on the paper. Just let them flow. Randomly add yellow-green as well. Apply more Dioxazine Purple under the berries. Remove extra water with the brush or a napkin and soften the edges with a damp brush.

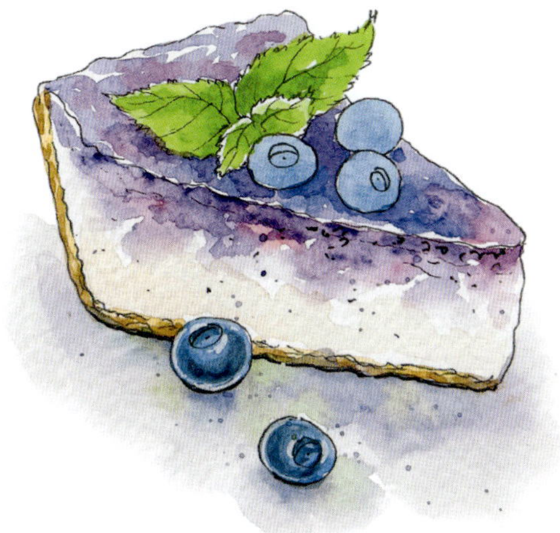

4

5. When the paper is dry, mix Phthalo Blue and Sap Green in equal parts to get dark green, then paint shadows on the leaf centers and carefully blend with a damp brush. Mix Phthalo Blue and Dioxazine Purple in equal parts to get a dark blue. Paint shadows under the leaves and under all the berries with thin lines and strokes. Also apply this color as shadows on the berries, not reaching their contour, and slightly blend with a damp brush. Add splatters of Dioxazine Purple and Sap Green. Well done! Now, let's wait for the paper to dry.

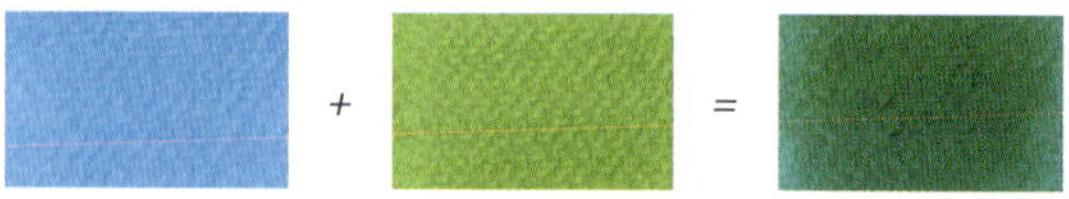

phthalo blue + sap green

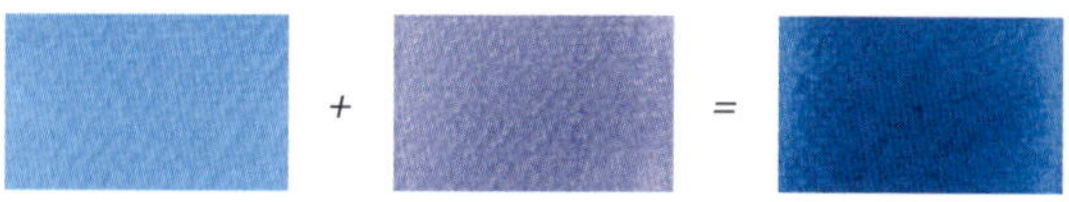

phthalo blue + dioxazine purple

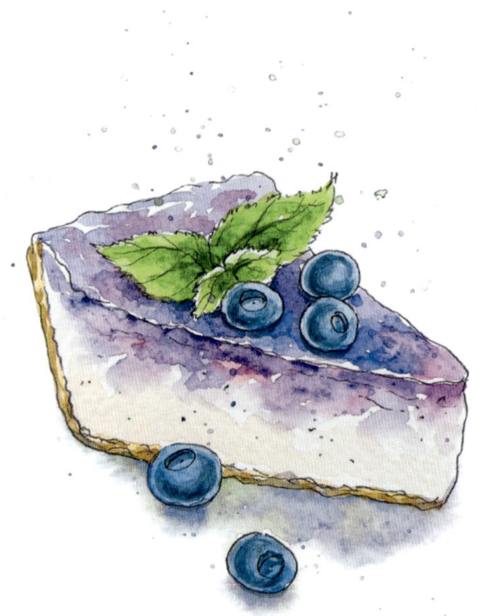

5

6. Use the black waterproof liner to make some of the outlines bolder, especially under the cheesecake, under the berries and under the mint leaves. Use a white gel pen to add uneven lines at the cheesecake's side edge to highlight its shiny surface. Also add semi-oval lines inside the berries, next to the contour and next to the oval centers. Add thin, smooth lines on the leaf veins and zigzag lines on the edges of the leaves.

Excellent work! Our sketch is ready!

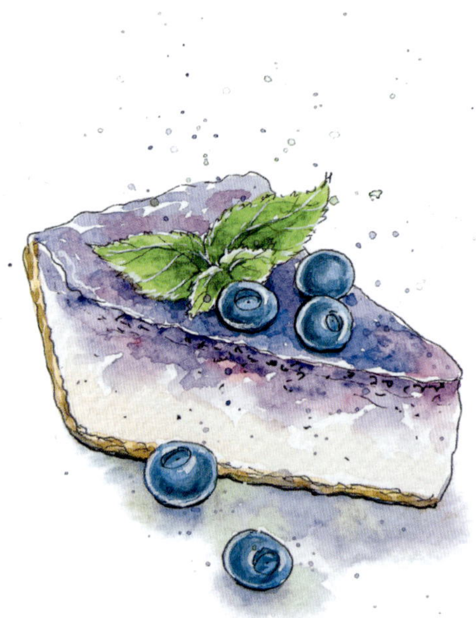

6

Lesson 27. Bottled Beauty Perfume

Dive into a world of sophistication and style with this lesson on drawing a perfume bottle. You'll learn how to use watercolor to create the transparency of glass and the shine of metal, making your bottle literally sparkle on paper. Practice your skills in creating fine gradients and delicate color flows that will transform your sketch from a simple drawing into a true work of art. Let's begin!

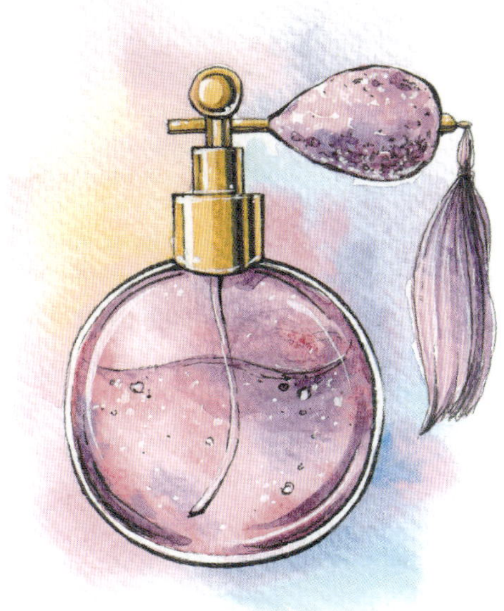

Paint Colors

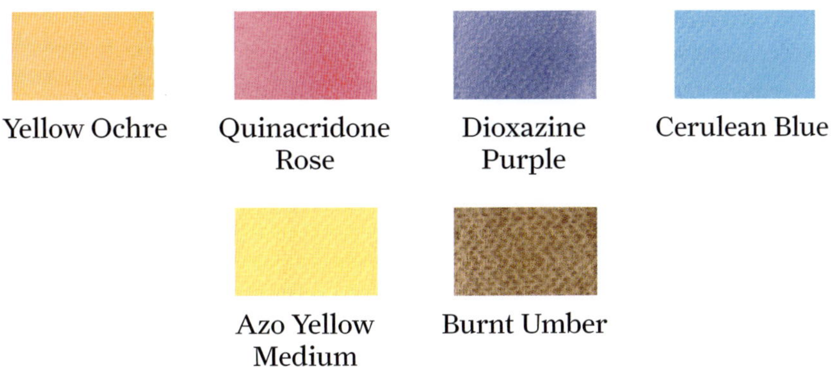

1. Use a pencil to draw a medium-size circle at the bottom of the paper. Draw a small rectangle on it. At the bottom of the rectangle, from the outer points, draw a semi-oval line. Draw a slightly curved line downward from the center of the semi-oval line. Above the rectangle draw a smaller rectangle, and above that, an even smaller one. At the top of the small rectangle, draw a circle. Draw a short line through the smallest rectangle. Draw a large drop to the right of the line. On the right side of the drop, draw a small circle and then make wavy lines to depict a tassel. It's okay if your lines are a bit different; you are just learning, and I'm sure you will do great with practice!

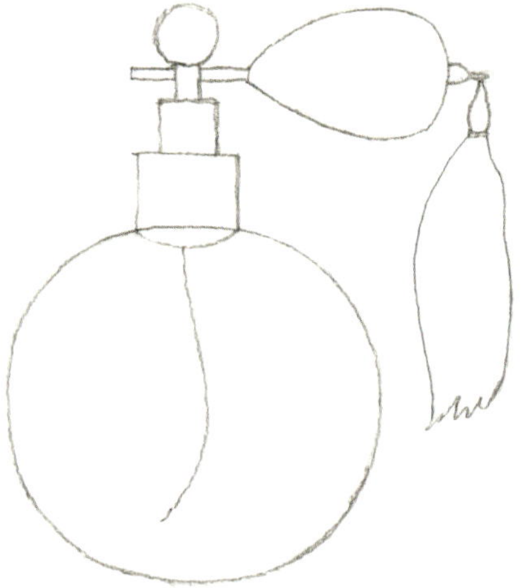

1

2. Use a black waterproof liner to outline the glass perfume bottle using a thin line. Add a small thickness to the glass with a similar line inside along the contour of the bottle, then add curved lines at the top left and bottom right. Just above the middle part of the bottle, draw a wavy line for the waterline and add several circles and dots for bubbles. Outline the spray stem inside the bottle. Outline the top of the bottle and the spray head. Add bold, black vertical lines on the right part of the lid and a thin line on the left. Also draw an inverted C on the round end. Randomly add small dots and short lines at the bottom of the droplet-shaped sprayer bulb and a few at the top. Outline the tassel with wavy lines and add hatches inside. Erase the pencil marks.

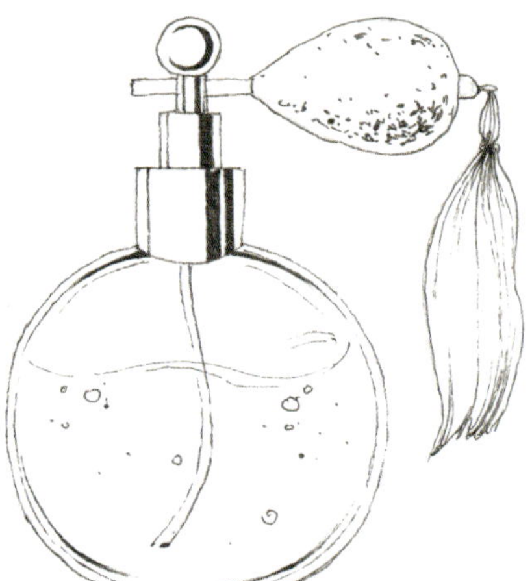

2

3. Dilute Yellow Ochre with a little water and paint the metallic gold parts, leaving lines of white paper on the left side. Prewet the paper with clean water inside the bottle except for the glass-thickness area. Paint inside the bottle with Quinacridone Rose and a little Dioxazine Purple, making the color lighter in some places and darker in others. Enjoy the process! Let the paints flow into each other! Also paint the sprayer with these colors using small strokes, using more Quinacridone Rose at the top and more Dioxazine Purple at the bottom. Try to leave spots of white paper. Paint the tassel using the same colors with long strokes, lighter on the left and darker on the right. Wait for the paper to dry.

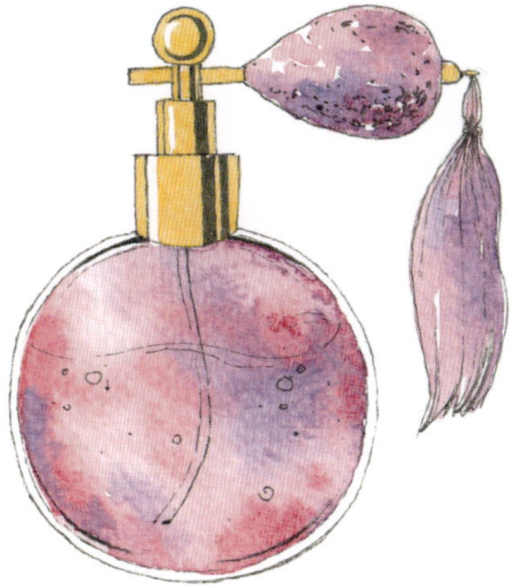

3

4. Add Quinacridone Rose, Cerulean Blue and Azo Yellow Medium to your palette and mix each color separately with water to get light shades. Prewet the paper around the perfume with clean water and paint the background around the bottle with these light shades, randomly adding pure Quinacridone Rose and Cerulean Blue. Let the magic happen! Let the colors freely flow into each other! Mix Yellow Ochre and a few drops of Burnt Umber and apply a second layer to the metal parts of the lid with even, vertical lines on the right side and around the ball on the lid. Great! Wait for the paper to dry.

yellow ochre + burnt umber

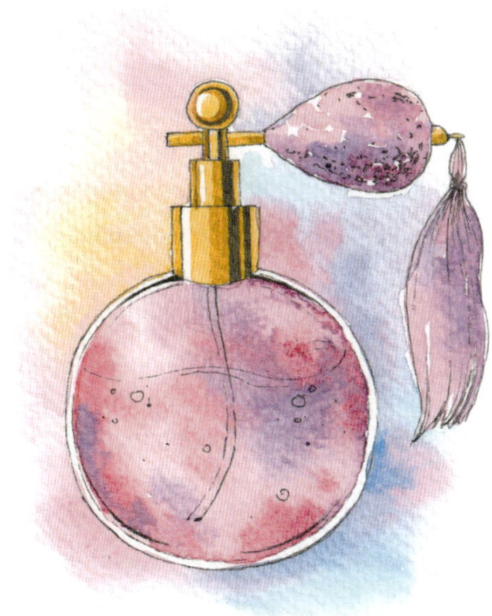

4

5. Mix Quinacridone Rose and a few drops of Dioxazine Purple to get a lilac color. Paint some thin, curved strokes with this color next to the edges of the bottle. Add small individual strokes to the sprayer at the bottom. Make several long, wavy strokes on the tassel on the right side. Under the waterline of the perfume, make some strokes of lilac and randomly soften with a damp brush. You are doing well! Again, let's wait for the paper to dry completely.

quinacridone rose + dioxazine purple

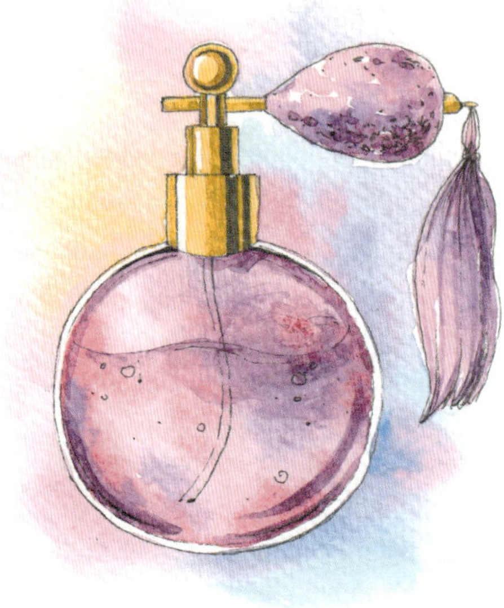

5

6. Use the black waterproof liner to make some of the outlines bolder, especially at the bottom and top of the bottle and at the bottom and top of the glass. Also make the lines bolder on the right side of the metal parts, on the sprayer on the right and left, on the tassel on the right top and bottom and on the spray stem at the bottom. To create a shine on the sprayer's metal ball, use a white gel pen to draw a small dot on the bottom right and add a semicircular line underneath that dot. Draw horizontal lines on the other metal parts and a semicircular line at the lid's bottom. Randomly place dots on the sprayer, a bit more at the top. Add a few wavy lines to the tassel's left side. Randomly draw small circles and dots of different sizes inside the bottle and add highlights on the glass along the contour. Draw a white line on the spray stem as well.

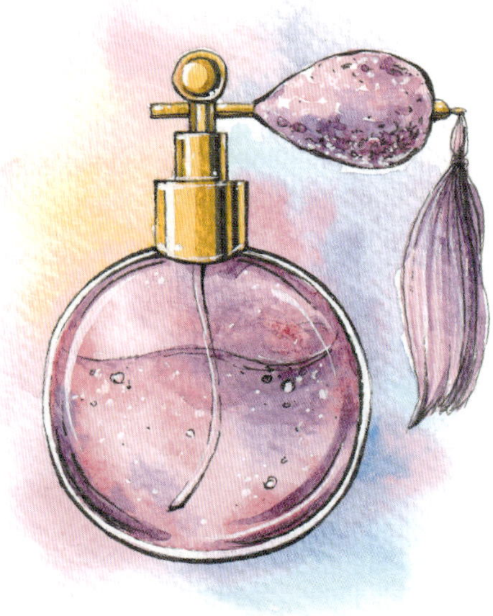

6

Fantastic! Our sketch is ready!

Lesson 28. Wooden Door and Whispering Flowers

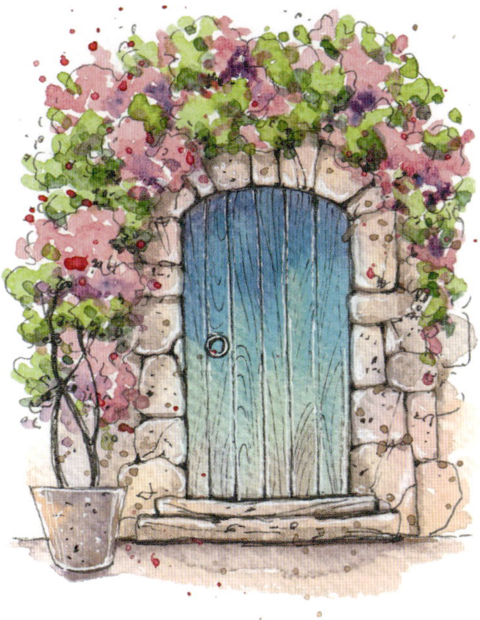

Get inspired by the Mediterranean atmosphere in this watercolor painting, where you'll capture a bright turquoise door and flowering bougainvillea. In this lesson, you will explore how to use black liner to depict the textures of stone and wood. You'll also learn how to mix subtle hues and apply delicate washes to bring out the architectural and natural beauty of the scene. Let's begin!

Paint Colors

Dioxazine Purple

Yellow Ochre

Quinacridone Rose

Cerulean Blue

Phthalo Green

Burnt Sienna

Permanent Lemon Yellow

Sap Green

Ultramarine Deep

1. Use a pencil to draw a rectangle slightly to the right of the paper's center. Then draw a semi-oval above this rectangle. Below the door, draw steps in the form of two elongated rectangles. Draw a horizontal line under the lower step. Then draw a pot in the shape of a trapezoid on the left side. Around the door draw a frame contour in a loose, semi-oval shape. Draw curved lines for the stem and branches of the bougainvillea, starting from the pot. With curly lines draw a cloud-like shape to show flowers and foliage, slightly overlapping the frame and door.

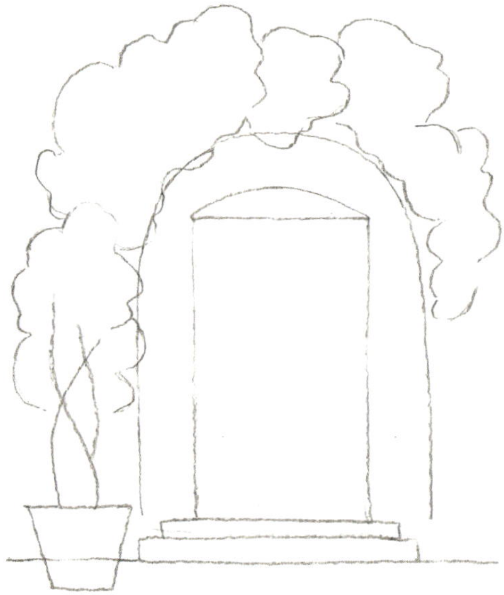

1

2. Use a black waterproof liner to outline the greenery and flowers growing from the pot up onto the wall, randomly grouping them with thin, curly lines. Next, outline the stem and pot, adding a semi-oval line at the bottom of the pot. Outline the door with simple lines and draw the round handle. Use thin lines to draw wooden boards on the door. Then outline the stone steps with uneven lines, making the steps slightly slanted. Draw stones of different sizes and slightly irregular shapes on the doorframe. On the right side, draw some stones on the wall area with thin, curved and uneven lines. Slightly mark the bottom line of the house. Great! Erase the pencil drawing.

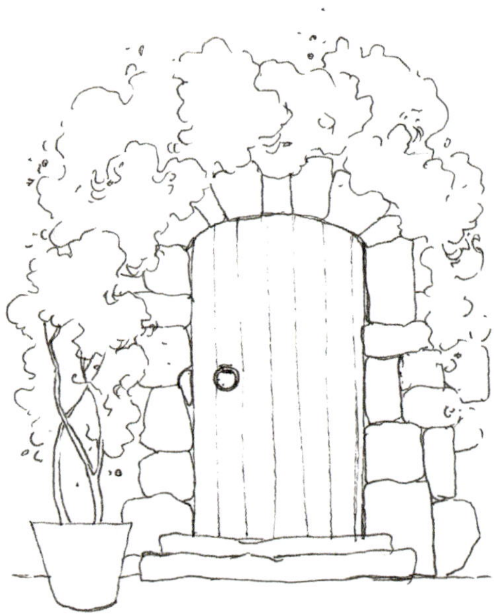

2

3. Prepare Dioxazine Purple, Yellow Ochre and Quinacridone Rose on your palette and mix some of each separately with water to get lighter shades. Mix Cerulean Blue and Phthalo Green in equal parts to get turquoise. Prewet the door with clean water and paint from the top with Dioxazine Purple, then turquoise, and toward the bottom with light purple and light ochre. Let the colors smoothly blend into each other. Then wait for the paper to dry. Paint the frame, walls around the frame and steps with broad, random strokes of light ochre, light purple and light rose, leaving areas of white paper. Use more Dioxazine Purple and Quinacridone Rose closer to the bougainvillea. Randomly soften the strokes with a damp brush. Well done! Let's wait for the paper to dry.

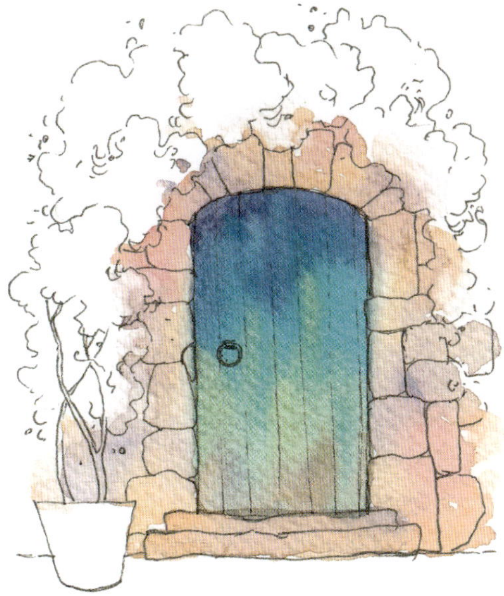

3

cerulean blue + phthalo green

4. Paint groups of flowers with small strokes, using Quinacridone Rose and Dioxazine Purple, sometimes skipping a bit of white paper and leaving space for greenery. Make smooth transitions from Quinacridone Rose to Dioxazine Purple, allowing some colors to blend a bit. The beauty of watercolor lies in its blend—like life, it's about merging the colors to create harmony. Mix Yellow Ochre and a few drops of Dioxazine Purple to paint the soil under the steps and under the pot. Paint the pot with a smooth gradient of Burnt Sienna and Dioxazine Purple. Mix Permanent Lemon Yellow and Sap Green in equal parts to get yellow-green and paint the foliage in groups with loose strokes, leaving white paper and drawing some individual leaves with small strokes.

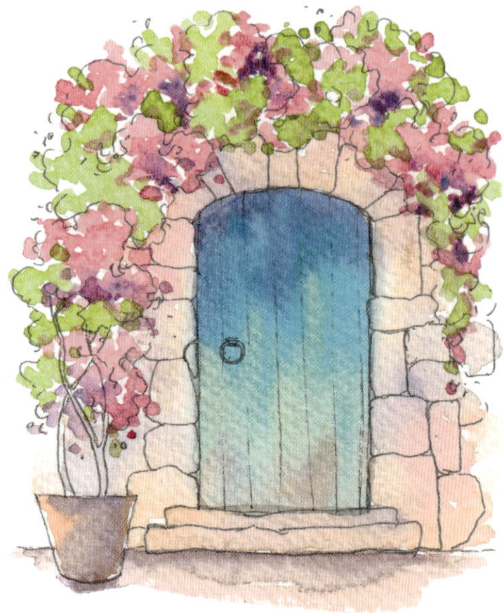

4

yellow ochre + dioxazine purple

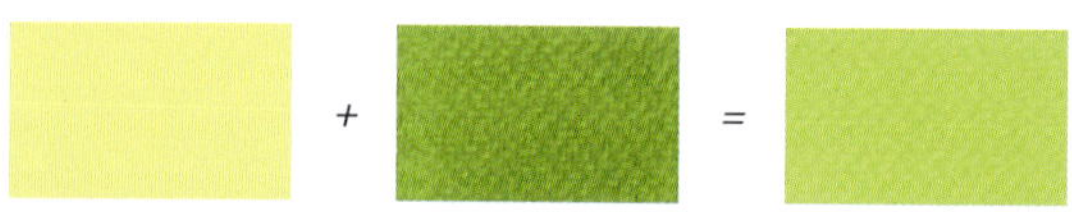

permanent lemon yellow + sap green

5. When the paper is dry, mix Sap Green and Ultramarine Deep in equal parts to get dark green and add shadows to the foliage. Paint the shadows on the lower and right parts of the green groups with small, random strokes. Mix Burnt Sienna and Dioxazine Purple in equal parts to get a violet-brown. Use this color to add shadows with short strokes to the contours between the stones, sometimes making strokes on the stones as well. Use the same color to add shadows on the steps. Add splatters to the flowers with Quinacridone Rose and to the stones with Burnt Sienna.

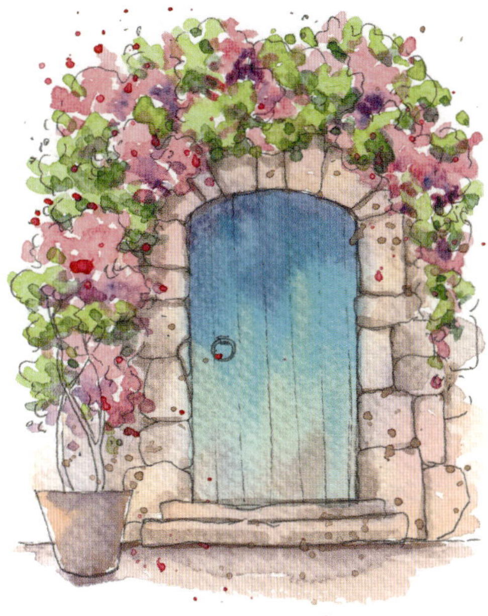

5

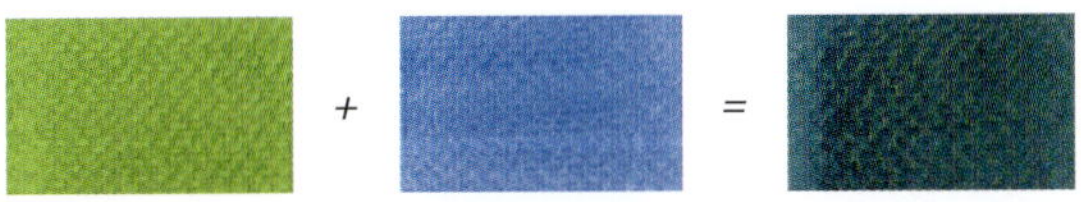

sap green + ultramarine deep

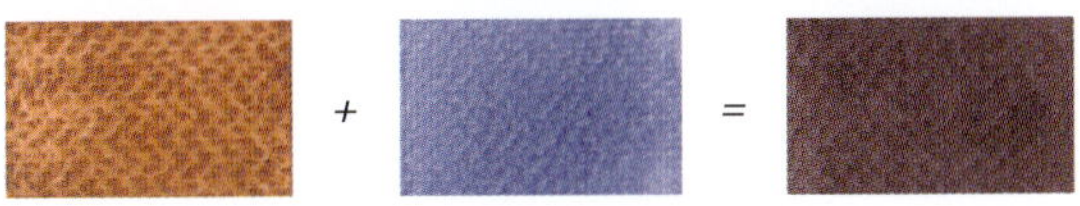

burnt sienna + dioxazine purple

6. Use the black waterproof liner to make some outlines bolder, especially on the frame, under the door and under the steps. Use long, wavy, slightly visible lines to draw wood grain on the door. Some lines can be a bit oval-like, some closer together and others further apart. Randomly place small dots, doodles and thin lines on the stones to show the rough texture. Add curls and dots on the greenery and flowers. Use a white gel pen to randomly place small dots, doodles and thin lines on the stones. Draw long stripes between the boards on the door. Add bright white lines on the pot and the door handle.

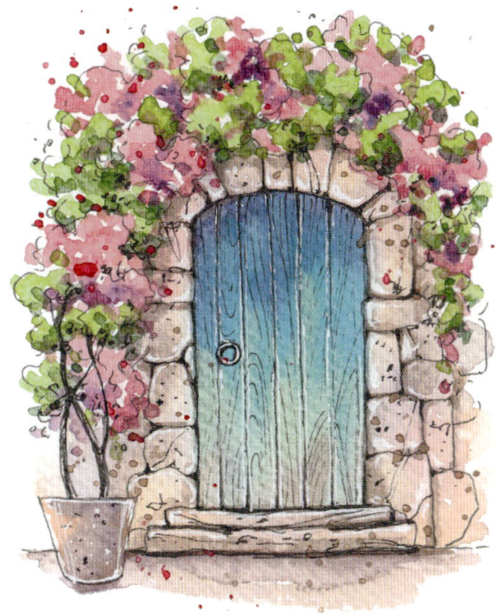

6

You are doing great! Our sketch is ready!

Lesson 29. Countryside Cottage Romance

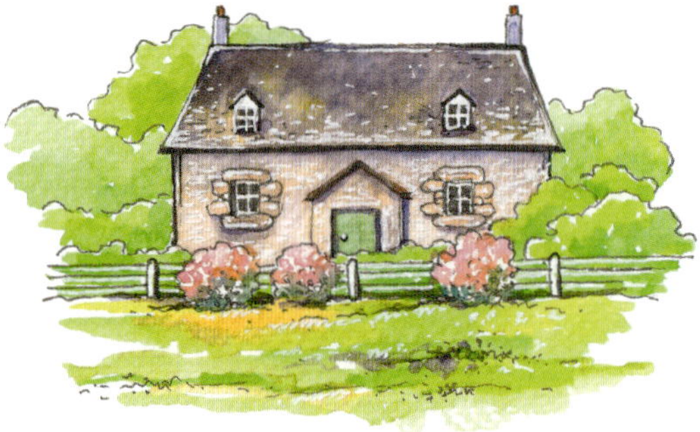

Let's dive into the charm of the countryside! In this lesson, we'll continue to practice combining different graphic and watercolor techniques to depict various details, such as the old roof, chimneys and cozy windows. You will learn how to create a rustic cottage surrounded by lush foliage and flowering bushes, capturing the essence of a serene, romantic rural setting. Get your brushes and let's start!

Paint Colors

- Permanent Lemon Yellow
- Cerulean Blue
- Sap Green
- Yellow Ochre
- Quinacridone Rose
- Dioxazine Purple
- Burnt Sienna

1. Use a pencil to draw a horizontal line slightly below the center of the paper. Place a rectangle on this line. Draw a trapezoid, with the wider side at the bottom, on top of the rectangle—this is our cottage. Draw a small, vertical rectangle at the bottom center of the cottage to depict the porch. Above it draw a triangle for the porch roof. Inside the larger rectangle at the bottom, draw another vertical rectangle for the door. Draw small rectangular windows on either side. Add smaller windows on the roof, with a small triangle above each. Draw chimneys on the top sides of the roof. Draw another horizontal line slightly above the first line for a fence in front of the cottage. Use curly lines to draw foliage next to the cottage. Draw bushes out of three circles in front of the fence.

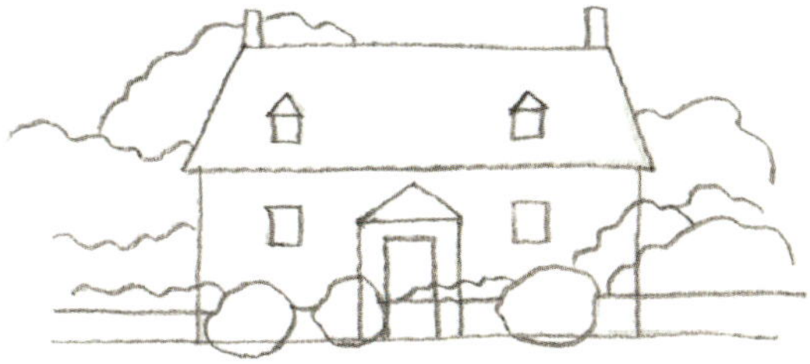

1

2. Use a black waterproof liner to outline the bushes, greenery and trees with thin, wavy lines. Draw vertical fence posts and connect them with slightly uneven horizontal lines to complete the fence. Outline the house, chimneys, windows and porch with slightly uneven lines. Add a small rectangle on top of each chimney. Make the lines under the cottage roof and the porch roof bolder. Inside the windows, draw four small squares and color them black with the liner to show frames. Draw soft rectangular stones of different sizes around the first-floor windows. Randomly draw uneven wavy lines and sometimes zig-zag-like lines to depict grass. Add dots and lines on the roof, grass and bushes. Erase the pencil drawing.

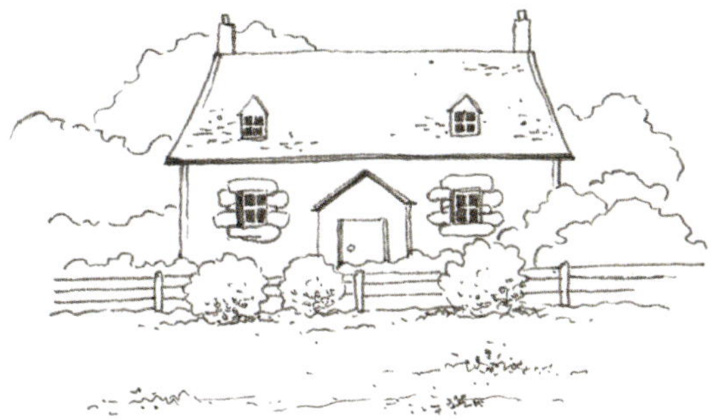

2

3. Mix Permanent Lemon Yellow and Cerulean Blue in equal parts to get a yellow-green. Also mix Cerulean Blue and Sap Green in equal parts to get a blue-green. Paint the trees and bushes behind the cottage from the top with yellow-green, gradually transitioning to blue-green at the bottom. Use blue-green to paint the greenery behind the fence and the door. Add a few drops of Permanent Lemon Yellow to the yellow-green and paint from the top of the bushes right in front of the cottage, transitioning to blue-green at the bottom. Paint the grass below the fence with Yellow Ochre, Permanent Lemon Yellow, yellow-green and Sap Green using large horizontal strokes, leaving areas of white paper. Use more Sap Green closer to the lines of the grass.

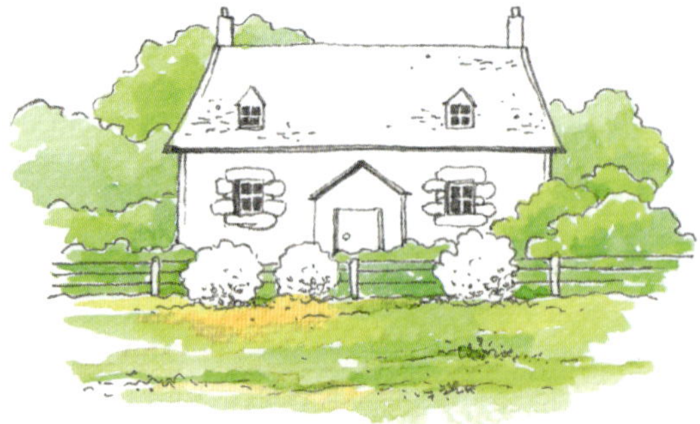

3

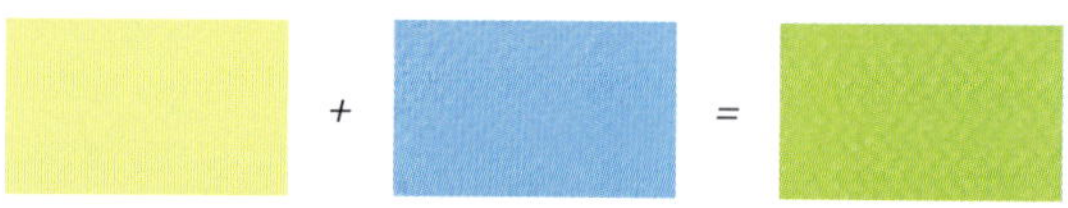

permanent lemon yellow + cerulean blue

cerulean blue + sap green

4. Paint the flower bushes starting with Quinacridone Rose and Yellow Ochre on top, transitioning smoothly to the blue-green at the bottom, leaving spots of white paper. Mix Dioxazine Purple and Yellow Ochre separately with water to get lighter shades. Use the light purple to paint on the cottage under the roof and transition smoothly to light ochre, skipping the window frames. Once the paper is completely dry, use Burnt Sienna to paint the top tips of the chimneys and the porch roof. Mix Sap Green and a few drops of Dioxazine Purple and use this color to add shadows under the flower bushes with long strokes and sometimes short separate strokes on the grass below. Also paint the door with Sap Green. So many details! But I'm sure you are doing great!

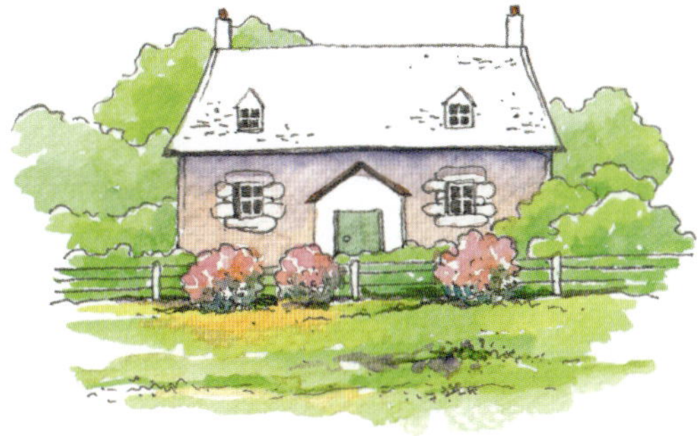

4

sap green + dioxazine purple

5. Mix Burnt Sienna with water to get a lighter shade and use this to paint the stone framing of the windows, adding a few strokes of the light purple on your palette at the bottom. Use light ochre and light purple to paint the porch. Prewet the roof with clean water and paint it with Dioxazine Purple, Yellow Ochre and Permanent Lemon Yellow. Use Dioxazine Purple on top, adding Yellow Ochre and Permanent Lemon Yellow below, mixing them a bit on the paper. And again, enjoy the flow! Let the colors blend naturally. Once the paper is dry, use Dioxazine Purple to paint the chimneys and draw shadows under the windows on the roof, to the right of the porch and around the door.

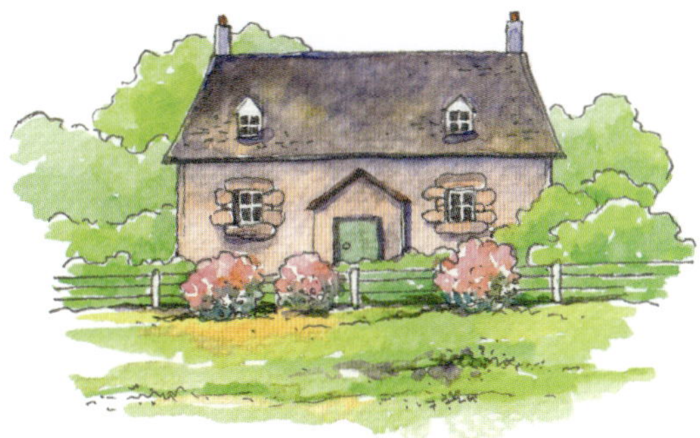

5

6. Use the black waterproof liner to make some of the outlines bolder, especially the corners of the roof, under the house and porch roof, under the stone window framing and under the flower bushes. Use a white gel pen to draw short, uneven hatches and dots on the roof, the house, the flower bushes and the grass. Add short, broken lines along the inner contour of the roof. Draw white lines next to the fence lines. Add one vertical line to the chimneys and one horizontal line to the window-frame stones.

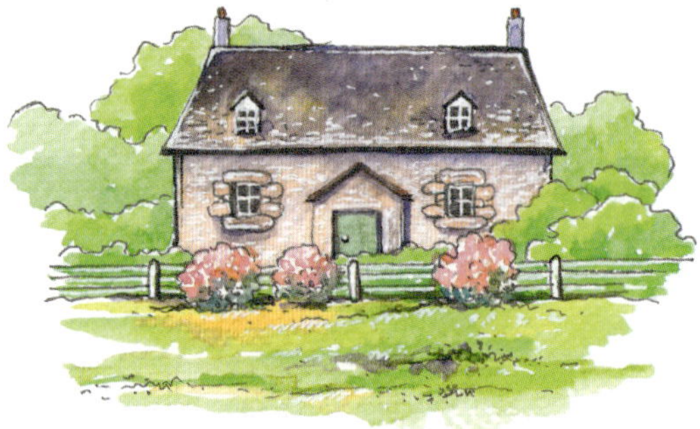

6

Well done! Our sketch is ready!

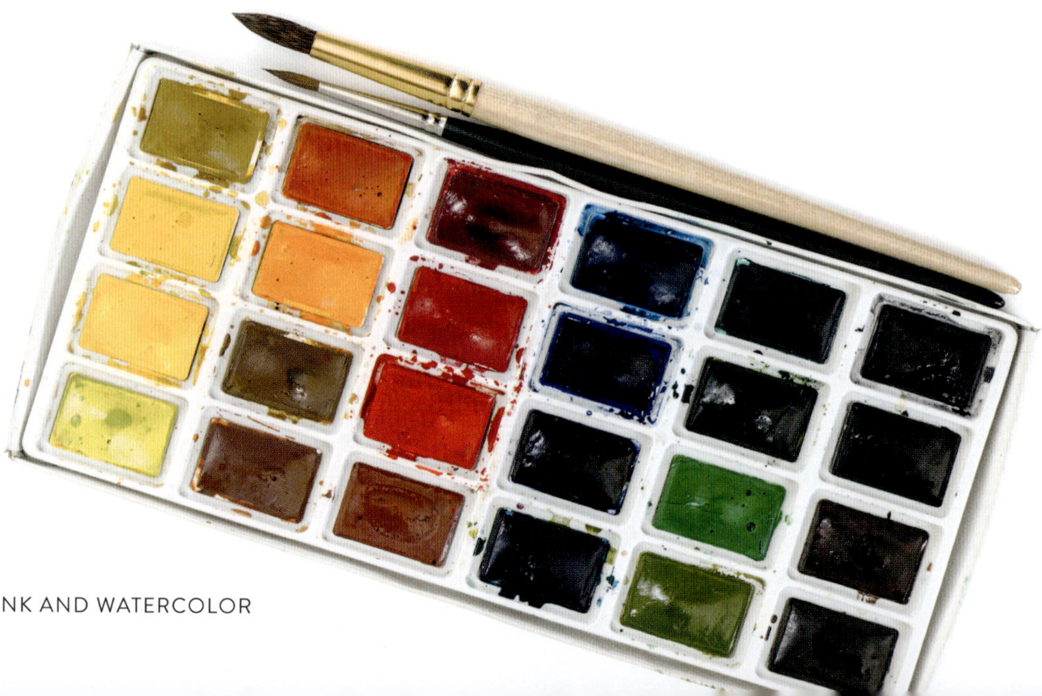

Lesson 30. Seascape Serenade

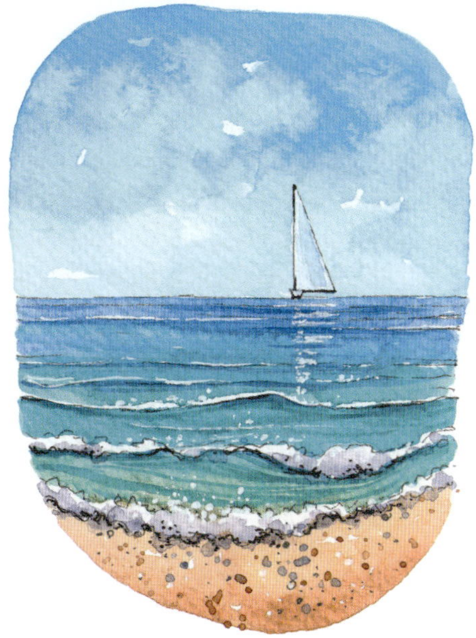

Unleash your creativity with this watercolor painting that captures the serene and dynamic essence of a seascape. This lesson will help you depict a tranquil yet vibrant seaside using black liner and watercolor washes. You will learn how to draw waves, foam and sand. Get your brushes ready and immerse yourself in a world of color and movement!

Paint Colors

Cerulean Blue

Yellow Ochre

Burnt Sienna

Phthalo Green

Ultramarine Deep

Dioxazine Purple

1. Use a pencil to draw a curved oval shape in the center of the paper; this is the background shape for the sketch. Draw a line just above the center to represent the horizon. Slightly above that line, draw a small elongated triangle; this will be a sailboat. Add a vertical line for the mast and a small trapezoid beneath it to make the boat. At the bottom of the background, draw three slightly different wavy lines at approximately the same distance apart, one above the other. These are the lines for the coastal waves.

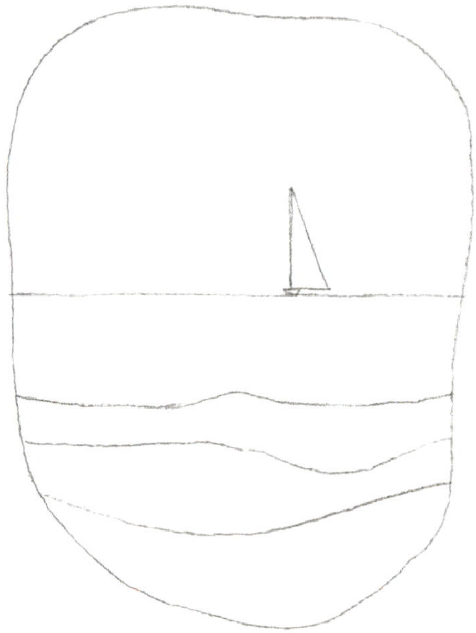

1

2. Use a black waterproof liner to outline the horizon with a thin line. Outline the sailboat with simple straight lines. Use interrupted horizontal lines for the waves farthest away; increase the distance between each wave as they move closer to the shore. Also draw more wavy lines for the water in the distance, moving toward more continuous curly waves by the shore. Draw the foam on the two closest waves with curly lines, adding another similar line above it to show the volume of the foam. Add small dots and doodles on the sand below the first wave.

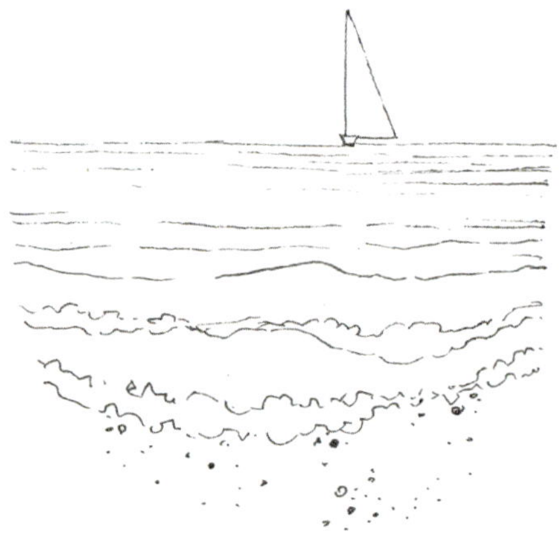

2

3. Paint the sky with Cerulean Blue, making it darker at the top and randomly blending and diluting it with water as you move downward, leaving spots of white paper. Use Yellow Ochre and Burnt Sienna to paint the sand with smooth transitions. Use more Yellow Ochre near the wave and more Burnt Sienna toward the bottom. Mix a turquoise color from equal parts of Cerulean Blue and Phthalo Green and prepare a lighter shade of turquoise separately. Use the light turquoise and a bit of Yellow Ochre to paint the area between the first and second waves, skipping the foam. Near the first wave, paint a few strokes of Yellow Ochre, diluted slightly with water, and then make a smooth transition to the light turquoise. Paint the area between the second and third waves just with light turquoise.

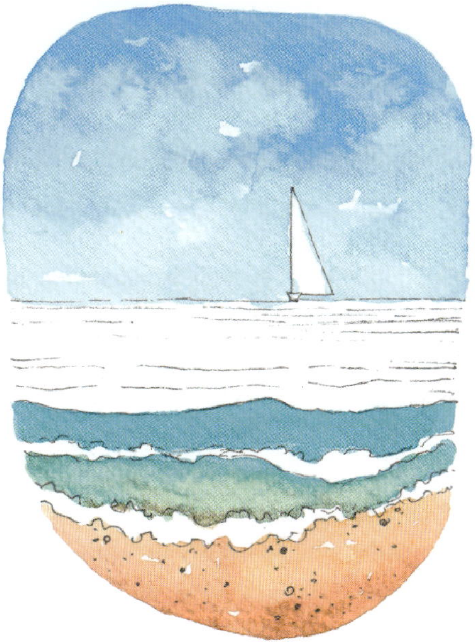

3

cerulean blue + phthalo green

4. Great! Now let's add the blue expanses of the serene sea! Mix Ultramarine Deep with some water to get a lighter shade. Paint the water from the third wave to the horizon line, starting with light turquoise at the bottom and gradually adding light ultramarine as you move up. Leave thin horizontal lines of white paper on the third and fourth waves. Paint the sailboat with a flat wash of light ultramarine. Wait for the paper to dry.

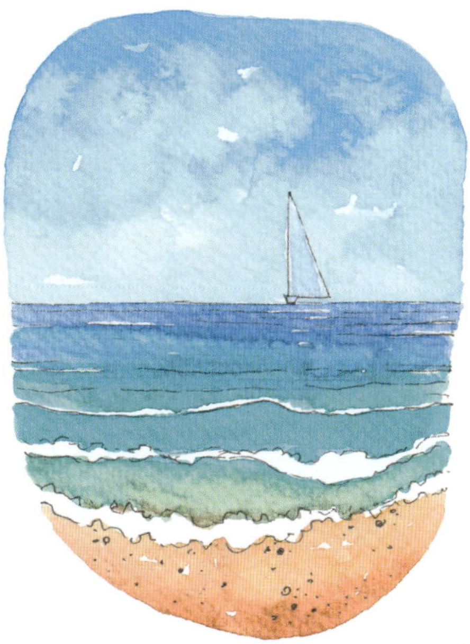

4

5. Use turquoise to paint thin, slightly wavy shadows under the second wave and a few semi-oval lines from the second wave to the first. Soften these strokes with a damp brush. Do the same under the third wave but with less curved strokes. Next use light ultramarine to paint thin shadows under the fourth wave and randomly use the same color to make thin strokes under the waves near the sailboat. Mix Dioxazine Purple with water to get a lighter shade and use random, detached, oval-like strokes to add shadows on the foam of the first and second waves, leaving white paper spots visible. Add a few strokes under the foam on the sand with the same color. Splatter Burnt Sienna and light purple on the sand.

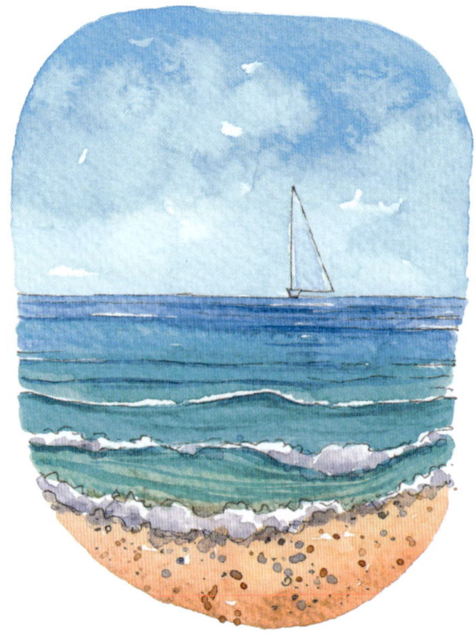

5

6. Use the black waterproof liner to make some of the outlines bolder, especially on the closest waves and the sailboat. Use a white gel pen to draw a white line on the left side of the sailboat and reflections in the water below it, slightly skipping the wave lines. Add a few thin, horizontal lines on the water between the fourth wave and the horizon. On the third wave, above the liner add a thin, light line. Randomly draw dots and small circles on the foam on the second and third waves to depict foam splashes. Draw small dots randomly on the sand to make the sand texture.

Fantastic! Our sketch is ready!

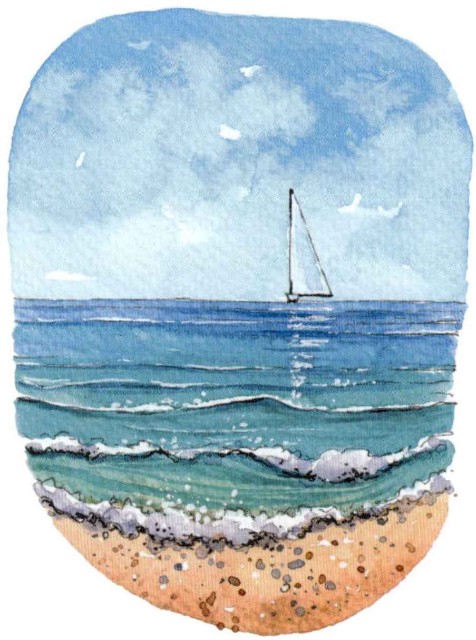

6

Acknowledgments

I would like to express my sincere gratitude to everyone who supported me in creating this book. First and foremost, my deepest appreciation goes to my husband, whose constant support and encouragement were invaluable throughout this journey. His patience and understanding allowed me to dedicate myself fully to this project.

A special thank-you to my family and foremost my mother, whose love for art and culture has profoundly inspired me since childhood. Her belief in my talents and her endless encouragement have always motivated me to follow my passion for art.

I am also incredibly grateful to my publishing team, especially my editor Alexandra, for their guidance and expertise. Their commitment to excellence has significantly improved the quality of this book, making it something I am truly proud of.

To all my friends, colleagues and the artistic community who have offered their valuable insights and feedback, thank you for helping me sharpen my vision and techniques.

Finally, I thank you, the reader, for your interest in this book. It is my sincere hope that it inspires you to explore and develop your own artistic path.

About the Author

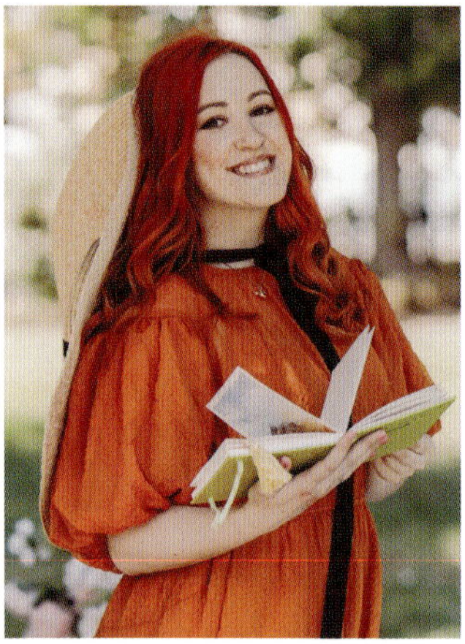

Anastasia Kozlova is a watercolor artist and educator based in London. She completed her education as a Fine Art Teacher from NRIAPE and completed a course at University of Arts London, Central Saint Martins. She is a proud member of the International Watercolor Society, the Professional Union of Artists and an artist member of the Society of Scottish Artists. She is a dedicated practitioner, enthusiast and explorer of new artistic techniques and styles. She has created more than 2,500 works on her personal drawing challenge and taught over 50,000 students.

Anastasia specializes in watercolor sketching and painting and has showcased her work in numerous exhibitions across the UK, Kazakhstan and Russia. With 11 years of teaching experience, she is a cofounder of the Dream and Draw Art School, organizing numerous online art marathons and courses. She has also held several charity art events and online art challenges, engaging thousands of artists worldwide.

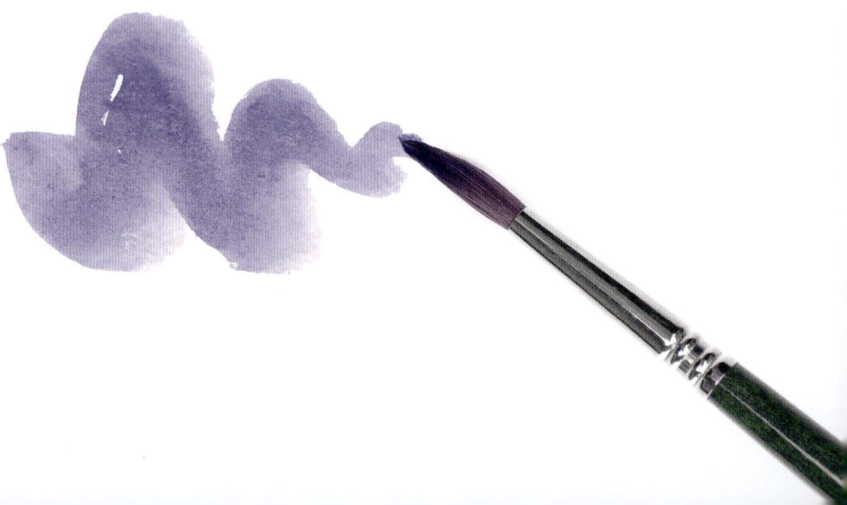

Index